dinner at the
AUTHENTIC CAFE

dinner at the AUTHENTIC CAFE

roger hayot with sheila linderman

MACMILLAN • USA

MACMILLAN
A Simon & Schuster Macmillan Company
15 Columbus Circle
New York, NY 10023

Library of Congress Cataloging-in-Publication Data

Hayot, Roger.
Dinner at the Authentic Cafe/Roger Hayot with Sheila Linderman.
p.   cm.
Includes index.
ISBN 0-02-549525-9
1. Cookery.   2. Authentic Cafe.   I. Linderman, Sheila.
II. Title.
TX714.H393   1995   94-43367   CIP
641.5--dc20

Design by Amy Peppler Adams, designLab, Seattle
Photography by Roger Hayot

Manufactured in the United States of America

10 9 8 7 6 5 4 3 2 1

This book is for my grandmother,
Hanina Hayot

Acknowledgments

Without my mentor, David Overton, I would never have had the chance to experiment, and to expand my repertoire and understanding of the restaurant business, and life in general. I will always be grateful to him.

To everyone at the Authentic Cafe, past and present, a heartfelt thank-you for taking this journey with me and for your very hard work.

To Louie and Annette Ryan, who always seem like an extension of myself and who keep me on the right track, I can't repay you both enough.

Thank-you to my friend and confidant, Greg Kling, for getting all the business aspects together, for making the money end of things so easy, and for being a true friend.

I can't thank my mother and father, Erna and Abner Hayot, enough for always letting me do my thing. I love you both very much.

To my old friend Jerry Burgos, who helped me in so many areas, including building the restaurant, thanks for all the great times and for your commitment to make the restaurant as consistent as it is.

Very special thanks to Sheila Linderman for making this project so damn easy. I didn't think it would go so painlessly. I can't wait to do the next book with you.

To my agents, Maureen and Eric Lasher, thank you for taking the time to guide me through the process of writing a book and allowing me to grow with it.

To my editor, Jane Sigal, thank you for your enthusiasm and spirit, which show up in these pages.

I want to thank all my relatives for the happy times around the dinner table while I was growing up. You taught me that breaking bread with family is one of life's best expressions of sharing.

We are lucky to have such great purveyors and farmers, whose work and know-how make the finest products available, and who challenge my skills and deepen my appreciation of the land.

Finally, I want to thank my grandmother, Hanina Hayot, rest in peace, who never spoke English, but who was always able to guide and prod me in the right direction. She taught me about my culture and the meaning of treating ancestors with respect and love.

Contents

Introduction

Although I grew up in Chicago, my parents' German and Moroccan families played a huge role in the development of my rather eclectic food tastes. Walking into my grandmother's apartment building on a Friday night, even before reaching the front door, I would be welcomed by wonderful Mediterranean aromas that wafted through the hallway. Once inside her home, I was bombarded with the colors and variety of foods on the table: roasted eggplant salad, carrot-cumin salad, braised chicken with cracked green olives and preserved lemons, and fragrant mint tea, to name a few.

On weekends, my family went to my aunt and uncle's apartment on Chicago's North Side, where my aunts and grandmother were always in the kitchen, preparing the many different foods of Morocco. I can still smell the aromas of peppers being scorched over an open flame, and of roasted cumin and coriander, that permeate

Moroccan cooking. Even today the remembered scent of freshly baked anise-flecked bread makes me smile.

My mother's cooking was German. Her father and brothers were butchers and experienced sausage makers. I remember the ropes of handmade sausages that my grandfather would bring home on weekends, and how proud he was of them. I remember, too, the leisurely, sometimes raucous times we would spend together. They always seemed to center on great, freshly prepared food.

Music was another big influence on my youth. Watching the Beatles on the *Ed Sullivan Show* made me want to play the drums. To buy a set, I went to work. It happened that my first job was at a restaurant—working at a great hot-dog stand, Fluky's, in Chicago, a city where the hot dog is not maligned but revered. Since I was only thirteen years old, I had to get a work permit from school. Little did I know that this was the beginning of a totally

different career.

Strange as it may seem, it was at Fluky's that I began to learn about quality food. We peeled our own potatoes for the french fries. We sliced everything the same day that we cooked it. People used to line up day and night just to eat there. Whenever I go back to Chicago, I stop by to say hello to Jack Drexler and eat one of those dogs. His father, Fluky himself, was a real card who always told wild stories as we peeled onions together. He would try to show me all the different ways not to cry. This, while tears streamed down our faces! I will never forget those days.

As I got older, I still wanted to be a musician but went on cooking to support myself. However, when I moved to Los Angeles at the age of twenty in 1977, I began working in better restaurants. I started to take cooking more seriously, and it came easily to me. Suddenly, cooking looked more like a career, and playing the drums more like a great way to unwind.

My first job in Los Angeles was at a country club. There I learned the old-time basics of the restaurant business: ice carving, buffets, banquets. But it was also the beginning of "nouvelle cuisine," with its radical idea of presenting food on a plate instead of a platter, its whimsical flavor pairings, and its emphasis on fresh ingredients and simple preparations. I adopted many of the new ways, although I must say that the portions I offer are far from "nouvelle."

I began to develop my own cooking style while working at the Cheesecake Factory for David Overton. I started there as a line cook, but David

allowed me to experiment, even encouraging me as he tasted the dishes I was creating. This is crucial to my personal philosophy of food: The greatest delicacies are the result of experimentation.

Eventually, those dishes were served as specials at the Cheesecake Factory. Then they made their way onto the regular menu. These very ethnic and eclectic creations were a striking departure from the restaurant's deli-like format.

David's encouragement never waned. We subscribed to cooking and restaurant magazines. Under the restaurant's auspices, I took classes from such cooks as Jeremiah Tower, Mark Miller, Paul Prudhomme, and Richard Olney. These classes introduced me to a new level of professionalism and inspired me to strive for more in my own career.

While still working as a line cook at the Cheesecake Factory, a tenure that lasted for ten years, I started working for a large-scale caterer, Michael Fuerste, as a sideline. Here was another person who was 110 percent into his profession, and who also pushed me to develop my own personal style. My repertoire expanded considerably and I began to cater a few events on my own. It started to feel like time to strike out by myself.

Coincidentally—or perhaps it was fate—my father, who had moved to

L.A. from Chicago in 1978, decided to go into semi-retirement around this time. His kosher butcher shop, located in an ethnic area on Beverly Boulevard, in the heart of the Fairfax District with its wonderful Middle Eastern markets, seemed like the perfect starting spot for my own catering kitchen.

He already had a walk-in refrigerator; I would just have to build the kitchen. But why stop there? Why not put in seats? So, once again with the help of David Overton, the 27-seat, 800-square-foot Authentic Cafe opened in 1987.

I knew what kind of restaurant I wanted. I wanted to make my own recipes. I did not want to compromise on the quality of my ingredients. And I didn't want to substitute ingredients in ethnic dishes just for the sake of saving time or money, even if this meant frequent trips to specialty markets (which I have come to love). In short, I wanted to provide the freshest and highest quality *authentic* food at reasonable prices, to nourish souls as well as bodies.

After two months, I received my first good reviews from local critics. From then on, the reviews came every week. Every night there would be thirty to forty-five people waiting in line for seats, often in the rain. Two years later, we expanded and took over the space next door. Now, after almost eight years, we *still* have a line out the door almost every night.

The crowd includes execs from CBS across the street as well as young locals who consider the Authentic Cafe to be their neighborhood restaurant. Some customers I see in the restaurant every single day.

Actually, dinners at the Authentic Cafe aren't very different from my family dinners. My father, who was also a butcher in Morocco and Paris, makes sausages in the back. They may be jerk pork sausage and chicken sausage with cilantro and chilies, but he is doing what he does best and loves most. The room is as animated as the weekend family gatherings I remember. When I sit in the dining room of my restaurant, I feel like I am at a party that has moved from my grandmother's house to mine.

The food isn't architecture on a plate. It's rustic and homey. But there's nothing homebound and prim about the flavors—they are exotic and bold. The menu is like a culinary jaunt through the United States, Latin America, Asia, the Mediterranean, and the Caribbean—what I like to call the "sun" countries—with common ingredients and flavors providing the paths between these countries and their cuisines. I hope that the recipes in this book will inspire you to accompany me on this journey in the kitchen, and perhaps take a trip on your own.

Exotic Foods Used in This Book:
What They Are, Where to Get Them, How to Use Them

We live in a culturally varied country and we are blessed with a burgeoning number of ethnic markets, not only in urban areas but in small towns as well. And because the population continues to diversify, products that were either unavailable in the past, or available only in specialty markets, can now be found in many supermarkets.

Although some of the ingredients in this book have foreign names, they are all accessible. Some may require a trip to specialty or ethnic markets, but that's half the fun of cooking and experiencing new foods.

Talk to the people who use these ingredients and find out about their foods. To get you started, here's a glossary of exotic ingredients found in the pantry at the Authentic Cafe, with information on where to find them. I urge you to go out and discover the thrill of what is probably in your own backyard.

Achiote Paste. This paste is made from a combination of vinegar, ground annato seeds (small, brick-red seeds of a tree, used mostly in the Caribbean's Yucatán), cumin, oregano, and several other spices. It is commonly used for adding color and an earthy flavor in the Yucatán region of Mexico. Achiote paste is available in Latin groceries.

Adobo. A vinegary sauce (*en adobo* means "pickled") from Mexico that is used in meats, chicken, and vegetables. It is available in Latin groceries.

Allspice. Allspice berries are a reddish-brown spice widely used in Caribbean foods. The wood of the allspice tree is used in Jamaican jerk pits as a fragrant smoking and fire source for foods. Allspice berries are available in most supermarkets.

Balsamic Vinegar. Made in Modena, Italy, this vinegar has a smooth, mellow flavor. It is made from unfermented grape juice that is aged in wooden casks. It can be very costly, but it is definitely worth the price to have this vinegar on hand as a staple. It is available in Italian groceries, specialty food shops, and most supermarkets.

Banana Leaves. Many countries use banana leaves to wrap food, primarily before steaming. Wash the leaves and remove the tough stems. Toast each leaf above a low open flame or directly on the burner of an electric range set on low for about 20 seconds on one side, moving it constantly, then for about 15 seconds on the other side. The leaf will shrink slightly and deepen in color, but it will be more pliable. Banana leaves are available in Latin and some Asian groceries.

Black Beans. Also called turtle beans, these are from the central and Yucatán regions of Mexico. They are also widely used in the Caribbean. They are available in health food shops and most supermarkets.

Brown Sugar. The brown sugar in the United States is actually a blend of molasses and sucrose, or table sugar, with molasses being a by-product of the sugar refining process common in the United States. The difference between light and dark brown sugar is defined by the percentage of molasses they contain. The brown sugar found in Europe is the result of a different refining process and does not contain molasses per se, nor is it moist, as is the brown sugar here.

Cactus (Nopale). The pads of the prickly pear cactus are edible. First remove the little spines. Gloves must be worn when handling cactus. Using a knife, cut out the spines, which are sometimes hard to see. Grill the prepared pads or blanch them in water. They are great pickled. Their flavor is a cross between green beans and okra. They are available in Latin groceries as well as supermarkets that carry Latin ingredients.

Calamata Olives. These are the best-quality Greek olives packed in a wine-vinegar brine. Each usually has a slit to allow the marinade to penetrate. Calamata olives are a purplish-black color with a tangy flavor. They are available in Greek groceries, some specialty food shops, and most supermarkets.

Candied Red Ginger. Made in China, this ginger is very sweet and spicy at the same time. It is sold in glass jars in Asian groceries.

Capers. The flowering buds of the caper bush. They are usually pickled or packed in salt, and are common to Mediterranean cuisines. The bush itself grows best in the salt air. Capers are available in specialty food stores and most supermarkets.

Caraway. This crescent-shaped seed with a slight flavor of anise or licorice is used in curry pastes and rye bread. It is available in most supermarkets.

Cellophane (Mung Bean) Noodles. These noodles (a.k.a. glass noodles or saifun), which need only soaking in warm water to be eaten, are made from the starch of the green mung bean. They are quite common to Thai and Chinese cuisines and can be found in Asian groceries, as well as supermarkets that carry Asian ingredients. They should be soaked for about 20 minutes in warm water (no cooking required).

Champagne Vinegar. This vinegar is made from, of course, champagne, and has a pale color and a light flavor. I use champagne vinegar routinely in cooking because of its mild flavor rather than take a chance on white wine vinegar, which can be so raw as to be overwhelming to other ingredients. Champagne vinegar is available in specialty food shops and some supermarkets.

Chayote. A pale green squash about the size of a large pear, chayote (or mirliton squash in the South) is excellent when stuffed or sautéed. It is popular in Mexican and Central American cuisines. It is available in Latin groceries and some supermarkets.

Cheeses.

Feta. A soft, crumbly sheep cheese that is usually cured and packed in brine. Relatively low in fat, this cheese is widely used in Mediterranean cooking. Feta cheese is available in specialty food stores and most supermarkets.

Fontina. A buttery, mild-flavored cheese with a slightly creamy texture; the netted varieties are made in Italy or Denmark. It is available in specialty food stores and most supermarkets.

Gorgonzola. A sheep's milk cheese, with origins in Lombardy and Piedmont, Italy; it is a blue cheese with a very spicy aroma. Usually comes in foil-wrapped wheels and is available in specialty food stores.

Mascarpone. A fresh, creamy Italian cheese that is the major ingredient in tiramisú. It is available in Italian groceries and cheese shops.

Oaxaca Cheese. A braided string cheese with a tangy flavor, from the Oaxaca region of Mexico; a fresh cheese made from cow's milk. Oaxaca cheese is available in Latin groceries and some supermarkets.

Parmesan. A hard, rather salty cow's milk cheese, originally from Reggiano, Italy, that is usually used finely grated or very thinly sliced. Parmesan is a classic cheese that should be purchased in chunks and freshly grated or sliced. The best, Parmigiano-Reggiano cheese, is available in specialty food stores and some supermarkets.

(Pecorino) Romano. A hard, dry sheep's milk cheese with a sharp flavor, used much the same way that Parmesan, a similar Italian cheese, is used. It is available in specialty food stores and most supermarkets.

exotic foods…

Queso cotija añejo. A dry, aged Mexican cheese that crumbles easily and has similar flavor characteristics to those of Parmesan. Available in Latin groceries and some supermarkets.

Ranchero Cheese. A part-skim cow's milk cheese with a crumbly texture, somewhere between that of fresh mozzarella and ricotta. Available in Latin groceries and some supermarkets.

Smoked Gouda. Cold-smoked Dutch cheese with a mild flavor and a slightly creamy texture. A semi-hard cow's milk cheese that is great for cooking. Smoked gouda is available in cheese shops, specialty food shops, and some supermarkets.

Chick-Peas (Garbanzo Beans). These legumes are yellowish in color with an irregular (roughly round or heart) shape. Dried, they take about 2 hours to cook. Do not add tomatoes, acids, or salt during the initial cooking of dried chick-peas, as salts and acids tend to harden them. Dried chick-peas are available in Middle Eastern groceries, other specialty food shops, and some supermarkets. Canned chickpeas can be found in most supermarkets.

Chicken Tenders. These are the 1-inch strip of white meat that sits in the groove next to the sternum under the breast.

Chile (Satay) Oil. This flavored oil is made by adding red chilies to any mild oil, such as peanut, soy, or canola. The oil absorbs the chilies' flavor and color. Let the chilies sit in the oil for 3 weeks, then strain. Chile oil is available in Asian groceries and some supermarkets.

Chile-Garlic Paste, Vietnamese. A spicy condiment made with garlic and red chilies. The brand with the rooster on the label is very good. It is available in Asian groceries and other specialty food shops.

Chilies.

Ancho Chile. A dried poblano chile, 3 inches wide and $4\frac{1}{2}$ to 5 inches long, it has a reddish-brown color, a flavor between raisins and tobacco, and medium heat. Ancho chilies are available in Latin groceries and some supermarkets.

Chipotle Chile en Adobo. Smoked and dried jalapeños packed in cans with vinegar and tomato. They are very hot and have a strong smoky flavor. Cans of this condiment are available in Latin groceries and some specialty food shops.

Dried Pasilla Chile. Very dark—almost black—this medium to hot chile is also called chile negro. Toasting the chile brings out its plum and raisin flavors. Dried pasilla chilies are available in Latin groceries and some supermarkets.

Habanero Chile. One of the hottest chilies, yet with a fruity flavor, it is grown in the Yucatán, the Caribbean, and now in California. The chile is lantern-shaped and green, yellow, or orange. Available in Latin groceries and some supermarkets.

Jalapeño Chile. One of the best known chilies around, the jalapeño is 1 to $1\frac{1}{2}$ inches long with a full flavor and medium heat. As with most chilies, the heat is concentrated in the seeds. Available in Latin groceries and most supermarkets.

Morita Chile. A brick-red dried jalapeño chile, it has a sharp, smoky flavor and is very hot. Morita chilies are available in Latin groceries.

Poblano Chile. This chile measures 4 to 5 inches in length and 2 to 3 inches in width. When dried, it becomes the ancho chile. This medium-hot chile is ideal for stuffing, as in Chiles Rellenos. Available in Latin groceries and some supermarkets.

Red Thai Chilies. Tiny dried chilies that are very hot. They are excellent for infusing spice into oils. Available in bags or spice jars in Asian groceries, gourmet shops, and some supermarkets.

Serrano Chile. This green or red chile is about 2 inches long and $\frac{1}{4}$ inch wide. It has a fairly sharp, clear flavor, and is medium to hot. Available in Latin groceries and some supermarkets.

Cider Vinegar. This is apple cider that has turned into vinegar. It has a very sharp flavor. It is available in most supermarkets.

Cinnamon. Familiar cinnamon is really the bark of a tropical tree. The flavor is sweet with spicy overtones. It is used whole (in infusions) and ground.

Coconut, Fresh. This fruit of a very prolific tree that grows throughout the Pacific and South America has a smooth, hard shell, a brown inner husk covered with hair-like strands, and a light brown skin. The coconut has many uses. Place three holes in the end of a fresh coconut to drain out the coco water, then place the coconut in a 350° oven for 25 minutes. Cool the coconut, crack the shell, then peel. You can now grate or slice the meat.

Coconut Milk, Unsweetened. The liquid squeezed from grated coconut that has been soaked. It is frequently used in Thai curries and dishes from the Caribbean. Coconut milk is available canned in some supermarkets, Asian and Latin groceries, and other specialty food shops.

Coriander Seeds. These seeds come from the cilantro plant. They have a strong fragrance and flavor. Toast them first, then grind them to take full advantage of their flavor. Coriander is available, whole or ground, in most supermarkets.

Cornmeal, Blue. Similar in texture to yellow cornmeal, this blue-gray counterpart is milled from the dried kernels of blue corn (contrary to what some people think, it has not been dyed). Blue corn is native American and has a religious significance for the Hopis. It has a much earthier flavor than yellow corn. Because of the high protein content, it must be handled more carefully than yellow corn. Blue cornmeal is available in health food shops.

Cornmeal, Yellow. A somewhat coarse flour milled from dried yellow corn. Stone-ground cornmeal is dried corn ground between stones, leaving some of the germ. It is widely available in supermarkets.

Cornstarch. Unlike cornmeal, this is a finely milled flour taken only from the inner part of the corn kernel. Because it cooks very quickly in hot liquids, it is preferable to flour as a thickening agent for soups and sauces.

Couscous. This dish is made from semolina and used extensively in North African cuisine. It is usually steamed over water or broth. In Morocco, Algeria, and Tunisia, couscous is available as a whole dish, topped with grilled or stewed meats, vegetables cooked in broth, and beans. The pasta couscous, in the original and instant varieties, is available in most supermarkets and Middle Eastern groceries.

exotic foods...

Cracked Wheat (Bulgur). This grain is made by cracking wheat in boiling water, then drying and crushing it. It makes a fine alternative to plain rice. Cracked wheat is available in supermarkets, health food shops, and Middle Eastern groceries.

Creole Mustard. This is a pungent, grainy mustard from Louisiana that combines brown mustard seeds, vinegar, and horseradish. Zataran's is a very good brand. It is available in specialty food shops and some supermarkets.

Cumin. Cumin seeds have a robust flavor often used in the cuisines of the Middle East, Asia, and Latin America. Try to grind the seeds for each dish, but be sure to toast them in a dry frying pan first. This will release their oils and increase their flavor. Cumin is available, whole and ground, in most supermarkets.

Curry Powder. A mixture of many spices, most notably cumin, coriander, turmeric, and fenugreek. I recommend Dawsen's or another Madras-style curry powder. It is widely available in supermarkets.

Dijon Mustard. A smooth mustard made from mustard seeds, white wine, and spices; it is mild in flavor. Dijon mustard imported from France is considerably more pungent. It is widely available in supermarkets.

Dried Corn Husks. The outer skins of corn ears, used to wrap tamales before steaming. They must be soaked in warm water first to make them more pliable. They are available in Latin groceries and some supermarkets.

English (Hothouse) Cucumbers.
These are very long cucumbers with few seeds; choose firm fruit. They are available in most supermarkets.

Enoki Mushrooms. These cultivated mushrooms have extremely long, thin stems and tiny white caps; their texture is crisp and their flavor mild. Cut away the base of the mushroom cluster before using. Enoki mushrooms are available in specialty stores and some supermarkets.

Extra-Virgin Olive Oil. Cold, first-pressing "juice" of olives, this oil is low in acidity and has a fruity flavor. It is the finest, and most expensive, grade of olive oil sold. To make the most of this luxurious, fragrant oil, I like to serve it uncooked. Extra-virgin olive oil is available in specialty food shops and most supermarkets.

Fava Beans. These resemble large lima beans with a tough skin that is usually peeled after cooking. Fresh favas are usually sold in their long (8- to 10-inch) pods in the spring and summer. They are available in Middle Eastern groceries and other specialty food shops.

Fennel Bulb (Sweet Anise). Raw fennel, which is very high in iron, has a licorice flavor. The bulb is used extensively in Mediterranean cooking, while the thin, dill-like leaves are used in Asia. Try this vegetable, cooked or raw, anywhere you would use celery. Fennel is available in most supermarkets.

Fennel Seeds. These crescent-shaped seeds resemble cumin but are pale green in color and impart a sweet, aniselike flavor. They are available in most supermarkets.

Five-Spice Powder, Chinese. This fragrant seasoning is a blend of ground star anise, cloves, Szechwan peppercorns, anise seed, and cinnamon. It is available in some supermarkets, Asian groceries, and other specialty food shops.

Flageolet Beans.   Pale green dried beans, about the size and shape of a child's fingernail, flageolets are popular in French home cooking, where they are served alongside roast beef or leg of lamb. They are available in specialty food shops.

Garlic.   Also known as "the stinking rose," garlic is a member of the onion family. I like to use granulated garlic in some crusts. Garlic bulbs may be white or purple. Try to choose hard, shiny heads when buying fresh garlic. (Actually, the "fresh" garlic we commonly use has been dried slightly to increase shelf life; true, fresh garlic is sweet and juicy, and has a very short shelf life.) Garlic's flavor mellows considerably when roasted.

Ginger.   This rhizome, or branching, noded root, has been cultivated for over 3,000 years in Asia. It has a pungent, fresh flavor. Fresh ginger is preferred to ground ginger, which is relatively tasteless. Ginger should be kept refrigerated and is best when very fresh. It is available in some supermarkets, Asian groceries, and other specialty food shops.

Ginger, Japanese Pickled (Sushi).   Pickled ginger is a common accompaniment to sushi, and is used between tastings to cleanse the palate. It is available in Japanese groceries and other specialty food shops.

Green Onion (Scallion).   A staple of Chinese cooking, this onion, which is actually the shoot of a growing yellow onion, has a long green stem and a very fresh flavor. Remove the roots and use the white and light green parts only.

Gyoza Wrappers.   Basically, round won ton wrappers, made of wheat flour and water, these are used to make gyoza, or Japanese pot

stickers. They can be found in the refrigerated section of Asian markets and some supermarkets.

Haas Avocado.   A variety of avocado with a dark, mottled skin, Haas avocados have more oil in their flesh. They are creamier and have a more complex flavor than other varieties. Haas avocados are available in most supermarkets.

Harissa.   A red chile paste used as a condiment in Middle Eastern cuisines. This is a spicy mixture of chilies, vinegar, and other spices. It is readily available in Middle Eastern groceries.

Herbs.

Basil.   This member of the mint family is one of the most important herbs used in many cuisines, from Italian to Thai. It has a mild anise flavor and comes in many varieties (e.g., lemon, Thai, cinnamon, sweet, and globe). This herb is very easy to obtain.

Cilantro (Fresh Coriander).   Also known as Chinese parsley, cilantro's flavor is pungent. It is best bought with roots attached and should be stored with water covering the entire root.

Hoja Santa.   This is an herb that tastes like sarsaparilla or anise. It has a very broad leaf, so you can wrap food in it as well as take advantage of its aromatic capacity. If you live in a warm to hot climate with moderate humidity, it is worth growing. It is available in Latin groceries, or frozen, by mail order.

Italian (Flat-leaf) Parsley.   This common herb is dark green in color and has a milder flavor than the curly-leaf variety.

Marjoram.   A delicate, pungent herb with a slightly hot flavor.

exotic foods…

Oregano. In the same family as marjoram and with similar characteristics, oregano is a staple herb in Mediterranean cooking.

Sage. A pungent herb with a slightly bitter flavor, sage is a favorite in winter cooking, especially during the holiday season. Try to buy fresh sage, as it has considerably more flavor than dried.

Thyme. With oval, light green leaves that have a pungent, spicy flavor, this herb is indispensable for flavoring stocks and sauces. Lemon thyme has a lighter, more citrus-like flavor than its English or French cousins.

Hoisin. A sauce made from soybeans, red beans, sugar, vinegar, and other ingredients. Hoisin is traditionally used as a Chinese barbecue sauce. I recommend Koon Chun brand. It is available in some supermarkets, Asian groceries, and other specialty food shops.

Hot Sauce. I recommend any Mexican brand, such as Bufalo or Cholula.

Jicama. A tuber (or underground stem) with a light brown skin, this vegetable has a sweet flavor with a potatolike texture. Always peel the brown skin and the woody layer beneath the skin before using. It may be eaten raw or lightly cooked. It is available in some supermarkets.

Kaffir Lime Leaves. These fragrant leaves of the kaffir lime tree are used to flavor many of the dishes of Southeast Asia. They are available in Asian groceries.

Ketjap Manis. This is a thick, sweet soy sauce (made from soy sauce and molasses) from Indonesia. It's great for dipping. Ketjap manis is available in Asian groceries.

Kosher Salt. This coarse salt has no additives and a clean flavor, and is the salt that I prefer to use as a seasoning. It is used to prepare meats and poultry according to Jewish dietary laws.

Lemongrass. Very common in Southeast Asia, lemongrass, which resembles a pale-colored green onion, has an inimitable citrus flavor. Remove the tough outer leaves and use the bottom 3 or 4 inches only, as this is the most tender part. You can use the tough tops to flavor soups or stocks, but remove them before serving. Lemongrass is available in Asian groceries and other specialty food shops.

Mango. Originally from India, the mango has an oblong shape. When mangoes are still green, they are often cut into thin strips and eaten in salads. When ripe, the skin is yellow-orange with a reddish blush. It has a single, fairly large seed, which makes the fruit rather tricky to split. The flesh is orange with an exotic, fragrant flavor. As the fruit ripens, fibers develop in the flesh, so that an overripe mango may be quite fibrous. If you purée the pulp, strain it before using. Mangos are available in Asian groceries and other specialty food shops.

Masa Harina. Ground dried cornmeal used in many dishes from Mexico and the Southwestern United States. This staple is the base for corn tortillas, tamales, and other Latin preparations. Quaker makes a masa harina that can be found in most supermarkets.

Mirin. This Japanese cooking wine is made from sake (rice wine) and sugar. It is an excellent glazing agent when reduced. Do not confuse mirin with plain rice wine, which contains no additional sugar. Mirin is available in some supermarkets, Asian groceries, and other specialty food shops.

Nam Pla (Thai Fish Sauce). A thin, salty liquid made from salted anchovies fermented in wooden casks. It is used in place of salt in Thai cooking. It is available in Asian groceries and other specialty food shops.

Nutmeg. The seed of the nutmeg tree. The covering of the seed is called mace. Nutmeg has a spicy-sweet flavor and aroma. For best flavor, buy the whole seed and grate it before using. It is available in most supermarkets.

Orange Honey. This mild honey is produced by bees that are cultivated on orange blossoms. The pollen gives the honey a sweet, citrus flavor, which is much less astringent than that of clover honey. Orange honey is available in gourmet shops, health food stores, and most supermarkets.

Pancetta. This unsmoked Italian bacon comes rolled up like a log. It is available in Italian groceries and some specialty food shops.

Pankow Rice Bread Crumbs. These dry crumbs are made from a Japanese bread that is made of rice flour. They are neutral and have a very light texture, but add a nice crunch to a crust. They are available, boxed, in Japanese groceries and some supermarkets.

Papaya. This fruit grows in warm, tropical climates. When ripe, it can be eaten raw, and is delightful in salads. Depending on the variety, the fruit may be bright yellow or orange when ripe, and the flesh can range from yellow to salmon-colored. When in season, it is widely available in supermarkets and Latin groceries.

Pecans. Translation: "imprisoned nuts." They are grown in northern Mexico, and are used mostly in desserts and cakes.

Pepper, Black. Peppercorns that are picked when the berries are not completely ripe, then allowed to dry. Tellicherry is one of the best available.

Pepper, White. Peppercorns that are allowed to ripen fully before they are dried. White peppercorns have a milder flavor than black peppercorns.

Phyllo Dough. Phyllo is a paper-thin dough that is used extensively in Greek cooking and baking, as well as in Middle Eastern desserts. The dough can be bought in 1-pound packages, which contain 18 to 24 sheets (average dimensions: 14 x 18 inches), depending on the brand. I prefer Athens Foods brand. Boxes of phyllo are available in the freezer section of most supermarkets. Thaw it before using; be sure to thaw it slowly in the refrigerator, or it may crack. Also, keep the dough covered so it doesn't dry out.

Pine Nuts (Pignoli). The white seeds (once hulled) from the cones of a Southwestern (Piñones) pine tree; also used extensively in Italian cuisine. They are available in Italian groceries and other specialty food shops, and most supermarkets.

Pinto Beans. The most frequently used beans in Mexico; *pinto* literally means "painted." They are typically used in refried beans. Pinto beans are available in Latin groceries, health food shops, and most supermarkets.

Plantains. These are a tropical relative of bananas. When ripe (i.e., when the skin is black), their starch turns to sugar and they are eaten as a fruit. When green, plantains can be used much like potatoes. They are available in some supermarkets, Latin groceries, and other specialty food shops.

Plum Tomatoes. Also called roma tomatoes, these are oval and can be red or yellow. They have smaller and fewer seeds (and therefore more pulp) than their round counterparts, and when at their peak have a full, rich flavor. Avoid refrigerating tomatoes, if you can, as refrigeration changes their texture and flavor.

Plum Sauce, Chinese. A reduction of plums, vinegar, chilies, and spices, typically used with poultry. I recommend Koon Chun brand. It is available in Asian groceries and other specialty food shops.

Posole. Another name for hominy, which is made by soaking corn in a alkaline solution until it bursts. Posole is also the name for a traditional Southwestern stew. It is available in Latin groceries, and in most supermarkets as "hominy."

Preserved Lemons. Used as a condiment in Moroccan cooking, these lemons are made by splitting the fruit and mixing them with their juices and salt. The preserving process takes about 3 weeks. Use the rind only. They are available in Middle Eastern groceries, but make your own if you can. They store well.

Pure Olive Oil. This oil is extracted from olives by using solvents. It is light in flavor and color, good for cooking, and much cheaper than the extra-virgin variety. It is available in most supermarkets.

Rice Flour. Flour made from ground white rice; powdery and fine in texture. It is available in health food shops, Asian markets, and some supermarkets.

Rice Noodles. These noodles are made from rice flour and are quite common to Thai and other Asian cuisines. They can be rehydrated in boiling water, or fried in very hot oil until they expand. Rice noodles are available in fine (like angel hair) or thick (like fettuccine) widths in Asian groceries.

Rice Vinegar. Made from fermented rice wine, the Japanese variety is very mellow, while the Chinese version has a sharp flavor. It is available in some supermarkets, Asian groceries, and other specialty food shops.

Rock Shrimp. These small shrimp have extremely hard shells (hence their name), which are usually removed before they are sold. They have a firm, lobsterlike texture and a nice, sea-salt flavor. I use rock shrimp from Florida.

Saffron. The orange stigma (or stamen) from the crocus flower. This is the most expensive of all spices (although technically, it is an herb), as it takes about 17,000 of the hand-picked stigma to make one pound of saffron. The best saffron comes from Spain, and fortunately, very little is needed to impart a great deal of flavor. Saffron threads must be infused in hot liquid or oil to release their flavor. Saffron is available often in vials in specialty food shops.

Saifun (Mung Bean or Glass Noodles). See CELLOPHANE (GLASS) NOODLES.

Shallots. These small members of the onion family have a more subtle flavor than brown or white onions. They have a light brown skin and are usually about $\frac{1}{2}$ to 1 inch in diameter. The finest shallots are the gray variety. They are available in most supermarkets.

Sherry Vinegar. Vinegar made from—of course—sherry wine; it has a slightly sweet and very rich flavor. Sherry vinegar is available in specialty food shops and some supermarkets.

Soy Sauce. There are many varieties of this fermented soy bean condiment, the most commonly available being the Japanese and Chinese types. The former is lighter and somewhat cleaner, while the latter is richer, thicker, and more complex. I recommend the Pearl River Brand for heavy (Chinese) soy sauce.

Straw Mushrooms. Light brown mushrooms with an umbrella (half-open) shape. These mushrooms are sold, peeled, in cans, in most supermarkets.

Sun Choke. The true name for this brown-skinned tuber that resembles ginger root is Jerusalem artichoke. Despite this name, the sun choke bears no relation to regular artichokes. It has a sweet, nutty flavor, somewhat like a fresh water chestnut. When cooked, the sun choke's texture is like that of a potato. It is available in health food shops, Middle Eastern groceries, and some supermarkets.

Szechwan Peppercorns. This spice from China, sometimes called brown pepper, has a numbing quality, rather than the spiciness of black pepper. Dry toast these peppercorns in a skillet to release their flavor. They are available in some supermarkets, Asian groceries, and other specialty food shops.

Tahini. A paste made of ground toasted sesame seeds, commonly used in hummus, eggplant spreads, sauces, and a variety of other Middle Eastern dishes. Stir tahini before using it to incorporate the oil that naturally separates. It is available in Middle Eastern groceries and many supermarkets.

Tamale Masa. This fresh cornmeal dough is available in Latin groceries. You can also prepare it yourself using the recipe on most bags of masa harina.

Tamarind. A sour-tasting fruit that grows in a pod. The pulp is sold in 8-ounce blocks, which must be soaked and strained. Tamarind concentrate is also available in cans or jars in Asian groceries.

Taro. This is the starchy tuber, or underground stem, of a tropical plant (called *wu tao* in Chinese). When cooked, its flavor and consistency are a cross between cooked chestnuts and potatoes. Thinly sliced and deep-fried, taro chips are a sweet and delicate alternative to potato chips. Taro is available fresh in Latin and Asian groceries, as well as some supermarkets.

Toasted Sesame Oil. An amber-colored oil made by pressing roasted sesame seeds. Kadoya brand is very good. Store this oil in a dark, cool place as it can turn rancid easily. It is available in Asian groceries and some supermarkets.

Togarishi Spice Mix. A traditional Japanese spice mix, including different chilies and pepper, togarishi mix is sprinkled on miso soup or mixed into spicy tuna sushi rolls. Togarishi spice mix is available in small bottles in Japanese groceries.

Tomatillo. A small fruit that is green in color with a papery tan husk, which must be peeled before eating. Tomatillos have a lime-like flavor. Choose very firm fruits when purchasing. They are available in some supermarkets, Latin groceries, and other specialty food shops.

Tortillas, Corn. Flat, cooked disks of corn masa (dough); used in many dishes of Latin cooking, such as tacos and flautas. Corn tortillas have become commonplace. They are available in most supermarkets, Latin groceries, and other specialty food shops.

exotic foods...

Tortillas, Flour. Thin, flat, cooked disks of wheat flour dough, used in Mexican cuisine. They are available in some supermarkets, Latin groceries, and other specialty food shops.

Turbinado (Raw) Sugar. This coarse-grained sugar is available in health food shops and some supermarkets.

Wasabi (Japanese Horseradish Powder). This extremely pungent condiment is normally mixed with water and served in paste form as an accompaniment to sushi. It can also be used to give a spicy Asian flavor to a variety of dishes. If too much wasabi is added to a given recipe, it may impart a bitter taste. Available in small cans in Asian groceries, gourmet shops, and some supermarkets.

Won Ton Skins. Made of wheat flour, and available square and round, large and small, fresh won ton skins are used as wrappers in such dishes as spring rolls, ravioli, dumplings, pot stickers . . . even won tons. They can also be cut into strips and deep fried for use in salads or as a garnish. They are available in Asian groceries and some supermarkets.

Yuca (Cassava). A starchy tropical root with a bland potato-like flavor. Cook yuca as you would potatoes, removing the fiber that runs down the middle of the root after cooking. It is available fresh or frozen in some supermarkets, Latin groceries, and other specialty food shops. Fresh yuca takes much longer to cook than the frozen variety.

Zante (Dried) Currants. Tiny dried raisins made from the very small and delicate champagne grapes. These are not to be confused with fresh red currants, which are in the gooseberry family, or with black currants (cassis). Zante currants are available packaged or in bulk in health food and gourmet shops.

Shopping List of Exotic Ingredients

Here is a list of the more exotic ingredients you will need to make most of the recipes in this book. These ingredients won't spoil quickly, so you can buy them all at one time, at fancy grocery stores or local ethnic markets, or by mail order, and then you can prepare most of these recipes whenever the mood strikes. To make shopping easier, the list is organized by type of food shop.

Specialty Food Shops and Some Supermarkets

Champagne vinegar
Creole mustard
Flageolet beans
Phyllo dough
Quick grits
Saffron threads

Asian Groceries

Candied red ginger
Cellophane (mung bean) noodles
Chile (satay) oil
Coconut milk, unsweetened
Five-spice powder, Chinese
Ginger, Japanese pink pickled
Kaffir lime leaves
Ketjap manis
Hoisin sauce
Mirin (Japanese cooking wine)
Nam pla (Thai fish sauce)
Plum sauce, Chinese
Rice flour
Rice noodles
Rice vinegar
Szechwan peppercorns
Soy sauce, heavy (Chinese)
Tamarind concentrate
Toasted sesame oil
Togarishi spice mix (Japanese)
Vietnamese chile-garlic paste

Latin Groceries

Achiote paste
Ancho chilies
Banana leaves
Blue cornmeal
Chipotle chile en adobo
Dried corn husks
Dried pasilla chilies
Hoja santa
Masa harina

Middle Eastern Groceries

Tahini (toasted sesame paste)
Dried chick-peas (garbanzo beans)
Harissa
Preserved lemons

Note *Refrigerate all canned or bottled food after opening. Store the hoja santa, banana leaves, kaffir lime leaves, and phyllo dough in the freezer, well wrapped.*

exotic foods...

Mail Order and Shopping Sources

409 Vanderbilt Street
Brooklyn, NY 11218
(718) 436-8565
(800) 316-0820
Prepared curries, a variety of spices, and chilies available by mail order.

607 A. Juan Tabo Blvd.
Albuquerque, NM 87123
(505) 275-6902
Hoja santa and posole.

4757 Melrose Avenue
Los Angeles, CA 90029
(213) 662-9705
Thai products.

4725 Santa Monica Blvd.
Los Angeles, CA 90029
(213) 663-1503
Indian and Middle Eastern products.

560 Broadway
New York, NY 10012
(212) 431-1691
Oils, vinegars, spices, and a variety of dried beans.

821 Washington Street
Oakland, CA 94607
(519) 836-2250
Phyllo dough, spices, olives, olive oils, etc., mostly from Greece and Italy. Ratto's also has a variety of cooking utensils.

Broadway and Third Street
Los Angeles, CA 90013
(213) 749-0645
Produce from around the world, fresh meats, fish and seafood; lots of ethnic (mostly Latin) food stalls.

P.O. Box 4136
San Luis Obispo, CA 93403
(800) 462-3220
Over 500 hot and spicy items, including curries, chutneys, dried chilies, hot sauces, cooking sauces, marinades, and spicy condiments, available by mail order.

3939 Brooklyn Avenue
Los Angeles, CA 90063
(213) 263-2143
Mexican products, including chilies, chipotle chile en adobo, and bottled salsa.

Pepper Gal
**10536 119th Avenue N
Largo, FL 33543**

This seed company carries only hot and sweet peppers.

Redwood City Seed Company
**P.O. Box 361
Redwood City, CA 94064**

This company specializes in vegetable and herb seeds from Europe, Mexico, and Asia.

Specialty World Foods
**84 Montgomery Street
Albany, NY 12207
(800) 233-0913 (outside NY State)
(518) 436-7603 (within NY State)**

Wide variety of chilies, nam pla (Thai fish sauce), Vietnamese chile-garlic paste, saifun (mung bean or glass noodles), etc., all available by mail order.

Sunrise Enterprises
**P.O. Box 10058
Elmwood, CT 06110**

This company specializes in Asian vegetables and herbs. In addition to vegetable seeds, it carries ginger and taro tubers and Chinese chive plants.

Authentic Cafe Basics

At the Authentic Cafe, we always have these basic recipes on hand for making our wide-ranging repertoire of dishes. To be sure, most of the stocks, spice mixes, and other preparations included here are available in supermarkets or specialty food shops. But if you want to enjoy food with the full flavor of the Authentic Cafe, try making the fundamentals yourself.

Most good soups begin with a flavorful stock, or broth, and, of course, the best stocks are homemade. They are simple and inexpensive to make, and can be frozen in small quantities so that you won't have to chip away at a block of ice when a recipe calls for only 1 cup. As for the other basics, I like to control the quality of all the elements as much as possible. These preparations all just seem to taste better when you know that the best ingredients have gone into making them.

chicken stock

MAKES ABOUT 10 CUPS

4 pounds (12 cups) raw chicken bones, fat trimmed

16 cups cold water

3 large carrots, coarsely chopped (2½ cups)

3 celery ribs, leaves removed, coarsely chopped (1½ cups)

1 large onion, coarsely chopped (2 cups)

1 tablespoon black peppercorns

1 teaspoon kosher salt

3 large egg whites, lightly beaten (optional)

What's in a Shape?

Traditional stockpots are tall and narrow. Shaped in this way, with little surface exposed to the air, the pot lets the stock simmer for a long time, developing the flavor without losing too much liquid to evaporation. (Compare this to a braising pan, which is short and wide.)

Most soups and many sauces and stews are based on a stock of some sort, so the flavor of a finished dish often depends on the quality of the stock. If you want your cooking to shine, always start with the best.

For my chicken stock, I use raw chicken bones—the bones of a raw chicken that has had all the meat removed. Ask for them at the butcher's or supermarket. Or, if you bone your own chickens, freeze the carcasses until you accumulate enough to make stock.

1. Combine the chicken bones and water in a large stockpot and bring to a boil over medium heat. Skim the foam.

2. Add the carrots, celery, onion, peppercorns, and salt and return to a boil. Reduce the heat to low and simmer until the liquid reduces by half, 2 to 3 hours. Skim every 30 minutes.

3. Strain the stock twice through a cheesecloth-lined strainer or a fine-mesh china cap. Discard the contents of the strainer. If the stock has been well skimmed, it should be clear.

4. If the stock is cloudy, clarify it if desired: Pour the stock into a clean pot. Add the egg whites and bring the liquid to a gentle simmer over very low heat. The egg whites will form a filter on the surface and trap any impurities and much of the fat that may be clouding the stock. The stock must barely simmer for about 15 minutes. If the stock boils too hard or it is stirred, the filter will break, and small particles of egg white may cloud the stock further. After 15 minutes, carefully skim the egg whites and any fat off the surface.

5. Let the stock cool completely before covering and storing it. The stock can be refrigerated for up to 2 days, or it can be frozen for up to 3 weeks.

vegetable stock

MAKES ABOUT 8 CUPS

- 5 large garlic cloves, unpeeled
- ¼ cup plus 1 teaspoon pure olive oil
- 2 small fennel bulbs, coarsely chopped (2 cups)
- 5 or 6 celery ribs, leaves removed, coarsely chopped (3 cups)
- 1 medium-size onion, coarsely chopped (1½ cups)
- 3 large carrots, coarsely chopped (2½ cups)
- 2 ounces white mushrooms, sliced ⅛ inch thick (1 cup)
- 3 small or 2 large plum tomatoes, seeded and coarsely chopped (1 cup)
- 1 teaspoon black peppercorns
- 1 tablespoon kosher salt
- 12 cups cold water

Salting Stock

I like a rich, flavorful stock. Our stocks are only lightly seasoned so that they won't overwhelm sauces and soups. In the final recipes, we adjust for the salt in the stock. In general, if a finished stock is going to be reduced further, less salt should be used in the stock's preparation.

Many of my recipes are meatless, except that they might call for chicken stock. If you prefer strictly vegetarian fare, here is a flavorful substitute for chicken stock that won't compromise on taste.

1. Preheat the oven to 350°. Rub the garlic cloves with 1 teaspoon of the oil and arrange them in a small shallow baking pan. Roast them until they are soft and just beginning to brown, about 20 minutes. Do not overcook the garlic, or it will be bitter. Let the garlic cool, then peel off the skin or squeeze the cloves out of the skin. Set aside.

2. Heat a medium-size stockpot over medium heat. Add the remaining ¼ cup oil and heat it, about 2 minutes. Add the fennel, celery, onion, carrots, and mushrooms and cook, stirring occasionally, until they begin to soften, about 5 minutes. Cover the pot, reduce the heat to low, and "sweat" the vegetables, stirring occasionally, until soft, about 10 minutes.

3. Remove the lid, add the tomatoes and roasted garlic, and cook, stirring occasionally, until the tomatoes start to release some of their liquid, about 5 minutes. Add the peppercorns, salt, and water, increase the heat to medium, and bring to a boil. Reduce the heat again to low and simmer the stock until the liquid reduces by about half, about 2 hours. If any foam rises, skim it off.

4. Strain the stock twice through a cheesecloth-lined strainer or a fine-mesh china cap. Discard the contents of the strainer. Let the stock cool completely before covering and storing it. The stock can be refrigerated for up to 2 days, or it can be frozen for up to 3 weeks. Skim any fat off the surface before using.

shrimp stock

MAKES 4 CUPS

2 tablespoons pure
   olive oil

6 ounces (about 4 cups)
   shrimp shells
   (*see* Note)

1 medium-size carrot,
   coarsely chopped
   (¾ cup)

2 celery ribs, leaves
   removed, coarsely
   chopped (1 cup)

1½ teaspoons freshly
   ground black pepper

½ cup canned or home-
   made tomato sauce

2 cups dry white wine,
   preferably
   Chardonnay

2½ cups cold water

2¼ teaspoons kosher salt

Freezing Tricks

You can easily freeze small quantities of stock in ice-cube trays. Store frozen cubes in a plastic bag or in an airtight container. Or freeze small batches of stock in resealable bags.

To use the frozen stock, simply remove as many cubes from the tray as needed. Or, if you have used a plastic bag, cut it open and peel it away from the stock. When thawing frozen stock in a bag in the refrigerator, be sure to put a dish underneath in case the bag leaks.

Much more complex than fish stock, Shrimp Stock gives a fuller, richer flavor to seafood dishes. I prefer not to substitute anything else for the unique flavor of this stock—nothing compares. For the choice of dry white wine in the stock, I like an oaky Chardonnay; its flavor complements seafood.

1. Heat a medium-size stockpot over medium heat. Add the oil and heat it, about 1 minute. Add the shrimp shells and cook, stirring, until they turn pink, about 5 minutes.

2. Reduce the heat to low, add the carrot, celery, and black pepper, and cook, stirring occasionally, until soft but not brown, about 10 minutes.

3. Stir in the tomato sauce. Cook, stirring, for 1 minute. Add the wine, water, and salt. Bring to a boil over medium heat, then reduce the heat to low and simmer until well flavored, about 45 minutes. Skim every 15 minutes.

4. Strain the stock twice through a cheesecloth-lined strainer or a fine-mesh china cap. Discard the contents of the strainer. Let the stock cool completely before covering and storing it. The stock can be refrigerated for up to 2 days, or it can be frozen for up to 3 weeks. Skim any fat off the surface before using.

Note *It takes about 5 pounds of shrimp in the shell to yield about 6 ounces of shrimp shells. Every time you make a dish that calls for peeled fresh shrimp, reserve the shells and freeze them. That way, when you have the urge, you can make this wonderful stock. Or ask your fishmonger to save shrimp shells for you.*

preserved lemons

6 firm lemons, washed, dried, and quartered (cut once crosswise and then lengthwise)

½ cup freshly squeezed lemon juice

1 cup kosher salt

A Moroccan staple, these lemons bring a special salty and very sour flavor to a dish. They are typically used in *tagines*, or Moroccan stews, but I like to use them in salads and to flavor crusty breaded fish.

It is worth the small effort it takes to make them. I quarter my lemons to speed up the preserving process and to make the pieces easier to handle. When a recipe calls for preserved lemons, use the rind only. The pulpy flesh will be too briny and will not be subtle in the dish you're preparing. The pulp pulls away easily from the rind.

1. Combine the lemons, lemon juice, and ¼ cup of the salt in an 8-cup nonporous container. Cover with a plate that just fits inside the container, and place cans of food or another weight on the plate so that it presses down on the lemons.

2. Let the container sit at room temperature for 7 days, adding 2 tablespoons of salt and stirring the lemons daily.

3. Refrigerate the lemons. Stir them every 3 days for 15 days. When the lemons exude their juice and stay submerged, remove the plate and weights. After this period, the lemons will be ready to use, but they can be refrigerated, covered, for up to 2 months. Use the rind only. Discard the pulp.

special szechwan salt

3 tablespoons
Szechwan pepper-
corns, stems removed

¾ cup kosher salt

2 tablespoons Chinese
five-spice powder

I first learned about the virtues of Szechwan peppercorns (aromatic without the heat of regular peppercorns) and kosher salt (much purer than table salt) from Barbara Tropp in San Francisco. Barbara studied in China and shares her encyclopedic knowledge of that country's food and culture through her books, classes, and restaurant, China Moon.

For my Special Szechwan Salt, I merely added Chinese five-spice powder to the mixture of Szechwan peppercorns and kosher salt. A standard ingredient in the coating of my fried calamari, this seasoned salt is also good rubbed on duck and meats destined for the grill.

Combine all the ingredients in a small frying pan and set it over medium heat. Cook, stirring occasionally, just until the mixture begins to smoke, about 5 minutes. Remove the pan from the heat and process the mixture to a fine powder in a blender or food processor. Transfer it to a small airtight container. The mixture stays fresh for about 1 month. Stir it well before using.

green curry paste

MAKES ABOUT ¾ CUP

Seven   2-inch serrano chilies, seeded and chopped (3 to 4 tablespoons)

3   medium-size garlic cloves, minced (4¼ teaspoons)

3   medium-size shallots, minced (¼ cup)

One   1-inch piece ginger, peeled and minced (2½ teaspoons)

¼   cup minced cilantro (fresh coriander)

1¼   teaspoons ground coriander

1¼   teaspoons ground caraway

⅛   teaspoon freshly ground black pepper

¾   teaspoon ground cumin

¾   teaspoon ground nutmeg

⅛   teaspoon ground cloves

2   teaspoons finely grated lemon zest

½   teaspoon kosher salt

3   tablespoons mild vegetable oil, such as peanut

I like to use this smooth and spicy Thai paste in Green Curry–Coconut Sauce, naturally, but I also add it as an Asian accent to Chicken Sausage with Serrano and Cilantro. For a few simple uses, try a dab of this versatile condiment in chicken soup, or stir a teaspoonful into mayonnaise.

Place all the ingredients in a blender or food processor and purée to a smooth paste. Transfer the paste to a small airtight container. The paste can be refrigerated for up to 3 days, or it can be frozen for up to 3 weeks.

Chile Alert

When handling fresh chilies and their seeds, shield your eyes from any juice, however fine a mist, that may spray up from the chilies, and be sure to rinse the knife and cutting board thoroughly after chopping. Wash your hands well and do not rub your eyes!

authentic cafe spice mix

MAKES 2½ CUPS

- 1 cup ground cumin
- ½ cup dried oregano leaves
- ½ cup granulated garlic
- ½ cup kosher salt
- 2 tablespoons ground cayenne pepper
- 2 tablespoons freshly ground black pepper

We use this spice mix as a basic seasoning salt in some of the Latin dishes at the restaurant. While we usually avoid dried herbs and granulated garlic, this is a dry seasoning mix, stored at room temperature, and fresh herbs and garlic would spoil.

Combine all the ingredients in a small airtight container. The mixture stays fresh for about 1 month. Stir it well before using.

corn tortillas

MAKES ABOUT EIGHTEEN 6-INCH TORTILLAS

- 2 cups masa harina
- 2 cups warm water
- 2 teaspoons kosher salt

If you cannot get fresh tortilla masa, or tortilla dough, from a *tortillaria* (where tortillas are made), preparing your own is the next best alternative.

To make tortilla dough, you need tortilla flour, or masa harina. This special cornmeal is made by first boiling dried corn kernels with unslaked lime, then drying and grinding the corn. Quaker makes masa harina, available in supermarkets.

1. Prepare the tortilla dough: Combine all the ingredients in a large, nonporous bowl and mix well with a spoon or your fingers. Cover with plastic wrap, pressing the wrap directly on the surface of the dough, and let sit until the masa harina absorbs the water, about 20 minutes. The dough can be made ahead and refrigerated for up to 4 hours.

2. Shape and cook the tortillas: Measure out 1½-ounce, or ¼-cup, pieces of dough. Shape the pieces into balls. Place them on a large plastic-lined platter or baking sheet, and cover immediately with plastic wrap to prevent the dough balls from hardening.

3. Heat a *comal* or 10-inch nonstick frying pan over medium-high heat. Lay 1 plastic sandwich bag flat on the bottom of a tortilla press. Place 1 dough ball on the plastic bag. Take care to re-cover the other dough balls with plastic. Lay another sandwich bag on the dough in the press and close the press with medium pressure to obtain a tortilla ¹⁄₁₆ inch thick.

4. Peel the top plastic bag off the tortilla, then carefully but quickly remove the other bag and place the tortilla in the hot pan. Cook the tortilla until firm but not dried out or leathery, with a toasty fragrance, about 30 to 45 seconds on each side. The tortilla should puff during cooking. If it does not, raise the heat slightly. The tortilla should not color. If it does, reduce the heat. Repeat with the remaining dough balls.

5. As the tortillas are done, remove them and stack on a plate. Cover them with a lint-free towel and continue shaping and cooking tortillas.

6. Of course tortillas hot out of the pan are best. But cooled tortillas can be refrigerated, in resealable plastic bags for up to 3 hours. If making them ahead, undercook them slightly and finish cooking in a *comal* or frying pan.

Evoking the Land of Tortillas

The first time I was in Mexico, I was walking down the streets of Puerto Vallarta. There, among the many street vendors, was a flatbed with six people working frantically. They were grilling seafood and meats. One woman was making the most fragrant tortillas I've ever tasted.

At the Authentic Cafe, I try to re-create the same flavors and romantic atmosphere I encounter in my travels. So besides using "authentic" ingredients in my cooking, I use authentic cooking tools. When I make tortillas, for instance, I use a tortilla press, a simple Mexican utensil that flattens tortillas to an even thickness, and a *comal*, a heavy cast-iron griddle that heats evenly and cooks tortillas quickly without browning them.

dry jerk spice rub

MAKES 1½ CUPS

- ¼ cup dried onion flakes
- ¼ cup onion powder
- 2 tablespoons dried thyme leaves
- ¼ cup kosher salt
- 2 tablespoons ground allspice
- 1½ teaspoons ground nutmeg
- 1¼ teaspoons ground cinnamon
- ¼ cup sugar
- 2 tablespoons freshly ground black pepper
- 4½ teaspoons dried chives
- 1 tablespoon dried habanero chile flakes

The Anawak Indians first marinated meats and slow-cooked them in a pit covered with allspice wood. My first taste of this kind of cooking—jerked food—was at Janet's, a small, funky restaurant in south-central Los Angeles. The flavors exploded in my mouth and inspired me to make the trip to Jamaica to taste the real stuff. There, I sampled the offerings at about fifteen jerk stands and subsequently came up with this spice rub. The habanero chile flakes are extremely spicy, yet they have a fruity flavor.

Combine all the ingredients in a small airtight container and store. The mixture stays fresh for about 1 month. Stir it well before using.

Breakfast Dishes

I hesitate to refer to the following dishes as being for breakfast. The fact is, we have these dishes on our menu all day, and it never ceases to amaze me that people do, in fact, order them throughout the day. Perhaps it is because some folks are just happy to find a decent breakfast after 11 A.M. Or maybe they believe that breakfast really is the most important meal of the day, no matter what time it is eaten. Personally, I believe that these foods can be among the most comforting, especially the hot cereals. I know I always appreciated a hot breakfast when I was a child, and if it happened to involve pancakes, so much the better.

These recipes all have some sort of classic, familiar base with my own twist, be it ethnic or some sort of fantasy. I believe that no foods lend themselves better to experimentation than those we eat for breakfast, and it is very satisfying for me to see that so many people seem to enjoy the results of these experiments.

warm breakfast couscous

Makes four 1-cup servings

5 cups milk (whole, low-fat, or nonfat)

12 dried calmyrna figs, tough ends removed, thinly sliced (³/₄ cup)

6 to 8 dried apricot halves, thinly sliced (¹/₂ cup)

¹/₂ cup dark raisins

1¹/₈ teaspoons ground cinnamon

3 tablespoons mild honey, such as orange

¹/₄ teaspoon kosher salt

1¹/₂ cups coarse rapid-cooking couscous

¹/₄ cup slivered almonds, lightly toasted (see Note)

The virtues of hot cereal for breakfast are numerous, but many hot cereals lack texture. This variation on a Moroccan theme is loaded with texture and interesting flavors. And, if made with low-fat milk, it makes a nutritious, low-fat, high-fiber breakfast with lots of staying power. These particular dried fruits are traditional in Moroccan cooking, but you may substitute your favorites.

1. Combine 3 cups of the milk, the dried fruits, ¹/₈ teaspoon of the cinnamon, the honey, and salt in a large, nonreactive saucepan. Bring to a simmer over very low heat, and continue to barely simmer to plump the fruit, about 5 minutes. Do not let the liquid boil or it will curdle.

2. Remove the pan from the heat and stir in the couscous. Cover, and let the couscous rest for 5 minutes.

3. Meanwhile, in a medium-size saucepan, heat the remaining 2 cups of milk over medium heat until bubbles appear around the edge.

4. Spoon the couscous into bowls, mounding it in the center. Sprinkle with the almonds and the remaining cinnamon, then ladle the hot milk around the couscous. Serve immediately.

Note *To lightly toast almonds, bake them in a 350° oven until pale gold, about 8 minutes.*

warm breakfast polenta with chocolate, mascarpone, cinnamon, and almonds

MAKES FOUR 1-CUP SERVINGS

1 cup water

2¼ cups milk

3 tablespoons granulated sugar

½ teaspoon kosher salt

¾ cup fine yellow cornmeal

2 tablespoons mascarpone cheese, stirred to loosen

2 ounces good-quality bittersweet chocolate, finely grated (8 teaspoons)

About ¾ ounce shelled almonds, lightly toasted (see Note, page 34) and chopped medium-fine (8 teaspoons)

¼ teaspoon ground cinnamon

Four 3-inch cinnamon sticks

4 fresh mission figs, if in season, ends trimmed and quartered lengthwise (optional)

I have been addicted to polenta ever since the first time I tasted it at the Zuni Cafe in San Francisco. It always reminds me of being in a warm place on a cold and rainy day, and has the same comforting quality of the hot cereal my mother used to make for me when I was a child growing up in Chicago.

1. Bring the water, milk, sugar, and salt to a boil in a medium-size saucepan over medium heat. Reduce the heat to low and add the cornmeal in a thin stream, stirring constantly with a wooden spoon. Cook the cornmeal, pressing out any lumps with the spoon and stirring constantly, until it thickens and all the grains seem cooked and slightly swollen, about 10 minutes. Taste the polenta; it should be soft, not gritty. The polenta should be thick, but not stiff—you should still be able to serve it with a ladle.

2. Ladle the polenta into soup plates. Use a spoon to make a small, ½-inch-deep depression in the center of each portion. Drop 1½ teaspoons of mascarpone into each depression, then sprinkle with the chocolate. Combine the almonds and cinnamon in a small bowl and sprinkle the mixture over all the polenta. Place a cinnamon stick in each portion, so that your guests may use it to swirl the mascarpone and chocolate.

3. If you are using figs, place 4 quarters around each portion of polenta and serve immediately.

huevos pan de maiz

Sauce

   4   tablespoons (½ stick)
       unsalted butter

   1   large garlic clove,
       minced (1 tablespoon)

   3   small shallots, minced
       (¼ cup)

   ¼   cup all-purpose flour

1¾   cups chicken stock,
       preferably homemade
       (page 24)

2 to 3   teaspoons puréed
       chipotle chile en
       adobo, or to taste
       (see Note)

   ½   teaspoon freshly
       ground black pepper

   ½   teaspoon kosher salt

   1   teaspoon minced
       fresh sage or ½
       teaspoon dried

   1   teaspoon minced
       fresh thyme or
       ½ teaspoon dried

   ⅓   cup heavy cream, at
       room temperature

   ¼   cup pure olive oil

   8   large eggs

Four   freshly baked
       4 x 4–inch cornbread
       squares *(see* Note)

   ¼   cup chopped cilantro
       (fresh coriander)

My biggest seller at breakfast, this hearty and spicy dish arrives at the table accompanied by our homemade Chicken Sausage with Serrano and Cilantro, which when mixed with the fried eggs, cornbread, and chile-infused sauce is just about Heaven. I'd also recommend any good, spicy chicken or turkey sausage you can get your hands on.

1. Preheat the oven to 250°.

2. Prepare the sauce: Heat a small saucepan over low heat. Add the butter, melt it, and then add the garlic and shallots. Cook, stirring, for 2 minutes. Add the flour and cook, whisking constantly, for 2 minutes more to cook the flour without browning it.

3. Still whisking, add the stock to the pan. Continue to whisk, still over low heat, as the stock heats until the mixture thickens, about 5 minutes.

4. Add the chipotle chile, pepper, and salt to the pan. Bring the sauce to the brink of boiling over medium heat, without letting it come to a full boil. Remove the pan from the heat and whisk in the sage, thyme, and cream. Taste and adjust the seasonings. Cover the sauce and keep it warm while preparing the eggs.

5. Prepare the eggs: Heat a medium-size nonstick frying pan over medium heat. Add 1 tablespoon of the oil and heat, about 1 minute. Fry 2 of the eggs just until the whites are set, about 1 minute. Flip the eggs and cook them for about 30 seconds more.

6. Place 1 of the cornbread squares on an ovenproof plate or platter and set the fried eggs on top. Pour $\frac{1}{2}$ cup of sauce over the eggs. Keep the plate warm in the oven while frying the remaining eggs and preparing the other plates.

7. Garnish with the cilantro and serve immediately. Pass any remaining sauce separately.

Note *For the chipotle chile en adobo, purée the entire contents of the can. The unused portion can be refrigerated, covered, for up to 2 weeks.*

For the cornbread, use your favorite recipe. If you make a batch in an 8-inch square pan, which will probably be about 1 inch thick, just cut the cornbread into 4 squares.

Raw Egg Alert

With an alarming incidence of salmonella poisoning in this country, we must all take precautions. The only way to guarantee a safe egg is to thoroughly cook it. But if you still want to eat eggs poached, at least take care to use only the freshest eggs. In any case, never use cracked raw eggs as these cracks will allow aerobic bacteria to grow. Place *cold* eggs in either a hot frying pan or in boiling water. Don't keep cooked eggs warm for too long—eat them as soon as you have prepared everyone's portion.

huevos rancheros

MAKES 4 SERVINGS

2 cups Ranchero Sauce
(recipe follows)

4½ ounces Oaxaca
cheese, grated
(¾ cup)

6 ounces Ranchero
cheese, crumbled
(1 cup)

2 tablespoons
minced cilantro (fresh
coriander)

Eight 6-inch corn tortillas,
preferably homemade
(page 30)

½ cup mild vegetable oil,
such as peanut or corn

8 extra-large eggs

Huevos Rancheros is an extremely easy egg dish to prepare: You fry cheese tortilla "sandwiches" and then top them with fried eggs and Ranchero Sauce.

One of the cheeses in the tortilla "sandwiches" comes from Oaxaca, Mexico. It is braided and resembles string cheese with a somewhat tart flavor. The Cacique brand Oaxaca cheese made in California does not taste quite the same, but still has a nice creaminess. Ranchero cheese, the other cheese in the filling, has an even stronger flavor and a crumbly texture.

1. Preheat the oven to 250°. Warm the Ranchero Sauce in a medium-size saucepan over low heat, stirring often.

2. Combine the Oaxaca cheese, ½ cup of the Ranchero cheese, and the cilantro in a small bowl. Divide this cheese mixture among 4 of the tortillas, and then cover each with a second tortilla to make "sandwiches."

3. Heat a large frying pan over medium heat. Add ¼ cup of the oil and heat, about 2 minutes. Fry the tortilla "sandwiches" until crispy, 2 to 3 minutes on each side. Drain on paper towels.

4. Heat a medium-size nonstick frying pan over medium heat. Add 1 tablespoon of the remaining oil and heat, about 1 minute. Fry 2 of the eggs until the whites are set, about 1 minute. Flip the eggs and cook for 30 seconds more.

5. Place 1 of the fried tortilla sandwiches on an ovenproof plate or platter and set the fried eggs on top. Cover with ½ cup of the sauce, then sprinkle 2 tablespoons of the remaining Ranchero cheese on top. Keep the plate warm in the oven while frying the remaining eggs and preparing the other plates.

6. When all the eggs are prepared, serve them immediately. Pass any remaining sauce separately.

ranchero sauce

MAKES ABOUT 3 CUPS

2 pounds ripe plum tomatoes

3 tablespoons pure olive oil

1 large onion, minced (1½ cups)

1 small green bell pepper, cut into ¼-inch dice

2 large jalapeño chilies, seeded and minced (4 teaspoons)

1½ teaspoons ground cumin

2 large cloves garlic, minced (2 tablespoons)

½ teaspoon freshly ground black pepper

¾ teaspoon kosher salt

¼ cup minced cilantro (fresh coriander)

Jerry Burgos, who is one of my best friends and helped me build the restaurant, gave me this recipe, a personal interpretation of classic Ranchero sauce. He has his own restaurant, the Galaxy Cafe, near Columbus, Ohio. Aside from its natural affinity for eggs, this sauce works well with grilled chicken or meat.

1. Preheat the oven to 400°. Rub 5 of the tomatoes with 1 tablespoon of the oil and arrange them in a small baking pan. Roast them until they are soft and the skins begin to split, 20 to 25 minutes. Heat the broiler and broil the tomatoes until the skins begin to blacken, 1 to 2 minutes on each side. Let the tomatoes cool, then peel and seed them. Purée them in a blender or food processor. You should have about 1 cup of purée. Set aside.

2. Seed the remaining tomatoes and cut them into ¼-inch dice. Heat a medium-size, nonreactive saucepan over medium heat. Add the remaining 2 tablespoons oil and heat, about 1 minute. Add the onion, bell pepper, diced tomatoes, and the chilies, along with the cumin, garlic, and pepper. Cook this mixture, stirring occasionally to prevent the vegetables from sticking and burning, until the tomatoes begin to release their juice, about 5 minutes.

3. Add the tomato purée to the pan and reduce the heat to low. Simmer, stirring often, until the sauce thickens slightly and the peppers are tender, 20 to 25 minutes. Remove the pan from the heat and stir in the salt and cilantro. The sauce can be refrigerated, covered, for up to 2 days.

One 12-inch square of banana leaf

1 pound tamale masa

4 cups Authentic Cafe Black Beans *(page 200)*, optional

1 cup Roasted Poblano Chile Sauce *(recipe follows)*

6 cups water

1 tablespoon cider vinegar

2 teaspoons kosher salt

8 very fresh large eggs

1$\frac{1}{4}$ ounces queso cotija añejo, crumbled ($\frac{1}{4}$ cup)

$\frac{1}{4}$ cup crème fraîche or sour cream, at room temperature

$\frac{1}{2}$ hoja santa, tightly rolled and then cut into $\frac{1}{16}$-inch strips

. . . because that's where I first ate poached eggs in masa cups, steamed on a banana leaf. Banana leaves lend an inimitable flavor to other ingredients. Toasting the banana leaf makes it even more fragrant.

Choose very fresh eggs for this recipe. The whites of the freshest eggs cling to the yolk and make shapely poached eggs. Vinegar in the poaching water also discourages the white from spreading. For the full flavor of Huevos de Mexico City as we serve it at the Authentic Cafe, serve Authentic Cafe Black Beans on the side.

1. Rinse the banana leaf and pat it dry. Toast it above a low open flame or directly on the burner of an electric range set on low, for about 20 seconds on one side, moving it constantly, then for about 15 seconds on the other side. The leaf will shrink slightly and deepen in color. Line the bottom of a steamer basket with the toasted leaf.

2. Measure out eight 2-ounce, or scant $\frac{1}{4}$-cup, pieces of masa. Flatten 1 piece of the masa between your hands and form a cup just the size to hold a poached egg, about 2$\frac{3}{4}$ inches wide, 1 inch high, and $\frac{1}{2}$ inch deep. Shape all the masa pieces in this way, and place them in the leaf-lined steamer basket.

3. Bring about $\frac{1}{2}$ inch of water in the bottom of the steamer to a boil over high heat. Verify that the water does not evaporate completely during cooking. Reduce the heat to low so the water simmers, place the steamer basket on top, and cover. Steam the tamale cups until they are firm and slightly swollen, about 20 minutes. They will droop a bit, but should still remain somewhat cup-like.

4. While the masa cups are steaming, gently heat the Authentic Cafe Black Beans, if using, and the Roasted Poblano Chile Sauce. Keep them warm in covered saucepans.

5. About 7 minutes before the masa cups are done, bring the 6 cups of water to a boil with the vinegar and salt in a large wide, shallow saucepan or sauté pan. Once the water boils, reduce the heat to low so that it barely simmers. Carefully crack one of the eggs into a small shallow bowl, taking care not to break the yolk. Slide the egg into the simmering water, then, using a wooden spoon or a skimmer, move the egg to one side of the pan. Quickly repeat this with 3 more eggs, keeping them separate in the pan. Poach the eggs for 3 to 5 minutes, depending on how well you like your yolk cooked. Obviously, the first eggs in the pan should be the first ones out, so try to keep track. Remove the eggs with a wire skimmer or a slotted spoon and drain them on paper towels. Repeat with the remaining eggs. Alternatively, if you have an egg poacher, poach the eggs according to the manufacturer's instructions.

6. If using the Authentic Cafe Black Beans, spread 1 cup of them on half of each of 4 plates and sprinkle them with the cheese. Place about 2 tablespoons of the warmed sauce on the other half of the plate. (The sauce need not cover the rest of the plate.) Using a spoon or a large wide spatula, carefully lift the steamed masa cups off the banana leaf and place 2, side by side, on the sauce. Spoon a little more sauce in each masa cup, then set 1 poached egg on top. Spoon the rest of the sauce over the eggs.

7. Stir the crème fraîche or sour cream to make it fluid. If you have a squeeze bottle (like an old-fashioned ketchup bottle), use it to squeeze lines of cream over the eggs. Or drizzle the cream from a spoon. Garnish with the hoja santa and serve immediately.

roasted poblano chile sauce

MAKES ABOUT 1½ CUPS

3 medium-size
poblano chilies

4 teaspoons pure
olive oil

4 large garlic cloves,
peeled

1 cup chicken stock,
preferably homemade
(page 24), warmed

¼ teaspoon freshly
ground white pepper

1 teaspoon kosher salt

2 tablespoons
chopped cilantro
(fresh coriander)

Try this sauce also with "chilaquiles." Scramble up some eggs and stir in leftover tortilla chips and sautéed vegetables (onions, mushrooms, and corn, for example). Spoon Roasted Poblano Chile Sauce over the top, sprinkle generously with Oaxaca, Ranchero, or Monterey Jack cheese, add a lid, and bake in a moderate oven until the cheese melts.

1. Preheat the oven to 450°. Rub the chilies with 1 tablespoon of the oil and arrange them in a small baking pan. Roast them until the skin begins to blister, about 20 minutes.

2. Once the chilies have roasted for 15 minutes, rub the garlic cloves with the remaining 1 teaspoon of oil, add them to the baking pan, and roast for 5 minutes.

3. Remove the baking pan from the oven. Place the roasted chilies in a small bowl, cover with plastic wrap, and let them "sweat" for about 5 minutes. Peel the thin outer skin from the chilies, then remove their stems and seeds.

4. Place the peeled chilies, roasted garlic, the stock, pepper, salt, and cilantro in a blender or food processor and purée until smooth. The sauce can be refrigerated, covered, for up to 2 days, or it can be frozen for up to 1 week.

sour cream–mango pancakes with candied pecans

Makes 4 servings,
3 pancakes each

Dry ingredients

1 tablespoon granulated sugar

1¼ cups sifted unbleached all-purpose flour

1 teaspoon baking powder

1 teaspoon baking soda

½ teaspoon kosher salt

Wet ingredients

3 large eggs, beaten

2 cups sour cream

3 tablespoons unsalted butter, melted

One 1-inch piece ginger, peeled and minced (1 tablespoon)

8 teaspoons mild vegetable oil

1 medium-size ripe mango, pitted, peeled, and cut into ¼-inch dice (1 cup)

28 Candied Pecans (page 125)

1 cup pure maple syrup, warmed

I love tropical fruit in the morning, and these pancakes will show you why. The pancakes themselves are light and fluffy, while the pecan crunch and smooth mango make for an eye-opening change that need not be enjoyed only for breakfast. Be sure to turn the pancakes only once, and don't overcook them or they will become tough. If mangos are not in season, or if you just prefer another fruit, try peeled, seeded, and diced papaya

1. Preheat the oven to 200°, or if it has a "warm" setting, use it.

2. Combine the dry ingredients in a large bowl and mix well with a whisk. Whisk together the wet ingredients in a medium-size bowl. Pour the wet ingredients into the dry ingredients and whisk until very smooth.

3. Heat a large nonstick griddle or frying pan over medium-low heat. Brush with 2 teaspoons of the oil. Pour ¼ cup of batter on the griddle for each pancake. It will spread to a diameter of 4 to 5 inches. If you can make more than 1 pancake at a time without crowding them, please do so.

4. Sprinkle the batter on the griddle with about 1 tablespoon of diced mango. Wait for the pancake to begin to bubble, about 1 to 1½ minutes. Flip the pancake with a wide metal spatula and cook until golden brown, another 1 to 1½ minutes. If it isn't browning, increase the heat under the pan. Remove the pancake to an ovenproof platter or plates and keep warm, covered loosely with aluminum foil, in the oven. Continue with the rest of the batter.

5. Sprinkle the pancakes with the Candied Pecans and serve immediately. Pass the maple syrup separately.

Starters

For me, the excitement over a meal starts at the very beginning. You can combine so many different options in order to create a memorable experience, and if you do that right from the start, tantalizing your guests with the anticipation of what is to come, so much the better.

I try to get people to use their hands as much as possible when eating at the restaurant. (No one has ever described the Authentic Cafe as a formal dining establishment.) I feel that this puts them in touch with foods from all around the world, very much as if they were traveling and tasting different foods at street stalls.

When I go out to eat, I often prefer to sample a variety of starters. Sometimes, I even make a whole meal of them. I enjoy combining different cuisines and types of food on one plate, or at least within the same meal. At the Authentic Cafe, we have a variety of small starter plates, giving people a chance to do the same. We also provide forks, just in case.

authentic guacamole

MAKES ABOUT 2 CUPS; 4 SERVINGS

2 large ripe avocados,
preferably Haas

3 tablespoons
minced onion

1 medium-size
serrano chile,
seeded and minced
(1½ teaspoons)

2 tablespoons
minced cilantro
(fresh coriander)

2 tablespoons freshly
squeezed lemon juice

2 large jalapeño chilies,
grilled (see Steps 1
and 2, page 63),
seeded, and minced
(about 2 tablespoons)

Pinch freshly ground
black pepper

1 teaspoon kosher salt

Haas avocados, the variety with the dark green, pebbly skin, are much richer and more buttery than other varieties. For this reason, they are the avocados of choice for guacamole. And here is the definitive guacamole recipe for using these superior avocados. It's a classic, with no tomatoes, and simply delicious.

If you are making guacamole ahead of time, save one of the pits and store it in the guacamole. It will prevent the guacamole from turning brown.

1. Cut the avocados in half lengthwise and remove the pits. Reserve 1 pit. Scoop the pulp of the avocados into a small, nonreactive bowl. Mash the pulp coarsely using a fork or a whisk.

2. Add the remaining ingredients to the bowl and mix, leaving the guacamole fairly chunky. The guacamole can be refrigerated for up to 2 hours. Place the reserved pit in the guacamole and cover with plastic wrap, pressing the plastic directly on the surface of the guacamole.

The Right Bowl

In general, we refer to glass or stainless-steel bowls as "nonreactive." Specifically, you want a bowl that will not react with whatever is being mixed inside. Furthermore, for some recipes you should use a nonporous bowl (unglazed ceramic or wood would *not* work), which will not absorb the oils from the avocados and chilies.

pan-asian guacamole

MAKES ABOUT 2 CUPS; 4 SERVINGS

2 large ripe avocados,
preferably Haas

1/4 cup pink sweet pickled
(Japanese) ginger,
chopped

1/4 cup plain low-fat
(or nonfat) yogurt

1 tablespoon wasabi
powder

2 green onions, white
and light green parts
only, chopped
(3 tablespoons)

2 tablespoons black
sesame seeds, toasted
(see Note)

1 teaspoon kosher salt

2 tablespoons freshly
squeezed lime juice

While in Hawaii, it came to me that these Pacific flavors would go well with any grilled fish or with freshly fried taro or potato chips. This version of guacamole can also be used as a vegetable dip.

1. Cut the avocados in half lengthwise and remove the pits. Reserve 1 pit. Scoop the pulp of the avocados into a small nonreactive bowl. Mash the pulp coarsely using a fork or a whisk.

2. In another nonreactive bowl, combine the remaining ingredients. Make sure that no lumps remain in the wasabi. Stir this mixture gently into the mashed avocado. The guacamole can be refrigerated for up to 2 hours. Place the reserved pit in the guacamole and cover with plastic wrap, pressing the plastic directly on the surface of the guacamole.

Note *If the package doesn't specify that they are toasted, toast sesame seeds by baking them in a 350° oven for 5 minutes.*

Trick of the Trade

To remove the pit of an avocado easily, first cut the avocado in half lengthwise with a large sharp knife, following the outline of the pit. Jab the pit with the knife, leaving the point of the knife in the pit. Twist the knife slightly and the pit will twist out with it.

thai chicken satay

MAKES 3 OR 4 SERVINGS

Marinade

⅓ cup ketjap manis

⅓ cup unsweetened coconut milk

One ½-inch piece ginger, peeled and minced (1 teaspoon)

1 small garlic clove, minced (1 teaspoon)

½ teaspoon freshly ground black pepper

½ teaspoon chile (satay) oil

1 pound chicken tenderloins ("tenders"), tendons removed

6 to 8 wooden skewers, soaked in warm water for at least 1 hour

Thai Peanut Sauce (recipe follows)

Marinating morsels of food and then grilling them on skewers has been used for centuries as a fast, easy, and delicious way to cook. I love the traditional recipes for skewer cooking, such as this Thai classic, as well as the new combinations you can create. With Chicken Satay, Indonesian Cucumber Salad is a natural.

Ketjap manis, which is called for in this marinade, is a sweet soy sauce. Take care in grilling not to burn the chicken because of the sugar in the soy sauce.

1. Combine all the marinade ingredients in a medium-size, nonreactive bowl and mix well. Add the chicken and stir until all the pieces are covered with marinade. Refrigerate, covered, for at least 4 hours and up to 1 day.

2. Just before serving, prepare a fire in a barbecue grill or preheat the broiler. Oil the grill/broiler rack. Drain the chicken, leaving any clinging marinade. Thread 2 chicken pieces onto each skewer, keeping them elongated, not bunched up.

3. Place the chicken skewers on the grill/broiler rack about 6 inches from the heat and cook just until done, 1 or 2 minutes on each side. Serve immediately. Pass the Thai Peanut Sauce and, if you like, Indonesian Cucumber Salad separately.

thai peanut sauce

½ cup crunchy
  peanut butter

⅓ cup unsweetened
  coconut milk

2 tablespoons
  tamarind concentrate

1 tablespoon nam pla
  (Thai fish sauce)

1 small garlic clove,
  minced (1 teaspoon)

One ¼-inch piece ginger,
  peeled and minced
  (½ teaspoon)

1 packed tablespoon
  light or dark brown
  sugar

1 lemongrass stalk,
  bottom 3 or 4 inches
  only, tough outer
  leaves removed,
  minced (2 tablespoons)

1 teaspoon chile
  (satay) oil

¼ cup very hot tap water

This is my version of a classic dipping sauce. In addition to Thai Chicken Satay, it goes well with everything from grilled vegetables to grilled tuna, catfish, and swordfish.

Mix all the ingredients, except the water, in a small, nonreactive bowl. Add the hot water and mix well. The sauce can be refrigerated, covered, for up to 2 days. Serve at room temperature. Stir just before serving.

49

hummus

One 15-ounce can chick-
       peas (garbanzo beans),
       drained (1½ cups)

  1   medium-size
       garlic clove, minced
       (2½ teaspoons)

  5   tablespoons tahini

  ¼   cup freshly squeezed
       lemon juice

  ½   teaspoon freshly
       ground black pepper

  1   scant teaspoon
       kosher salt

  5   tablespoons
       extra-virgin olive oil

This earthy, silken spread is great as a dipping sauce with Falafel, the deep-fried chickpea disks. You can also try wrapping hummus in a sheet of nori, or Japanese seaweed, with some shredded carrots, onion sprouts, and sunflower seeds for a Middle Eastern take on sushi.

Place all the ingredients in a food processor and purée until very smooth. The Hummus can be refrigerated, covered, for up to 1 day.

grilled shrimp, mango, and avocado cocktail

MAKES 4 SERVINGS

1/2 pound medium-size raw shrimp, peeled and deveined

1 teaspoon kosher salt, plus additional for seasoning the shrimp

1/4 teaspoon freshly ground black pepper, plus additional for seasoning the shrimp

6-inch bamboo skewers, soaked in water for 8 hours and drained

1 large serrano chile, seeded and minced (1 1/2 teaspoons)

1 small or 1/2 medium-size jicama, peeled and cut into 1/4-inch dice (1/2 cup)

1/4 small red onion, minced (1/4 cup)

One 1-inch piece ginger, peeled and minced (1 tablespoon)

2 tablespoons chopped cilantro (fresh coriander)

1/4 cup freshly squeezed lime juice

1/4 medium-size red bell pepper, cut into 1/16-inch dice (2 tablespoons)

1/4 cup extra-virgin olive oil

1 medium-size ripe mango, pitted, peeled, and cut into 1/2-inch dice (1 cup)

1 large ripe avocado, preferably Haas, pitted, peeled, and cut into 1/2-inch dice (1 cup)

If you have a barbecue in your backyard or on your balcony, try using some kind of fruitwood, such as applewood, to enhance the flavor of the shrimp. The smokiness of the shrimp cooked this way is fantastic with the sweet mango and the silky avocado.

1. Prepare a fire in a barbecue grill or preheat the broiler. Oil the grill/broiler rack. Butterfly the shrimp by cutting down their backs two-thirds of the way through to the belly side. Season them lightly with salt and pepper. Thread two shrimp on each of the skewers.

2. Place the shrimp on the grill/broiler rack about 6 inches from the heat and cook just until they turn pink, 1 or 1 1/2 minutes on each side. Let the shrimp cool. Discard the skewers.

3. In a medium-size, nonreactive bowl, combine all the ingredients, except the shrimp and the avocado, and toss well. Using a large rubber spatula or spoon, gently fold in the shrimp and avocado, making sure they are well coated with lime juice and oil. The cocktail can be refrigerated, covered, for up to 2 hours. Toss gently before serving.

grilled lemon squid

MAKES 4 SERVINGS

1 pound small cleaned
squid, with tentacles

7 tablespoons
extra-virgin olive oil

6 tablespoons freshly
squeezed lemon juice

2 small garlic cloves,
minced (2 teaspoons)

1/4 teaspoon freshly
ground black pepper

1/2 teaspoon kosher salt

3/4 teaspoon hot sauce

3 tablespoons minced
Italian (flat-leaf)
parsley

1 1/2 teaspoons minced
fresh oregano

This one's great for any simple barbecue. The flavors are very clean and bright. Mix up some margaritas and enjoy the sun!

1. Prepare a fire in a barbecue grill using fruitwood, if possible, or preheat the broiler. Oil the grill/broiler rack.

2. Cut off and discard the beak of each squid, the hard ball in the tentacles. Pull out and discard the clear, plastic-like "pen" from inside the body. Score the squid bodies in a cross-hatch fashion. In a medium-size bowl, mix the scored squid with 1/4 cup of the oil.

3. Place the squid on the grill/broiler rack about 6 inches from the heat and cook just until opaque and tender, about 2 minutes on each side. Do not overcook. Transfer to plates or a platter.

4. Meanwhile, in a small, nonreactive bowl, combine the remaining ingredients to make a sauce.

5. Once the squid is cooked, spoon the sauce over it and serve immediately.

Squid Success

Scoring squid before putting it on the grill allows it to cook more quickly without getting tough, and keeps it from curling.

If your grill grates are so wide that the squid may slip through, thread the squid onto skewers first, then lay the skewers crosswise on the grill. If the skewers are wooden, be sure to soak them in water for at least 1 hour to prevent them from burning on the grill.

2 cups mild vegetable oil, such as corn

Crust

1 cup rice flour

1/2 cup cornstarch

1 teaspoon baking powder

2 1/2 teaspoons Special Szechwan Salt *(page 28)*

1 tablespoon black sesame seeds, toasted *(see* Note, *page 47)*

1 pound small or medium-size cleaned calamari, with tentacles, bodies sliced into 1/4-inch rings (do not slice the tentacles)

1 cup milk, poured into a shallow bowl

I can't stop eating these calamari when I make them. By using a combination of rice flour and cornstarch, you will get a very crunchy coating. The Special Szechwan Salt, seasoned with Szechwan peppercorns and Chinese five-spice powder, gives the calamari a very special fragrance. Use these fried calamari in Crispy Calamari Salad, or serve them as an appetizer with Indonesian Ketjap Manis–Chile Sauce.

1. Heat the oil to 375° in a medium-size saucepan over medium heat. Use a candy thermometer to verify the temperature.

2. Combine all the crust ingredients in a 10-inch pie pan or medium-size shallow bowl and mix well. Dredge the calamari in the crust mixture, then dip it in the milk. Dredge the calamari in the crust mixture again and shake off any excess.

3. Fry the calamari, in 3 or 4 batches, in the hot oil until brown and quite crisp, about 1 minute per batch. Do not overcook or the calamari will be tough. Verify that the oil is still at 375° between batches. (If the oil is not hot enough, the calamari will take too long to cook and will toughen; if the oil is too hot, the crust will burn and the calamari may not cook through.) Using a slotted spoon or wire skimmer, remove the calamari from the oil and drain on paper towels. Serve immediately.

scallop ceviche

¾ pound medium-size sea scallops, rubbery white hinge removed, cut horizontally into ¼-inch-thick slices

½ small ripe mango, pitted, peeled, and cut into ½-inch dice (½ cup)

⅓ small red bell pepper, cut into ⅛-inch dice

½ large ripe avocado, preferably Haas, pitted, peeled, and cut into ½-inch dice (½ cup)

1 medium-size jalapeño chile, seeded and minced (2 teaspoons)

1 teaspoon minced cilantro (fresh coriander)

6 tablespoons freshly squeezed lime juice

2 tablespoons pure olive oil

½ teaspoon kosher salt

One ¾-inch piece ginger, peeled and minced (2 teaspoons)

¼ teaspoon freshly ground white pepper

I love to eat ceviche, which is simply marinated food, typically seafood, "cooked" by the acid in citrus juice. How long you let it marinate depends on how cooked you like your seafood. Scallops take well to this treatment, and here the sweetness of the mango plays against the scallops' clean, briny flavor. Chilies give the ceviche just the right bite.

Combine all the ingredients in a medium-size, nonreactive bowl and mix well. Refrigerate, covered, for at least ½ hour and up to 3 hours. Serve in sundae glasses.

crab and avocado napoleons

MAKES 4 SERVINGS

- $\frac{1}{2}$ pound lump crabmeat, carefully picked over
- 2 green onions, white and light green parts only, thinly sliced (3 tablespoons)
- 1 large shallot, minced (2 tablespoons)
- 1 lemongrass stalk, bottom 3 or 4 inches only, tough outer leaves removed, minced (2 tablespoons)
- One 1-inch strip red bell pepper, cut into $\frac{1}{8}$-inch dice (2 tablespoons)
- $\frac{1}{2}$ cup freshly squeezed lemon juice
- $\frac{1}{4}$ teaspoon freshly ground black pepper
- 1 teaspoon kosher salt
- $\frac{1}{4}$ teaspoon toasted sesame oil
- $3\frac{1}{2}$ teaspoons black sesame seeds, toasted (see Note, page 47)
- $1\frac{1}{2}$ cups mild vegetable oil, such as soy
- 12 small, square won ton skins
- $\frac{1}{4}$ pound firm, nutty-flavored sprouts, such as sunflower
- $\frac{1}{2}$ ripe avocado, preferably Haas, pitted, peeled, and cut length-wise into 12 slices

These are a playful takeoff on the traditional dessert specialty, with no sacrifice of elegance. Here, fried won ton skins stand in for the classic puff-pastry layers, and crabmeat and avocado replace the pastry cream filling. The crab and avocado combination reminds me of the California rolls eaten in sushi bars today.

1. In a large, nonreactive bowl, combine the crabmeat, green onions, shallot, lemongrass, bell pepper, lemon juice, black pepper, salt, sesame oil, $1\frac{1}{2}$ teaspoons of the sesame seeds, and $\frac{1}{2}$ cup of the vegetable oil. Toss gently, then let this mixture sit while preparing the won ton skins.

2. Heat the remaining 1 cup of vegetable oil to 360° in an 8-inch shallow pan. Use a candy thermometer to verify the oil temperature. Fry 2 or 3 of the won ton skins at a time, keeping them flat and turning them once with tongs, until golden, about 20 seconds on each side. Remove them and drain on paper towels.

3. Arrange the sprouts on plates. Place 1 fried won ton skin in the center of each plate, then top with 1 tablespoon of the crab mixture and 1 slice of avocado. Repeat the layering, ending with a layer of crab/avocado, until each plate has 3 stacked won ton–crab–avocado layers. Sprinkle with the remaining 2 teaspoons sesame seeds. Serve immediately.

poblano chilies stuffed with chicken, potatoes, olives, and raisins

MAKES 4 SERVINGS

1 cup mild vegetable oil, such as canola

4 medium-size poblano chilies

Stuffing

2 tablespoons pure olive oil

One 4-ounce skinless, boneless chicken breast half, cut into ⅓-inch dice

⅓ cup pitted Spanish green olives, sliced

⅓ cup dark raisins, soaked in warm water for ½ hour and drained

1 small red potato, unpeeled, cut into ¼-inch dice (⅓ cup)

1 large garlic clove, minced (1 tablespoon)

1 teaspoon ground cumin

¼ teaspoon freshly ground black pepper

½ teaspoon minced fresh oregano, or ¼ teaspoon dried

⅓ cup chicken stock, preferably homemade (page 24)

These chilies are full of contrasting flavors. The salty olives, combined with the sweet raisins, practically explode in your mouth. The Roasted Tomato Sauce is mild, so as not to overpower the ingredients in the chilies.

1. Heat the vegetable oil to 375° in a small saucepan. Use a candy thermometer to verify the oil temperature. Fry 1 chile at a time, using tongs to turn it every few minutes, just until the skin begins to blister, about 5 to 6 minutes total. Do not overcook the chilies, or the flesh will become too fragile to stuff. Be careful not to puncture the skin with the tongs.

2. Place the fried chilies in a small, nonreactive, nonporous bowl, cover with plastic wrap, and let them "sweat" for about 5 minutes. Peel the thin outer skin from the chilies. Leaving the stems intact, cut a slit lengthwise along 1 side of each chile and remove all the seeds. Set aside. The vegetable oil can be reused for frying. It will retain some spiciness.

3. Prepare the stuffing: Heat a 10-inch sauté pan or frying pan over medium heat until hot. Add the olive oil and heat it, about 1 minute. Place the chicken, olives, raisins, and potato in the pan, along with the garlic, cumin, black pepper, and dried oregano, if using. Stir quickly with a wooden spoon to keep the ingredients from sticking. Cook, stirring, for 1 minute.

4. Add the stock and cook over medium heat until the liquid has almost evaporated. Add the fresh oregano, if using, and the salt. Remove the pan from the heat and stir in the cilantro. Place the mixture in a large bowl and let it cool. Mix in the cheese.

1/4 teaspoon kosher salt

2 tablespoons minced cilantro (fresh coriander)

2 1/2 ounces queso fresco or Monterey Jack cheese, grated (1/2 cup)

Roasted Tomato Sauce *(recipe follows)*

2 tablespoons pure olive oil

4 lime wedges

5. Stuff the chilies, packing them tightly by hand, or use a small spoon. Overlap the edges of the slit to seal. Place them slit down on an oiled pie pan or a small shallow baking pan. The chilies can be stuffed and refrigerated, covered, for up to 6 hours. Bring them to room temperature before baking.

6. Preheat the oven to 400°. Warm the Roasted Tomato Sauce in a small saucepan over low heat, stirring occasionally. Rub the stuffed chilies with the 2 tablespoons olive oil and bake them, until a small sharp knife inserted in a chile comes out hot to the touch, 7 to 10 minutes.

7. Ladle the warmed sauce onto plates or a platter. Using a spatula, place the hot chilies on the sauce. Garnish each chile with a lime wedge and serve immediately. Pass any remaining sauce separately.

roasted tomato sauce

MAKES ABOUT 2 CUPS

2 tablespoons pure olive oil

8 large ripe plum tomatoes

2 tablespoons extra-virgin olive oil

1/4 cup freshly squeezed lime juice

1/2 teaspoon freshly ground black pepper

1/2 teaspoon kosher salt

This tomato sauce gains an intense flavor from roasting. Try it also with grilled snapper or another mild fish.

1. Preheat the oven to 400°. Rub the tomatoes with the pure olive oil and arrange them in a small shallow baking pan. Roast them until they are soft and the skins begin to split, 20 to 25 minutes. Heat the broiler and broil the tomatoes until the skins begin to blacken, 1 to 2 minutes on each side.

2. Remove the pan from the oven. Let the tomatoes cool, then peel and seed them. Purée them in a blender or food processor. Place the purée in a medium-size bowl and stir in the remaining ingredients. Serve at room temperature. The sauce can be refrigerated, covered, for up to 2 days.

MAKES 4 SERVINGS

1 cup mild vegetable oil, such as canola

4 medium-size poblano chilies

12 ounces Oaxaca cheese, grated (2 cups)

3 ounces smoked mozzarella cheese, grated ($\frac{1}{2}$ cup)

1$\frac{1}{2}$ ounces smoked Gouda cheese, grated ($\frac{1}{4}$ cup)

$\frac{1}{2}$ cup minced cilantro (fresh coriander)

Roasted Tomato and Chipotle Chile Sauce (recipe follows)

Blue cornmeal mixture

1 cup blue cornmeal

1 tablespoon ground cumin

2 small garlic cloves, minced (2$\frac{1}{2}$ teaspoons)

1 tablespoon freshly ground black pepper

1 tablespoon kosher salt

$\frac{1}{2}$ teaspoon minced fresh oregano, or $\frac{1}{4}$ teaspoon dried

$\frac{1}{2}$ teaspoon ground cayenne pepper

$\frac{1}{2}$ cup all-purpose flour, spread in a shallow bowl

3 eggs, beaten in a shallow bowl

4 lime wedges

This is my version of the classic Mexican dish. The chilies have a crisp crust, while the filling remains creamy. Serve these on Roasted Tomato and Chipotle Chile Sauce, and you will surely find that the richness of the cheese filling is complemented by the sauce's smoky spiciness.

1. Heat the oil to 375° in a small saucepan. Use a candy thermometer to verify the oil temperature. Fry 1 chile at a time, using tongs to turn it every few minutes, just until the skin begins to blister, about 5 minutes total. Do not overcook the chilies, or the flesh will become too fragile to stuff. Be careful not to puncture the skin with the tongs.

2. Place the fried chilies in a small bowl, cover with plastic wrap, and let them "sweat" for about 5 minutes. Peel the thin outer skin from the chilies. Leaving the stems intact, cut a slit lengthwise along 1 side of each chile and remove all the seeds. Set aside.

3. Combine the cheeses and cilantro in a small bowl and mix well. Stuff the chilies with this mixture, packing them tightly by hand or use a small spoon. Overlap the edges of the slit to seal. The chilies can be stuffed and refrigerated, covered, for up to 6 hours. Bring them to room temperature before proceding.

4. Preheat the oven to 375°. Heat the oil to 375° or verify the temperature. Warm the Roasted Tomato and Chipotle Chile Sauce in a small saucepan over low heat, stirring occasionally.

5. Combine all the cornmeal mixture ingredients in a shallow bowl. Dredge the stuffed chilies in the flour, dip them in the beaten eggs, and then roll in the cornmeal mixture. Make sure that each chile is well coated with flour, egg, and cornmeal mixture, and that the seam is well covered with coating as well.

6. Using tongs to turn the chilies as needed (they will not be submerged in this small quantity of oil), fry 1 or 2 chilies at a time, seam side down, in the hot oil until crispy, about 1 minute on each side. Drain on paper towels. The oil can be strained and reused for frying. It will retain some spiciness.

7. Place the fried chilies slit down in an oiled pie pan or a small shallow baking pan and bake them until a small sharp knife inserted in a chile comes out hot to the touch, 5 to 7 minutes.

8. Ladle the warmed sauce onto plates or a platter. Using a spatula, place the hot chilies on the sauce. Garnish each chile with a lime wedge and serve immediately. Pass any remaining sauce separately.

roasted tomato and chipotle chile sauce

MAKES ABOUT 2½ CUPS

- 10 large ripe plum tomatoes
- 1 small onion, halved
- 4 teaspoons pure olive oil
- 2 small garlic cloves, minced (1½ teaspoons)
- ¼ cup minced cilantro (fresh coriander)
- 1 tablespoon chipotle chile en adobo, puréed (see Note, page 37)
- ¼ cup freshly squeezed lime juice
- 2 teaspoons kosher salt
- 1¼ teaspoons freshly ground black pepper
- ¼ cup fruity extra-virgin olive oil

An essential element of Blue Corn Chiles Rellenos, this sauce is also delicious with grilled chicken or fish. The chipotle chilies lend a nice smoky flavor. The slightly charred skins of the tomatoes highlight the flavor of the chilies and give the sauce a rough look.

1. Preheat the oven to 400°. Rub the tomatoes and onion with the pure olive oil. Arrange the tomatoes and onion in a large shallow baking pan. Roast them until they are soft and the skins begin to split, about 20 to 25 minutes. Heat the broiler and broil them until the skins begin to blacken, 1 to 2 minutes per side.

2. Remove the pan from the oven. Let the tomatoes cool, then leave the skin on but seed the tomatoes. Whirl them with the onion in a blender or food processor to a medium purée.

3. Place the purée in a medium-size, nonreactive bowl and stir in the remaining ingredients. Let the sauce sit for about 20 minutes to allow the flavors to meld. Serve at room temperature. The sauce can be refrigerated, covered, for up to 2 days.

seafood tamales in a banana leaf with hoja santa

MAKES 4 SERVINGS

Four 6 x 8-inch pieces of banana leaf

1¼ pounds prepared tamale masa

½ pound medium-size sea scallops, rubbery white hinge removed, cut horizontally into ¼-inch-thick slices

¼ pound raw peeled rock shrimp

Roasted Poblano Chile Sauce *(page 42)*

Four 2 x 2-inch pieces of hoja santa

Four 6 x 6-inch squares of aluminum foil

These tamales, flavored with anise-like hoja santa and wrapped in toasted banana leaves, are simply fantastic. I first ate something similar to them in Oaxaca, Mexico, where Zapotec Indian women were serving tamales out of baskets in the outdoor markets.

1. Rinse the pieces of banana leaf and pat them dry. Remove the tough outer stems and outer edges. Toast each piece above a low, open flame or directly on the burner of an electric range set on low, for about 20 seconds on one side, moving it constantly, then for about 15 seconds on the other side. The leaves will shrink slightly and deepen in color

2. Lay 1 piece of banana leaf on a work surface. Place ¼ cup of the tamale masa in the center of the leaf and shape the masa into a rectangle approximately 2 x 3 x ¼ inches. Top with one-quarter of the sliced scallops and one-quarter of the shrimp, distributing the seafood evenly over the masa.

3. Drizzle 2 tablespoons of Roasted Poblano Chile Sauce over the seafood and top this with a piece of hoja santa. Flatten another ¼ cup of masa to a rectangle the same size as the first, and cover the tamale with it. Seal the edges. Drizzle 1 more tablespoon of sauce on top.

4. Wrap the long sides of the banana leaf over the tamale, then fold the short sides over the top. Set the leaf-wrapped tamale on a piece of aluminum foil and wrap it in the foil. Prepare the other tamales in the same way.

5. Bring about ½ inch of water in the bottom of a steamer to a boil over high heat. Verify that the water does not evaporate completely during cooking. Place the tamales in the steamer basket. Reduce the heat to low so the water simmers, place the steamer basket on top, and cover. Steam the tamales until they feel set when lightly squeezed, about 30 minutes, then remove the basket from the heat and let the tamales sit until they firm up slightly, about 1 minute.

6. Remove the aluminum foil and serve the tamales with the remaining sauce, allowing your guests to further unwrap their own tamales. Pass the remaining Roasted Poblano Chile Sauce separately.

chicken tamales in banana leaves

MAKES 12 TAMALES; 6 SERVINGS

- 1 small red bell pepper
- 4 jalapeño chilies
- 1 tablespoon pure olive oil
- Twelve 4-inch squares of banana leaf
- ½ pound (2 sticks) unsalted butter, at room temperature
- 2 cups masa harina
- ½ teaspoon baking powder
- ¼ cup dark raisins, soaked for ½ hour in warm water, then drained
- ¼ cup Spanish green olives, pitted and sliced
- 1½ cups chicken stock, preferably home-made (page 24)
- ½ pound cooked skinless, boneless chicken breast half, cut into ¼-inch dice or shredded
- 1 small garlic clove, minced (1 teaspoon)
- 1 teaspoon freshly ground black pepper
- 1 teaspoon kosher salt

In El Salvador, these tamales are wrapped in banana leaves, which add their unique flavor to the sweetness of the raisins and the briny flavor of the olives.

1. Preheat the broiler. Rub the bell pepper and the jalapeños with the oil and arrange separately on baking sheets or pie plates. Broil the bell pepper until the skin begins to blister, about 2 minutes on each side. Broil the jalapeños until the skin begins to blister, about 1 minute on each side. Place the broiled bell pepper and jalapeño in a small bowl, cover with plastic wrap, and let them "sweat" for about 20 minutes. Peel the thin outer skin from the bell pepper and jalapeños and remove the stem and seeds. Cut the bell pepper into matchstick strips. Cut the jalapeños into ⅛-inch dice.

2. Rinse the squares of banana leaf and pat them dry. Remove the tough outer stems and outer edges. Toast each piece above a low, open flame or directly on the burner of an electric range set on low, for about 20 seconds on one side, moving it constantly, then for about 15 seconds on the other side. The leaves will shrink slightly and deepen in color.

3. Whip the butter with an electric mixer for about 3 minutes at high speed. This will incorporate air into the butter. Place all the remaining ingredients in a large, nonreactive bowl and mix well. Using a large rubber spatula or a spoon, fold in the whipped butter.

4. Lay 1 square of banana leaf on a work surface. Place about ⅓ cup of the tamale mixture in the center of the leaf. Fold the sides of the banana leaf over the tamale mixture, compacting the tamale and forming a square. Set the leaf-wrapped tamale on a square of aluminum foil and wrap it in the foil. Prepare the other tamales in the same way.

Twelve 4-inch squares of
aluminum foil

Authentic
Guacamole *(page 46)*

Tomato Salsa
(recipe follows)

1 cup sour cream

5. Bring about ½ inch of water in the bottom of a steamer to a boil over high heat. Verify that the water does not evaporate completely during cooking. Place the tamales in the steamer basket. Reduce the heat to low so the water simmers, place the steamer basket on top, and cover. Steam the tamales until they feel set, about 30 minutes, then remove the basket from the heat and let the tamales sit until they firm up slightly, about 1 minute.

6. Remove the aluminum foil and serve the tamales with the Authentic Guacamole, Tomato Salsa, and sour cream.

tomato salsa

MAKES ABOUT 2 CUPS

5 medium-size ripe
tomatoes

2 tablespoons pure
olive oil

2 medium-size jalapeño
chilies

2 tablespoons
minced cilantro
(fresh coriander)

3 tablespoons finely
chopped red onion

Pinch freshly ground black
pepper

1 teaspoon kosher salt

2 tablespoons freshly
squeezed lemon juice

The charred flavor that the grilled tomatoes and chilies give this salsa is nicely balanced by the raw tomatoes. Try it with tortilla chips, any tamales, and soft tacos.

1. Prepare a fire in a barbecue grill and oil the grill rack. Rub 3 of the tomatoes and the jalapeños with the oil.

2. Place the tomatoes and jalapeños on the grill rack about 6 inches from the heat and cook, turning once, until the tomato skins split and the jalapeños are charred, 3 to 5 minutes on each side. Let cool. Seed the tomatoes. Whirl them in a blender or food processor to a coarse purée. You should have about 1 cup of pulp. Seed and chop the jalapeños.

3. Seed and cut the remaining 2 tomatoes into ¼-inch dice. You should have about 1 cup of diced tomatoes.

4. Place all of the ingredients in a food processor and purée coarsely. The salsa can be refrigerated, covered, for up to 2 days. Serve at room temperature.

chicken szechwan dumplings with soy-cilantro sauce

MAKES 16 DUMPLINGS;
4 OR 5 SERVINGS

Filling

6 ounces skinless, boneless chicken leg meat (2 drumsticks and 2 thighs), trimmed of excess fat

1 tablespoon finely diced carrot

1 green onion, white and light green parts only, minced (1 tablespoon)

1 medium-size garlic clove, minced (1½ teaspoons)

1½ teaspoons sugar

One ⅛-inch slice ginger, peeled and minced (½ teaspoon)

2 tablespoons toasted sesame oil

1 fresh water chestnut, cut into ⅛-inch dice

2 tablespoons heavy (Chinese) soy sauce

16 small square won ton skins

2 tablespoons cornstarch

The inspiration for these dumplings came from the dim sum houses in Chinatown, with their steaming carts filled with dozens of choices. They are very popular in my cooking classes because they are so easy to prepare and satisfying to eat.

Leg meat is used in this recipe because the dark meat of a chicken has more flavor than the breast. But I'm limited to stuffings when using dark meat. Curiously, when people can *see* dark meat, they don't like it!

1. Prepare the filling: Grind the chicken in a meat grinder, using the medium plate, and transfer the ground meat to a medium-size bowl. Or chop the chicken in a food processor, using the pulse button to obtain a rough texture. Add the rest of the filling ingredients to the ground chicken and mix well, either by hand or with a few pulses of the food processor.

2. Lay the won ton skins on a work surface. Place about 1 tablespoon of the filling, depending on the size of the skins, in the center of each skin. Lightly brush water on the edges of the skins and bring the edges up around the filling to close, pinching the skins at the top. Do not overfill or the dumplings will open during cooking. Dust the dumplings with cornstarch to prevent them from sticking to one another. The dumplings can be prepared to this point and refrigerated, covered, for up to 4 hours.

1½ teaspoons kosher salt

Soy-Cilantro Sauce
(recipe follows)

¼ cup chopped cilantro
(fresh coriander)

3. In a large pot, bring 12 cups of water to a boil over high heat and add the salt. Add the dumplings, reduce the heat to medium, and simmer until the dumplings float to the top, about 5 minutes. The won ton skins should be opaque and tender. Using a skimmer or a slotted spoon, remove the dumplings to a platter. Pour the Soy-Cilantro Sauce over the dumplings. Sprinkle with the cilantro and serve immediately.

soy-cilantro sauce

MAKES ABOUT ¾ CUP

¼ cup chopped cilantro
(fresh coriander)

3 to 4 green onions, white
and light green parts
only, chopped (¼ cup)

2 tablespoons heavy
(Chinese) soy sauce

2 tablespoons hoisin
sauce

½ teaspoon Vietnamese
chile-garlic paste

1 tablespoon distilled
white vinegar

1 medium-size
garlic clove, minced
(1½ teaspoons)

One ¼- to ⅜-inch slice
ginger, peeled and
minced (¾ teaspoon)

2 tablespoons toasted
sesame oil

The Chinese method for brewing soy sauce is quite different from that of the Japanese. Chinese soy sauce ages longer and has different ingredients, including molasses, giving it much more depth. For this sauce, the rich and full-bodied Chinese soy sauce is preferable. Pass this sauce with sautéed chicken breast or steamed catfish.

1. Place all the ingredients in a blender or food processor and process until almost smooth.

2. The sauce can be refrigerated, covered, for up to 2 days. Serve the sauce at room temperature, or warm it in a small, nonreactive saucepan.

shrimp won tons with orange-basil oil

Makes 12 won tons;
3 or 4 servings

Sauce

4 large basil leaves

¼ cup pure olive oil

1 dried red Thai chile

2 cups freshly squeezed orange juice

Pinch kosher salt

Filling

6 ounces raw medium-size shrimp, peeled, deveined, and cut into ¼-inch dice

1 to 2 green onions, white and light green parts only, chopped (2 tablespoons)

1 small garlic clove, minced (1 teaspoon)

One ½-inch piece ginger, peeled and minced (1 teaspoon)

½ teaspoon freshly ground black pepper

¾ teaspoon kosher salt

Finely grated zest from 1 orange (½ teaspoon)

1 large egg white

1 teaspoon minced basil

The won tons in this simple but elegant dish are shaped like ravioli. This is a fantastic combination of the shrimp's sea flavor with citrus and basil. The orange juice reduction adds an intense flavor. Try to use fresh, not frozen, shrimp.

1. At least 1 day ahead, begin the sauce: Prepare an ice bath with about 4 cups of cold water and about 6 ice cubes. In a small saucepan, bring 1 cup of water to a boil over high heat, add the basil, and let cook for 10 seconds. Remove this blanched basil using a slotted spoon and drop it into the ice bath to stop the cooking. Drain.

2. Place the blanched basil in a blender or food processor and purée. Place the puréed basil, the oil, and chile in a jar and shake well. Refrigerate the basil oil overnight in a covered jar. It can be refrigerated, covered, for up to 2 days.

3. Before serving: Bring the orange juice to a boil in a small saucepan over high heat, reduce the heat to medium, and continue to simmer until the juice reduces to ½ cup. Set aside.

4. Remove the basil oil from the refrigerator and let it come to room temperature. (It may appear cloudy when cold; this is okay.) Pour the oil through a fine-mesh strainer lined with cheesecloth, or through a coffee filter. Stir the basil oil into the orange reduction and add the salt.

5. Combine all the filling ingredients in a small bowl and mix well.

24 small square
won ton skins

1 egg white, lightly
beaten

1½ teaspoons kosher salt

1 tablespoon black
sesame seeds, toasted
(see Note, page 47)

1 tablespoon minced
basil

6. Lay half the won ton skins on a work surface. Place about 1 tablespoon of the filling, depending on the size of the skins, in the center of each skin. Lightly brush the egg white on the edges of the skins and cover the bottoms with the remaining won ton skins. Do not overfill or the won tons will open during cooking. Pat the edges together to seal, pressing out any large air bubbles that may remain around the filling. Trim the edges, if necessary, to make the bottom and top won ton skins approximately even.

7. In a large saucepan, bring 8 cups of water to a boil over high heat and add the remaining salt. Add the won tons, reduce the heat to medium, and simmer until the won ton skins are opaque and tender, about 2 minutes. (The shrimp will cook quickly.)

8. Scooping from the bottom of the sauce bowl so that the orange reduction and the oil will form separate pools on the plate, drizzle the sauce on the bottoms of plates or shallow soup bowls. Using a skimmer or a slotted spoon, remove the won tons to the sauced plates or bowls. Sprinkle with the sesame seeds and remaining basil. Serve immediately.

Inimitable Cheesecloth

Cheesecloth, or bouillon cloth, is one of those vintage household items that even the most modern cooks can't seem to live without. This loosely woven white cotton cloth, sold in continuous sheets, is indispensable for making yogurt cheese and wrapping up herbs and spices, such as pickling spices or parsley, thyme, and bay leaf for a bouquet garni, that you want to retrieve easily before serving a dish. It is also matchless for straining stocks and sauces. Cut a large swatch of this cloth, fold it over two or three times, and place it inside your strainer to trap fine particles.

grilled yuca cakes

MAKES 12 OR 13 CAKES;
4 TO 6 SERVINGS

1 tablespoon kosher salt

One 20-ounce bag frozen
yuca

6 to 8 green onions, white
and light green parts
only, thinly sliced
(½ cup)

2 medium-size
jalapeño chilies,
seeded and minced
(2 tablespoons)

3 tablespoons
minced cilantro
(fresh coriander)

¾ teaspoon ground
coriander

1 large garlic clove,
minced (1 tablespoon)

¾ teaspoon ground
cumin

½ teaspoon freshly
ground black pepper

1 teaspoon kosher salt

2 large egg whites,
lightly beaten

One 1-inch strip red bell
pepper, minced
(1 tablespoon)

3 tablespoons mild
vegetable oil, such as
corn

Pineapple Salsa
(recipe follows)

The potato-like qualities of yuca (cassava) make these cakes very creamy. This tuber is often used in the Caribbean; its neutral flavor allows it to be paired with many other, more complex flavors. Try these cakes also as a side dish, without the Pineapple Salsa.

1. In a large pot, bring 12 cups of water to a boil over high heat and add the 1 tablespoon of salt. Drop the still-frozen yuca in the water and bring back to a boil, then reduce the heat to medium and simmer until the yuca is tender, about 30 minutes. Drain the yuca, let it cool, and remove the fibrous core from each piece. (This will lift quite easily.) Cut the yuca into 1-inch cubes.

2. Place the cubed yuca and all the remaining ingredients, except the oil and Pineapple Salsa, in a large bowl and beat with an electric mixer on medium speed until well combined, about 1 minute. Measure out 4-ounce, or ¼-cup, pieces of the yuca mixture. Shape the pieces of mixture into cakes, about ½ inch thick and 2½ inches in diameter. Place the cakes on a plate and cover. The cakes can be refrigerated, covered, for up to 4 hours.

3. Heat a large nonstick frying pan over medium heat. Add the oil and heat it, about 1 minute. Without crowding the pan, fry the yuca cakes until they are golden brown and crispy, about 2½ minutes on each side. Serve immediately with the Pineapple Salsa.

pineapple salsa

MAKES 2 CUPS

- 1/2 large fresh pineapple, peeled, cored, and cut into 1/4-inch dice (2 cups)
- One 1-inch strip red bell pepper, cut into 1/8-inch dice (1 tablespoon)
- 1 small serrano chile, seeded and minced (3/4 teaspoon)
- 1/2 medium-size shallot, minced, (1 tablespoon)
- 1 tablespoon freshly squeezed lime juice
- 1 tablespoon minced cilantro (fresh coriander)
- 1/4 teaspoon freshly ground black pepper
- 1/4 teaspoon kosher salt

Pineapples always make me think of the sun and the tropics.

If you can find fresh habanero chilies, add them instead of the serranos in this recipe. Use only 1/3 teaspoon, though, unless you like it very hot! The chile has a nice fruit essence that complements the pineapple. Besides Grilled Yuca Cakes, you could serve this salsa with any grilled fish or chicken.

Mix all the ingredients well in a medium-size, nonreactive bowl. Let the salsa sit at room temperature for 1/2 hour to allow the pineapple to release its juice. The salsa can be refrigerated, covered, for up to 2 hours.

crab pupusas

MAKES 5 SERVINGS

Masa

- 2 cups masa harina
- 2 cups warm water
- 3 tablespoons mild vegetable oil, such as corn
- 2 teaspoons ground cumin
- 1/2 teaspoon freshly ground black pepper
- 1/2 teaspoon ground cayenne pepper
- 2 teaspoons kosher salt
- 1 small garlic clove, minced (1 teaspoon)

Crabmeat Filling

- 1/4 pound lump crabmeat, carefully picked over
- 2 1/2 ounces Oaxaca cheese, grated (1/2 cup)
- 1 1/2 ounces Ranchero cheese, grated (1/4 cup)
- 1 1/2 ounces queso cotija añejo, grated (2 tablespoons)
- 2 tablespoons minced cilantro (fresh coriander)
- 1 large serrano chile, seeded and minced (1 tablespoon)
- 1 large garlic clove, minced (1 tablespoon)

Many of the people who work with me at the restaurant are from El Salvador. One day, one of my prep cooks brought in pupusas, or disks of freshly grilled masa cakes. I decided that they would be fantastic stuffed with fresh crab. Serve these pupusas with Cabbage Escabeche.

1. Combine the masa ingredients in a medium-size, nonporous bowl and mix well. Cover with plastic wrap, pressing the wrap directly on the surface of the mixture, and let it sit at room temperature for 20 minutes.

2. Meanwhile, prepare the filling: In a medium-size bowl, combine the crabmeat, cheeses, cilantro, chile, and garlic. Mix thoroughly.

3. Measure out five 5-ounce, or 1/2-cup, pieces of the masa mixture. Lay a 12-inch square of plastic wrap on a work surface. With wet hands (you may want to keep a bowl of water next to where you are working), pat 1 piece of masa on the plastic wrap into a flat disk, about 1/2 inch thick and 5 inches in diameter. Make an indentation in the center of the disk and place one-fifth of the filling in the depression. Using the plastic wrap, bring the masa up around the crab mixture and pinch the seams closed, keeping the masa an even 1/2 inch thick all around the filling. With the pupusa still wrapped in the plastic, flatten it to an even 1-inch thickness. (It will still be about 5 inches in diameter.) Repeat this process with the remaining masa and filling. The pupusas can be refrigerated, wrapped, for up to 2 hours.

6 tablespoons pure olive oil

Cabbage Escabeche (*recipe follows*)

4. Heat a large nonstick sauté pan or frying pan over medium heat until hot. Add the olive oil and heat it, about 2 minutes. Gently unwrap the pupusas. Without crowding the pan, fry them until they are golden brown all over and the cheese melts, about 5 minutes on each side. Serve immediately over the Cabbage Escabeche.

cabbage escabeche

MAKES 5 SERVINGS

½ small head green cabbage, shredded (4 cups)

1 small carrot, grated (½ cup)

1 small jalapeño chile, seeded and minced (1 teaspoon)

One 1½-inch strip red bell pepper, cut into ¼-inch dice (3 tablespoons)

2 large garlic cloves, minced (2 tablespoons)

¼ cup champagne vinegar

¼ cup water

¼ teaspoon freshly ground black pepper

2 teaspoons kosher salt

1 teaspoon minced fresh oregano or ½ teaspoon dried

1 tablespoon sugar

This condiment can be served with Crab Pupusas or any grilled fish. As a variation, you can add diced mango or papaya.

Place the cabbage in a large, nonreactive bowl with the remaining ingredients and toss very well. Refrigerate the escabeche, covered, for at least 4 hours and up to 1 day. The longer it sits, the better. Serve at room temperature.

potato-calamata cakes on tomato-saffron sauce

MAKES 6 CAKES; 6 SERVINGS

Potato Mixture

1¼ cups mashed potatoes, preferably Idaho, cooled (*see* Note)

2 tablespoons minced onion

¼ cup pitted, quartered calamata olives

½ teaspoon chopped fresh rosemary, or ¼ teaspoon dried

2 tablespoons sour cream

1 small garlic clove, minced (½ teaspoon)

½ teaspoon kosher salt

⅛ teaspoon ground cayenne pepper

¼ teaspoon freshly ground black pepper

Bread-Crumb Mixture

½ cup fine dry bread crumbs

2 small garlic cloves, minced (1 teaspoon)

¼ teaspoon minced fresh rosemary, or ⅛ teaspoon dried

¼ teaspoon freshly ground black pepper

½ teaspoon kosher salt

¼ cup flour, spread in a shallow bowl

This is my favorite comfort food. It is also an excellent way to use up leftover mashed potatoes. The flavors are typically Mediterranean. The olives have a nice briny quality, which cuts through the potatoes. Sour cream adds a bit of richness. These cakes are also good served as a side dish, without the sauce.

If you wish to make small potato cakes as hors d'oeuvres, shape about 2 tablespoons of the potato mixture into ½-inch-thick cakes, about 1½ inches in diameter. Cook them for 1 minute on each side and then bake for 2 minutes. Pass the sauce separately. This recipe will make about 16 hors d'oeuvre–size potato cakes.

1. Preheat the oven to 350°. In a medium-size bowl, combine all the potato-mixture ingredients and mix thoroughly. Measure out ⅓-cup portions and, with lightly greased hands, form 1-inch-thick cakes, about 2 inches in diameter.

2. Combine the bread-crumb ingredients in a shallow bowl. Dredge the cakes in the flour, lightly tap off any excess, then dip them in the egg and coat with the bread-crumb mixture. Make sure they are evenly coated.

3. Heat a large ovenproof sauté pan or frying pan over medium heat. Add the oil and heat it, about 1 minute. Without crowding the pan, fry the cakes until they are golden brown, about 3 minutes on each side. Place the pan in the heated oven and bake the cakes for 4 minutes.

1 large egg, lightly
beaten in a shallow
bowl

3 tablespoons pure
olive oil

Tomato Saffron Sauce
(*recipe follows*)

6 fresh rosemary sprigs

4. Meanwhile, warm the Tomato-Saffron Sauce in a small saucepan over low heat, stirring often. Ladle the sauce onto plates or a platter. Using a large wide spatula, place the potato cakes on the sauce. Garnish each with a sprig of rosemary. Serve immediately. Pass any remaining sauce separately.

Note *Peel 2 small potatoes and boil them uncovered in salted water until tender, 30 to 35 minutes. Or use leftover unseasoned mashed or peeled baked potato.*

tomato-saffron sauce

MAKES ABOUT 1¾ CUPS

½ pound plum tomatoes

2 tablespoons pure
olive oil, plus 1
teaspoon for rubbing
the tomatoes

¼ small onion, minced
(¼ cup)

½ small garlic
clove, minced
(½ teaspoon)

⅛ teaspoon crumbled
saffron threads,
preferably Spanish

¼ teaspoon freshly
ground black pepper

¼ cup extra-virgin
olive oil

½ teaspoon kosher salt

Saffron has an exotic flavor that reminds me of my Moroccan roots. In addition to serving this sauce with Potato-Calamata Cakes, try it with other Mediterranean-style dishes, such as whole grilled snapper and roasted eggplant.

1. Preheat the oven to 350°. Rub the tomatoes with the 1 teaspoon of pure olive oil and arrange the tomatoes on a baking sheet. Roast them until the skins begin to split, but the tomatoes do not collapse completely, about 15 minutes. Remove the baking sheet from the oven. Let the tomatoes cool, then peel, seed, and crush them with a fork or a whisk; you should have about 1¼ cups of pulp.

2. Heat a small, nonreactive saucepan over medium heat. Add the 2 tablespoons pure olive oil and heat it, about 1 minute. Reduce the heat to low, then add the onion and garlic and cook, stirring, for about 30 seconds. Add the saffron and pepper to the pan and cook, stirring, for 1 minute to release the saffron's flavor. Add the crushed tomatoes and cook for 2 minutes.

3. Place the mixture in a blender or food processor, or leave it in the pan (off the stove) and use a hand-held blender. Purée the sauce. With the machine running, add the extra-virgin olive oil in a thin stream. Add the salt. Serve warm. The sauce can be refrigerated, covered, for up to 1 day.

falafel

MAKES 24 FALAFEL;
6 TO 8 SERVINGS

1¼ cups dried chick-peas
(garbanzo beans)

½ teaspoon baking soda

2 large garlic
cloves, minced
(2 tablespoons)

6 tablespoons minced
Italian (flat-leaf)
parsley

1 tablespoon plus
1 teaspoon kosher salt

2 teaspoons
ground cumin

½ teaspoon ground
cayenne pepper

1 teaspoon freshly
ground black pepper

6 tablespoons
whole-wheat flour

½ cup unsweetened
wheat germ

2 large eggs,
lightly beaten

Dash ground turmeric

½ cup plain yogurt
(regular, low-fat, or
nonfat)

2 cups mild vegetable
oil, such as peanut

Lemon-Tahini Sauce
(*recipe follows*)

These falafel have a lot of flavor, and the wheat germ gives them great texture. They are amazingly easy to prepare. For an assortment of Middle Eastern meze, serve the falafel with Tabbouleh and Hummus. Or get some pita bread and enjoy the falafel in a sandwich.

1. The night before you plan to serve the falafel, start preparing the chick-peas: In a medium-size, nonporous bowl, combine the chick-peas and about 3 cups of cold water. Stir in the baking soda, cover, and refrigerate.

2. The next day, drain the chick-peas thoroughly. You should have about 2½ cups of softer, but still uncooked, chick-peas. Place them in a food processor and grind finely. Add the remaining ingredients, except the oil and Lemon-Tahini Sauce, and mix with a few pulses of the food processor, or by hand. Let the mixture sit until the flour and wheat germ absorb the eggs, about 15 minutes.

3. Heat the oil to 360° in a small shallow saucepan. Use a candy thermometer to verify the temperature. Measure out 1-ounce, or 2-tablespoon, pieces of the falafel mixture. Shape the pieces of mixture into balls and flatten them slightly, so that they are about 2 inches in diameter and about ¾ inch thick.

4. Without crowding the pan, fry the disks until they are deep brown, but still greenish and moist inside, 4 to 5 minutes on each side.

5. Using tongs or a slotted spoon, remove the falafel and drain on paper towels. Verify that the oil is still at 360° between batches. Serve immediately. Pass the Lemon-Tahini Sauce separately.

lemon-tahini sauce

MAKES ABOUT 1 CUP

- ⅓ cup tahini
- ½ cup boiling water
- 3 tablespoons freshly squeezed lemon juice
- 1 teaspoon harissa
- ½ teaspoon ground cumin
- ¼ teaspoon freshly ground black pepper
- ¾ teaspoon kosher salt

You will often see this tangy sauce with Middle Eastern dishes such as falafel, or with grilled vegetables. It's also good on very fresh, flavorful chopped plum tomatoes, or on Belgian endive as a crudité dip. The harissa adds a nice flavor and some heat.

Whisk all the ingredients thoroughly in a small, nonreactive bowl. Serve immediately. The sauce can be refrigerated, covered, for up to 2 days. Serve it at room temperature and whisk before serving.

plantain fritters stuffed with fresh rock shrimp

Makes 24 fritters;
6 to 8 servings

Fritter Batter

3 semi-ripe plantains
(about 1 pound total),
peeled

1/4 small onion, minced
(1/4 cup)

1 large garlic clove,
minced (1 tablespoon)

1/2 cup rice flour

1 habanero chile,
seeded and minced
(1 tablespoon)

1/2 teaspoon
baking powder

1/2 teaspoon freshly
ground black pepper

1 1/4 teaspoons kosher salt

1 egg white,
lightly beaten

3/4 pound raw peeled
rock shrimp

3 cups mild vegetable
oil, such as corn

Spicy Papaya-Mustard
Sauce (recipe follows)
or Tomato Salsa
(page 63)

These fritters play a variety of flavors and textures off one another: Soft and slightly sweet plantains, very spicy habanero chile, and firm—lobster-like—rock shrimp (so-called because of their rock-hard shells; fortunately, they are usually available shelled). If you cannot find rock shrimp, you may substitute an equal weight of another firm, shelled and deveined raw shrimp.

1. Place the plantains in a medium-size saucepan and add enough water to cover. (You may cut them to fit, if necessary.) Bring the water to a boil over high heat, reduce the heat to medium, and simmer until the plantains are tender, about 10 minutes. Drain the plantains, let them cool, and then mash them with a fork. You should have about 1 1/2 cups of coarse purée.

2. Place all the fritter batter ingredients, except the egg white, in a large bowl. Using an electric mixer on its lowest speed, beat the ingredients to mix. Add the egg white and continue mixing until the egg white is incorporated and the mixture has the consistency of lumpy mashed potatoes, about 2 minutes.

3. Cover a baking sheet with plastic wrap or aluminum foil. Measure out heaping tablespoons of the fritter batter and place them on the baking sheet. If you have a small (1-ounce) ice-cream scoop, use it. With lightly floured hands, shape each piece of the mixture into a ball. Press 2 or 3 shrimp (or two or three 3/4-inch pieces of regular shrimp) into each ball, then reshape each into a ball, covering the shrimp with the fritter batter.

4. Heat the oil to 360° in a medium-size, nonreactive saucepan. Use a candy thermometer to verify the temperature. Fry about 4 fritters at a time, turning them as necessary for even cooking, until the fritters are golden brown, about 3 minutes. Using a skimmer or a slotted spoon, remove them and drain on paper towels. Verify that the oil is still at 360° between batches. (The fritters will absorb the oil if it is not hot enough, and will brown too quickly, leaving the shrimp raw, if it is too hot.)

5. Serve immediately. Pass the Spicy Papaya-Mustard Sauce or the Tomato Salsa separately.

spicy papaya-mustard sauce

MAKES ABOUT 2 CUPS

2 tablespoons mild vegetable oil, such as peanut

1½ teaspoons curry powder

¼ teaspoon ground allspice

¼ teaspoon freshly ground black pepper

One ¼-inch piece ginger, peeled and minced (¾ teaspoon)

1½ teaspoons dry mustard

2 large plum tomatoes, seeded and cut into ¼-inch dice (1 cup)

½ medium-size habanero chile, seeded and minced

1 medium-size ripe papaya, seeded, peeled, and cut into ¼-inch dice (1¼ cups)

¼ cup freshly squeezed orange juice

6 tablespoons aged red wine vinegar

1 tablespoon mild honey, such as orange

1½ teaspoons Worcestershire sauce

¼ cup Dijon mustard

¾ teaspoon kosher salt

This is a very flavorful condiment that I like to use on everything from Plantain Fritters and smoked chicken to Pecan–Cornmeal Crusted Catfish.

1. Heat a medium-size, nonreactive saucepan over medium heat. Add the oil and heat it, about 1 minute. Reduce the heat to low and add the curry, allspice, pepper, ginger, dry mustard, and tomatoes, and cook, stirring, for 30 seconds.

2. Add all of the remaining ingredients and simmer until the tomatoes are quite soft, about 30 minutes. Remove the pan from the heat and purée the sauce in a blender or food processor. Serve warm. The sauce can be kept refrigerated, covered, for up to 2 days.

coconut-curry chicken quesadillas

MAKES 8 SERVINGS

MAKES 8 SERVINGS

¼ cup dark raisins

¾ cup mild vegetable oil, such as peanut

¼ cup minced onion

2 tablespoons curry powder

1 large garlic clove, minced (1 tablespoon)

One 1-inch piece ginger, peeled and minced (1 tablespoon)

2 tablespoons packed light brown sugar

1 tablespoon Vietnamese chile-garlic paste

¼ cup chicken stock, preferably homemade (page 24)

½ pound peas in the pod, shelled, or thawed frozen (½ cup)

½ cup unsweetened coconut milk

¾ cup mashed potato, preferably Idaho (see Note)

One ½-pound skinless, boneless whole chicken breast, cut against the grain into ½-inch strips

1 tablespoon kosher salt

Eight 6-inch lard-free flour tortillas

8 ounces mozzarella cheese, grated (1½ cups)

Tomato Raita (recipe follows)

I got the idea for these quesadillas while eating samosas at one of my favorite Indian restaurants. Combining something sweet with something spicy allows the flavors to contrast with one another.

1. Place the raisins in a small bowl and cover them with hot water. Let the raisins sit for ½ hour. Drain.

2. Heat a large, nonreactive sauté pan or frying pan over medium heat until hot. Add ¼ cup of the oil and heat it, about 2 minutes. Reduce the heat to low, add the onion, curry powder, garlic, and ginger and cook, stirring constantly, for 2 minutes. Add the raisins, brown sugar, chile-garlic paste, stock, peas, and coconut milk to the pan. Increase the heat to medium and bring to a boil, then reduce the heat to medium again and let the liquid simmer until it reduces by half, about 15 minutes. Stir in the mashed potato.

3. Add the chicken to the pan along with the salt and simmer until the chicken is just done, about 5 minutes.

4. Heat a large frying until hot. For every tortilla that will fit in the pan, add 1 tablespoon of oil. Without crowding the pan, place the tortillas in the pan and cover each with about 3 tablespoons of cheese. Divide the chicken mixture evenly among the tortillas in the pan, placing it on only half the tortilla. Cook until the cheese melts and the tortillas are golden brown, about 1 minute. Do not allow the tortillas to burn. Fold them in half and serve immediately. Pass the Tomato Raita separately.

Note *Peel 1 small potato and boil it uncovered in salted water until tender, 30 to 35 minutes. Or use leftover unseasoned mashed or peeled baked potato.*

tomato raita

MAKES 2 CUPS

2   medium-size
    poblano chilies

2   teaspoons mild
    vegetable oil, such
    as peanut

3 or 4   medium-size plum
         tomatoes, seeded
         and cut into ¼-inch
         dice (1½ cups)

⅓   small onion, minced
    (⅓ cup)

1   teaspoon black
    mustard seeds,
    toasted (see Note)

½   teaspoon
    ground cumin

⅛   teaspoon freshly
    ground white pepper

2   tablespoons
    sour cream

½   cup plain yogurt
    (regular, low-fat, or
    nonfat)

1   tablespoon
    minced cilantro
    (fresh coriander)

1   teaspoon kosher salt

This is a delicious accompaniment to any curry dish; the yogurt helps cool the palate when eating a spicy dish.

1. Preheat the oven to 400°. Rub the chilies with the oil. Place them in a small shallow baking pan and roast until the skin begins to blister, about 20 minutes. Place the chilies in a small, nonreactive bowl, cover with plastic wrap, and let them "sweat" for about 5 minutes. Peel the thin outer skin from the chilies, then remove the stem and seeds. Cut the chilies into ⅛-inch dice; place them in a small, nonreactive bowl.

2. Add all the remaining ingredients to the bowl and stir well. Refrigerate the raita, covered, for 30 minutes and up to 2 hours to let the flavors meld. Serve slightly chilled, but not cold.

Note *To toast mustard seeds, heat a skillet over low heat. Add 2 teaspoons of mild vegetable oil, such as peanut, and heat, about 30 seconds. Add the mustard seeds and cook until they begin to pop out of the pan. Cover the pan, turn off the heat, and let the seeds cool.*

Soups

Soups remind me of Saturday lunches with my father at my grandmother's house. She always served us soup, many different kinds of soup, including a version of the Moroccan Eggplant and Lentil Soup in this chapter. To my way of thinking, soup is the ultimate comfort food; it always brings me back to an earlier time in my life.

Just about every culture has a special soup. For all of us, soup means breaking bread, and sharing. The gestures of ladling soup out of a big tureen and passing it around the table naturally seem to evoke feelings of contentment and community. And we all know that chicken soup can cure practically anything.

At the Authentic Cafe, soup always appears on the list of daily specials. I like to start with a great stock because you really can't compensate for a bad or weak one. I also like to keep it simple. I don't overly complicate the dish with endless ingredients or conflicting flavors. I like to taste

each component and not have any one overpower the others.

You will notice a scarcity of cream and butter in these soups. This is not an accident. I believe in generous portions and in being able to enjoy delicious things in whatever quantities you desire, without having to feel guilty. So, while these recipes are all rich in flavor, most are low in calories and fat.

moroccan eggplant and lentil soup

MAKES 4 SERVINGS

One 1¼-pound eggplant

¼ cup plus 2 teaspoons
    pure olive oil

5 large plum tomatoes

1 small onion, chopped
   (1 cup)

1 large garlic clove,
   minced (1 tablespoon)

¼ teaspoon freshly
   ground black pepper

1 teaspoon ground
   cumin

½ teaspoon ground
   coriander

3½ cups chicken stock,
    preferably homemade
    (page 24)

1½ cups lentils, picked
    over for stones

1½ teaspoons kosher salt

2 tablespoons minced
   Preserved Lemons,
   rind only *(page 27)*

1½ teaspoons harissa

1 tablespoon chopped
   fresh mint

Eggplant is one of my favorite vegetables. When roasted, it makes a great base for this soup, which was served to me on a trip to Rabat, Morocco. It is thick, creamy, and spicy, yet subtle. The preserved lemon makes it tangy.

1. Preheat the oven to 400°. Pierce the eggplant several times with a fork, then rub it all over with 1 teaspoon of the oil. Place the eggplant in a small shallow baking pan and roast it until it is tender and begins to shrink, about 45 minutes. Remove the pan from the oven. Keep the oven on. Let the eggplant cool just enough so that you can handle it. (The eggplant will be easier to peel when it is still warm, so don't let it cool completely.) Peel the eggplant, then cut it into quarters lengthwise and remove the seeds. Chop the eggplant coarsely. You should have about 1½ cups.

2. While the eggplant is baking, rub the tomatoes with 1 teaspoon of the oil and arrange them in a medium-size shallow baking pan. Roast them at the same temperature until the skins begin to split and the tomatoes are tender, 20 to 25 minutes. Heat the broiler and broil the tomatoes until the skins begin to blacken, about 5 minutes. Let the tomatoes cool, then peel and seed them. Chop them coarsely. You should have about 1 cup.

3. Heat a large saucepan over medium heat. Add the remaining ¼ cup of olive oil and heat it, about 2 minutes. Place the onion, garlic, pepper, cumin, and coriander in the pan and cook, stirring often, for about 2 minutes.

4. Add the stock, lentils, chopped tomatoes, and chopped eggplant. Bring the soup to a boil, then reduce the heat to low and simmer, stirring often, until the soup is smooth and the lentils are tender, about 50 minutes

5. Remove the pan from the heat and add the salt, lemon, and harissa. Ladle the soup into bowls, garnish with the mint, and serve immediately.

roasted butternut squash soup with green chile cream

MAKES 4 SERVINGS

One 2-pound butternut squash

3 tablespoons pure olive oil

2 medium-size shallots, minced (2 tablespoons)

¼ teaspoon ground nutmeg

¼ teaspoon ground cinnamon

¼ teaspoon ground white pepper

2½ cups water

¼ cup mild honey, such as orange

1 tablespoon plus 1 teaspoon kosher salt

Green Chile Cream (recipe follows)

Make this soup in the winter, when butternut squash is at the peak of its season. The spicy Green Chile Cream complements the soup's sweetness perfectly.

1. Preheat the oven to 400°.

2. Rub the squash with 1 tablespoon of the oil, place it in a small shallow baking pan, and roast until the skin splits and the squash is tender when pierced with a knife, about 1 hour. Let the squash cool slightly, then peel it, cut it in half, and remove the seeds and the inner membranes to which the seeds are connected. Mash the pulp. You should have about 3 cups.

3. Heat a large, nonreactive saucepan over low heat. Add the remaining oil and heat it, about 1 minute. Cook the shallots, stirring occasionally, until translucent, about 1 minute, then add the spices and cook, stirring, until fragrant, about 1 minute.

4. Place the squash pulp in the same pan and cook it, stirring constantly to prevent sticking, for 2 minutes. Add the water and bring the soup to a boil over medium heat. Reduce the heat to low and add the honey and salt.

5. Simmer the soup, stirring often to keep it from sticking, for 30 minutes. Purée the soup in a blender, food processor, or in the pan using a hand-held blender.

6. Ladle the soup into bowls and place a dollop of Green Chile Cream on top. (Or, if you have an empty ketchup or mustard squeeze bottle, place the cream in it and squirt the cream decoratively on top of the soup.) Serve immediately.

green chile cream

1 medium-size poblano chile

1 medium-size jalapeño chile

1 teaspoon pure olive oil

1½ tablespoons sour cream or crème fraîche

½ teaspoon kosher salt

Pinch ground white pepper

Drizzle this spicy cream on tacos, Authentic Cafe Black Beans (or black bean soup), or a tostada.

1. Preheat the oven to 400°. Rub the chilies with the oil and place them in a small shallow baking pan. Roast them until the skin begins to blister, about 20 minutes. (This may be done at the same time you are roasting the butternut squash for the Roasted Butternut Squash Soup.) Do not overcook the chile, or the flesh will become too fragile to handle. Place the chilies in a small, nonreactive bowl, cover with plastic wrap, and let them "sweat" for 5 minutes. Peel the thin outer skin from the chilies, and remove the stems and seeds.

2. Place all the ingredients in a blender or food processor and purée until very smooth. The Cream can be refrigerated, covered, for up to 2 hours.

A Different Blender

The inversion, or hand-held, blender helps you purée soups and sauces without the mess or burns you might encounter when using a conventional blender. With this little gem, you actually invert the blender (the whirring blade is at the protected end of a wand) into the pot in which you have cooked the soup or sauce. Take care to unplug the blender before cleaning it.

potato, escarole, fennel, and saffron soup

MAKES 4 SERVINGS

1   medium-size fennel
    bulb

4   medium-size Idaho
    potatoes, peeled and
    cut into $\frac{1}{4}$-inch dice (4
    cups)

8   cups cold water

1   teaspoon kosher salt

2   tablespoons mild
    vegetable oil

2   medium-size
    cloves garlic, minced
    (4 teaspoons)

1   teaspoon ground
    fennel

$\frac{1}{4}$ teaspoon freshly
    ground black pepper

$\frac{1}{8}$ teaspoon crumbled
    saffron threads,
    preferably Spanish

$\frac{1}{2}$ medium-size head
    escarole, cut into
    $\frac{1}{2}$-inch pieces

$\frac{3}{4}$ teaspoon red chile
    flakes

If you like classic potato-leek soup, try this fresh-tasting, chunky variation. It can be whipped up quickly, especially since the stock is prepared simply from fennel trimmings. The escarole gives the soup some crunch, while lending its slightly bitter flavor.

1. Trim the stems and tough outer ribs from the fennel bulb, reserving them and 2 tablespoons of fronds from the top. Cut the bulb into $\frac{1}{4}$-inch dice. You should have about 1 cup of dice. Set aside.

2. As you prepare the potatoes, place them in a large bowl filled with the cold water. Let them sit in the water for $\frac{1}{2}$ hour, then strain the water into a large, nonreactive stockpot. Add the fennel trimmings and salt to the pot, then bring it to a boil over high heat.

3. Once the liquid boils, reduce the heat to medium and simmer until reduced by half, about $1\frac{1}{4}$ to $1\frac{1}{2}$ hours. Strain the stock through a medium-mesh strainer. Set aside.

4. Heat a large, nonreactive saucepan over low heat. Add the oil and heat it, about 1 minute. Add the garlic, diced fennel, ground fennel, pepper, and saffron and cook, stirring constantly, until the fennel is just softened, about 3 minutes.

5. Pour the 4 cups of potato-fennel stock into the pan, increase the heat to medium, and bring to a boil. Add the potatoes and simmer until they are just tender, about 15 to 20 minutes.

6. Add the escarole to the pan and cook until it is slightly limp, 3 minutes. Remove the soup from the heat and adjust the salt, if needed. Ladle into bowls, sprinkle with the chile flakes and the reserved fennel fronds, and serve.

corn, coconut, lime, and basil soup

Stock

4 to 6 corn ears (as many
as it takes to yield 4
cups of corn kernels),
kernels scraped from
cob (see Note, page
147), cob broken in
half

8 cups cold water

1½ teaspoons kosher salt

2 tablespoons mild
vegetable oil, such as
corn

One ¾-inch slice ginger,
peeled and grated
(2 teaspoons)

1 medium-size
shallot, minced
(2 tablespoons)

1 large jalapeño chile,
seeded and minced
(1 tablespoon)

¼ teaspoon freshly
ground white pepper

3 kaffir lime leaves,
crumbled, or 1
tablespoon finely
grated lime zest

½ cup unsweetened
coconut milk

4 cups fresh corn
kernels (from above)

2 tablespoons thinly
sliced fresh basil

1 lime, cut lengthwise
into 8 wedges

This rich-tasting soup is actually quite light.
The corn's sweetness is a delicious foil for
the subtle tartness of the kaffir lime leaves.
But, if you cannot find kaffir lime leaves,
don't hesitate to make this light summer
soup—use grated lime zest instead.

1. Mix all the stock ingredients in a large, nonreactive
stockpot. (Be sure that the cobs are broken up, to expose
more surface area. This will give the stock more flavor.) Bring
to a boil over high heat, lower the heat to medium, and
simmer until the stock is reduced by half, about 1½ hours.
Skim off the foam on the surface, especially during the first
half-hour of the reduction.

2. Strain the stock through a fine-mesh strainer or through
cheesecloth.

3. Heat a large, nonreactive saucepan over low heat. Add the
oil and heat it, about 1 minute. Cook the ginger, shallot,
chile, and pepper over low heat, stirring often, until the
shallots are translucent, about 2 minutes.

4. Add the lime leaves or zest, along with the strained stock
and the coconut milk. Bring to a simmer over medium heat.
Reduce the heat to low and continue simmering for 5 minutes.

5. Add the corn and simmer for 5 minutes more. Ladle the
soup into bowls, garnish with the basil and lime wedges, and
serve.

rock shrimp won tons in lemongrass broth

Won Tons

6 ounces raw shelled rock shrimp, halved crosswise

1 sliver ginger, peeled and minced (¼ teaspoon)

1 teaspoon minced cilantro (fresh coriander)

¼ teaspoon freshly ground black pepper

¼ teaspoon kosher salt

1 or 2 green onions, white and pale green parts only, very thinly sliced (2 tablespoons)

2 tablespoons finely grated peeled carrot

24 round won ton skins or gyoza wrappers

¼ cup cornstarch

Broth

3¼ cups Shrimp Stock (page 26) or chicken stock, preferably homemade (page 24)

¼ small shallot, minced (1 teaspoon)

2 lemongrass stalks, bottom 4 inches only, tough outer leaves removed, bruised with a cleaver and halved lengthwise

This take-off on won ton soup is much lighter than the standard restaurant version. Lemongrass broth, with its clean, bright flavors, is a great match for the sea flavor of the fresh rock shrimp. Cooked rock shrimp have a texture and briny, yet sweet, flavor similiar to that of lobster.

1. Combine all the won ton ingredients, except the won ton skins and cornstarch, in a small bowl and mix well. Lay the won ton skins on a work surface and lightly brush 2 adjacent edges of each skin with water. Place a heaping teaspoon of filling in the center of each skin, then fold the dry edges up over the dampened edges to form a triangle. Pat to seal, pressing out any air at the same time, then fold the corners in and pinch together.

2. Cover a baking sheet with plastic wrap and sprinkle lightly with 2 tablespoons of the cornstarch. Place the won tons on the plastic, then sprinkle with the remaining 2 tablespoons cornstarch to prevent them from sticking. Cover the won tons with more plastic and refrigerate until ready to cook. The won tons can be refrigerated for up to 4 hours.

3. Combine the stock, shallot, lemongrass, and garlic in a large saucepan and bring to a boil over medium heat. Reduce the heat to low and simmer for 15 minutes, then remove from the heat, cover, and allow the broth to steep for 5 minutes more. Remove and discard the lemongrass.

1 small garlic clove, peeled (1 teaspoon)

1 tablespoon kosher salt

One 8-ounce can straw mushrooms, drained (¾ cup)

One 8-ounce can baby corn, drained and halved crosswise (¾ cup)

2 teaspoons chopped cilantro (fresh coriander)

4. Meanwhile, in a large saucepan bring 2 quarts of water to a boil over high heat and add the salt. Remove the won tons from the refrigerator and gently drop them into the boiling water. Poach the won tons until they float and the skins just turn opaque, about 5 minutes. Remove the won tons from the water using a slotted spoon, and drop them into the hot broth.

5. Add the mushrooms and corn to the broth, then simmer for 5 minutes over medium heat. Ladle the soup into bowls, sprinkle with the cilantro, and serve immediately.

spicy shrimp, scallop, and coconut soup

MAKES 4 SERVINGS

Coconut Broth

2½ cups Shrimp Stock (page 26)

One ⅛-inch piece ginger, peeled and minced (½ teaspoon)

1 small shallot, minced (1 tablespoon)

2 tablespoons tamarind concentrate

¾ cup unsweetened coconut milk

1 large serrano chile, seeded and sliced paper-thin (1 tablespoon)

½ pound raw medium-size shrimp, peeled and deveined

½ pound small sea scallops, rubbery white hinge removed

4 ounces saifun (mung bean, or glass, noodles), soaked in very warm tap water for 20 minutes, then drained (see Note)

1 tablespoon chopped cilantro (fresh coriander)

This Thai-inspired soup has bold, bright flavors—spicy chile, sour tamarind, and fresh, fresh seafood—all smoothed out and enriched by coconut milk.

1. Combine the stock, ginger, shallot, and tamarind in a large, nonreactive saucepan and bring to a boil over medium heat.

2. Reduce the heat to low and stir in the coconut milk, chile, seafood, and noodles. Gently poach the seafood until the shrimp turn pink, about 5 minutes.

3. Ladle the soup into bowls, sprinkle with the cilantro, and serve immediately.

Note *Saifun is usually packaged in 8-ounce bags, with four 2-ounce bundles to a package. So, for this recipe, use 2 of those bundles.*

hot and sour wild mushroom soup

MAKES 4 SERVINGS

- 2 tablespoons mild vegetable oil, such as peanut
- 1/2 pound fresh oyster mushrooms, tough stems removed, halved
- 5 ounces fresh shiitake mushrooms, stems removed, halved
- One 15-ounce can straw mushrooms, drained (1 1/2 cups)
- 1 1/2 teaspoons freshly ground black pepper
- 2 large garlic cloves, minced (2 tablespoons)
- One 1-inch piece ginger, peeled and minced (1 tablespoon)
- 1/3 cup rice wine
- 2 cups chicken stock, preferably homemade (page 24)
- 1/4 cup red wine vinegar
- 1/4 cup oyster sauce
- 1 tablespoon Vietnamese chile-garlic paste, or to taste
- 3 tablespoons warm water
- 3 tablespoons cornstarch
- 1/4 pound firm tofu, cut into 1/8-inch dice (3/4 cup)
- 2 teaspoons toasted sesame oil

There's nothing subtle about my hot and sour soup. You may want to reduce the amount of chile paste in this recipe, at least the first time you make it. The firm tofu adds a nice texture to the soup.

1. Heat a large, nonreactive saucepan over medium heat. Add the vegetable oil and heat it, about 1 minute. Add all the mushrooms, the pepper, garlic, and ginger and cook, stirring constantly, for 1 minute.

2. Add the rice wine to the pan, bring to a boil over medium heat, and then let it simmer for 1 minute.

3. Stir the stock, vinegar, oyster sauce, and chile-garlic paste into the pan. Bring the soup to a boil.

4. In a small bowl, stir the water into the cornstarch. Whisk this mixture gradually into the soup until it thickens, about 30 seconds. Add the tofu. Ladle the soup into bowls, drizzle sesame oil on top, and serve immediately.

Thrifty Cooking

Don't throw out those mushroom stems! When a recipe calls for mushroom caps only, save the stems for another use. You can even store them in the freezer until you're ready to cook them. (Thaw them before using.) Add the stems, chopped, to any recipe that includes a *mirepoix*—the chopped aromatic mixture of carrots, celery, onions, and, sometimes, fennel—when you "sweat" the vegetables, or cook them, covered, until they release their juices. These stems will give the dish even more depth of flavor.

smoked chicken, hominy, and triple-chile soup

Makes 4 to 6 servings

¼ cup pure olive oil

1 small onion, cut into ¼-inch dice (1 cup)

3 large garlic cloves, minced (3 tablespoons)

1 tablespoon ground cumin

2 medium-size ancho chilies, toasted (*see* Note) and cut into ¼-inch dice

1 medium-size dried pasilla chile, toasted (*see* Note) and cut into ¼-inch dice

1 medium-size poblano chile, seeded and thinly sliced (½ cup)

¼ pounds plum tomatoes, seeded and chopped (3 cups)

3 cups chicken stock, preferably homemade (*page 24*)

1 small ear corn, kernels scraped from cob (*see* Note, *page 147*), or thawed frozen kernels (1 cup)

1½ cups canned hominy, drained

6 ounces smoked chicken, cut into ¼-inch dice

1 teaspoon freshly ground black pepper

2 tablespoons pure maple syrup

1 teaspoon kosher salt

2 tablespoons chopped cilantro (fresh coriander)

On my earliest trip to New Mexico, one of the first dishes I ate was posole, a hearty stew of meats and hominy. This is my version, with smoked chicken standing in for the meat. Each of the three chilies contributes a different flavor component to the soup—smokiness, slight sweetness, heat. I like to add something sweet, such as maple syrup, to this recipe, to counter the bitterness of dried chilies. This gives the posole a well-rounded flavor.

1. Heat a large, nonreactive saucepan over medium heat. Add the oil and heat it, about 1 minute. Add the onion, garlic, and cumin and cook, stirring constantly, until the onion is translucent, about 2 minutes.

2. Add all the chilies to the pan, along with the tomatoes, and cook, stirring, for 1 minute. Add the stock and bring the soup to a boil. Reduce the heat to low and simmer for 10 minutes.

3. Add all the remaining ingredients, except the cilantro, and simmer for 2 minutes. Remove the pan from the heat, ladle the soup into bowls, and sprinkle with the cilantro.

Note *To toast dried chilies, remove the stems and seeds. You can toast these chilies easily in a toaster oven for about 30 seconds on each side, or in a shallow baking pan under a broiler for about 10 to 15 seconds on each side. Make sure they do not burn. Be careful when you remove them from the oven or broiler because any smoke or steam they might give off will be as spicy as the chilies themselves.*

pollo albondigas soup

Makes 4 servings,
each with 3 large meatballs

Meatballs

1/2 pound skinless, bone-
less chicken leg meat
(2 drumsticks and 2 thighs),
cut into 1/2-inch dice

3 tablespoons minced onion

1 large garlic clove, minced
(1 tablespoon)

2 teaspoons puréed chipotle
chile en adobo (see Note,
page 37)

1 tablespoon minced cilantro
(fresh coriander)

One 1-inch strip red bell pepper,
cut into 1/8-inch dice
(1 tablespoon)

1 egg white, lightly beaten

1/4 teaspoon freshly ground
black pepper

1/2 teaspoon kosher salt

1/4 cup cooked white rice

Soup

4 cups chicken stock,
preferably homemade
(page 24)

1/2 small corn ear, kernels
scraped from cob (see Note,
page 147), or thawed frozen
kernels (1/2 cup)

1/2 medium-size poblano chile,
seeded and thinly sliced
(1/4 cup)

1 small ancho chile, toasted
(see Note, page 92) and
thinly sliced (2 tablespoons)

1 large plum tomato, seeded
and cut into 1/4-inch dice
(1/2 cup)

1/2 teaspoon ground cumin

1 teaspoon kosher salt

1/4 teaspoon freshly ground
black pepper

This is a lighter version of the traditional Mexican meatball soup, made with chicken instead of beef or pork. Chipotle chilies give this soup a spicy and smoky flavor.

If you like, garnish the soup with lime wedges and chopped cilantro.

1. Prepare the meatballs: Grind the chicken in a meat grinder, using the medium plate. Or chop the chicken in a food processor, using the pulse button to obtain a rough texture. Place the ground chicken and the other meatball ingredients in a cold, medium-size, nonreactive bowl and mix well. Measure out heaping tablespoons of this mixture and shape them into 12 balls. The mixture will feel quite loose because of the egg white. Place the meatballs on a dish and set them aside while preparing the broth.

2. Heat a large, nonreactive saucepan over medium heat. Add the stock and the remaining ingredients. Bring the broth to a boil, then reduce the heat to low and simmer until the ancho chile softens, about 2 minutes. Taste the broth and adjust the seasoning, if necessary.

3. Using a spoon, gently drop the meatballs into the broth and simmer them until they float, about 7 minutes.

4. Ladle the soup and meatballs into bowls, placing 3 meatballs in each. Serve immediately.

thai chicken and straw mushroom soup

MAKES 4 SERVINGS

- 2 tablespoons mild vegetable oil, such as corn
- One 1-inch piece ginger, peeled and minced (1 tablespoon)
- 1 small garlic clove, minced (1 teaspoon)
- 1 medium-size shallot, minced (2 tablespoons)
- 2 small serrano chilies, seeded and thinly sliced (1 tablespoon)
- 1/4 teaspoon freshly ground white pepper
- 4 cups chicken stock, preferably homemade *(page 24)*
- 1 lemongrass stalk, bottom 4 inches only, tough outer leaves removed, minced (2 tablespoons)
- 6 kaffir lime leaves, or 1 tablespoon finely grated lime zest
- 2 tablespoons nam pla (Thai fish sauce)
- 1/2 pound skinless, boneless chicken breast half, cut against the grain into 1/4-inch strips
- One 15-ounce can straw mushrooms, drained (1 1/2 cups)
- 6 tablespoons freshly squeezed lime juice
- 3 large fresh basil leaves, cut into 1/8-inch strips (1 tablespoon)
- 1 tablespoon chopped cilantro (fresh coriander)
- 1 teaspoon chile (satay) oil

The combination of lemongrass and kaffir lime leaves in this soup brings out a natural sour flavor which plays off the spiciness of the two types of chilies. Adding the chicken at the end of the cooking process allows it to poach gently and remain tender.

1. Heat a large, nonreactive saucepan over medium heat. Add the vegetable oil and heat it, about 1 minute. Add the ginger, garlic, shallot, chilies, and pepper and cook, stirring, until the shallot is translucent, about 1 minute.

2. Add the stock and lemongrass to the pan. Bruise the lime leaves by crumpling them with your hand. Add them or the lime zest to the pan with the nam pla. Bring the soup to a boil, reduce the heat to low, and simmer for 20 minutes.

3. Add the chicken and the mushrooms and simmer for 5 minutes. Remove the pan from the heat and stir in the lime juice. Ladle the soup into soup bowls, sprinkle with the basil, cilantro, and chile oil, and serve immediately.

tortilla soup

MAKES 6 SERVINGS

- ¼ cup pure olive oil
- 1 small onion, coarsely chopped (1¼ cups)
- 3 large garlic cloves, minced (3 tablespoons)
- 1 tablespoon ground cumin
- ½ teaspoon dried oregano leaves
- ½ teaspoon ground cayenne pepper
- 1 teaspoon freshly ground black pepper
- 1 small zucchini, coarsely chopped (1 cup)
- ½ medium-size or large chayote, pitted and coarsely chopped (1 cup)
- ¼ pound white mushrooms, chopped (1 cup)
- 2 to 3 medium-size serrano chilies, seeded and minced (3 to 4 teaspoons)
- 1 pound plum tomatoes, seeded and chopped (2½ cups)
- ½ cup tomato sauce, homemade or canned
- 3 cups chicken stock, preferably homemade (page 24)
- 2 teaspoons kosher salt, or more to taste
- Six 6-inch corn tortillas, preferably homemade (page 30), cut into ¼-inch dice
- ½ cup chopped cilantro (fresh coriander)

Garnish

- Three 6-inch corn tortillas, preferably homemade (page 30), cut into ¼-inch strips and fried (see Note)
- 6 lime wedges
- 6 tablespoons chopped cilantro (fresh coriander)

This is not the traditional Mexican tortilla soup, but rather a Bolivian-style version. My customers like it so much they won't let me take it off the menu.

It is very thick, almost like a hot dip. The crunchiness of the fried tortillas gives the soup a great texture, while the spices lend a hot, tangy flavor. Although the list of ingredients is long, the soup is quite simple to make.

1. Heat a large, nonreactive saucepan over medium heat. Add the oil and heat it, about 2 minutes. Add the onion, garlic, cumin, oregano, cayenne, and black pepper and cook, stirring often, for 2 minutes.

2. Add the zucchini, chayote, mushrooms, and chilies to the pan and cook, stirring often, for 2 additional minutes.

3. Add the tomatoes, tomato sauce, and stock to the same pan. Stir and bring to a boil still over medium heat. Reduce the heat to low and let the soup simmer, uncovered, for 10 minutes. Add the salt and the diced tortillas and continue simmering for 5 minutes.

4. Remove the pan from the heat and transfer the soup to a blender or food processor. (You may want to do this in small batches, depending on the size of your food processor.) Pulse until the soup is nearly smooth, leaving a bit of texture. Stir in the ½ cup of cilantro.

5. Ladle the soup into bowls. Garnish with the fried tortilla strips, the lime wedges, and the remaining cilantro. Serve immediately.

Note *To fry tortilla strips, heat 1 cup of mild vegetable oil to 375° in a small saucepan. Fry the tortilla strips, in batches, in the hot oil until crisp. Drain on paper towels.*

Salads

When I was growing up, I went to my grandmother's house several times each week. She always seemed to have a wide variety of salads on hand, including the Moroccan Eggplant Salad and Carrot-Cumin Salad in this chapter.

At the Authentic Cafe, we also offer a broad range of salads, using the bounty of what California has to offer. I feel extremely lucky to be able to serve food that is very fresh. We often get produce that was picked the same morning!

Citrus is commonly used in many of our salads. It seems to bring an incredible amount of life to food. The play of different textures is also an important element. Serving a mixture of cool, crisp greens, which already have a variety of flavors, with warm vegetables, chicken, Angus beef, or seafood, as well as with slippery glass noodles or crispy won tons, creates a sort of push and pull of opposites within one salad. The Yin and Yang Chicken Salad is one of the best examples of this juxtaposition of flavors and textures.

romaine salad with pumpkin-seed dressing

MAKES 4 TO 6 SERVINGS
AS A STARTER

Dressing

 ½ cup pumpkin seeds, toasted (*see* Note)

 2 tablespoons plus 2 teaspoons champagne vinegar

 2 tablespoons plus 2 teaspoons freshly squeezed lime juice

 1½ teaspoons Dijon mustard

 1 large garlic clove, minced (1 tablespoon)

 ½ cup packed chopped cilantro (fresh coriander)

 1 small serrano chile, seeded and minced (1 teaspoon)

 ½ teaspoon freshly ground black pepper

 ½ teaspoon kosher salt

 ½ cup extra-virgin olive oil

 2 heads romaine lettuce

 4 tomatillos, husked and cut crosswise into ⅛-inch slices

 4 plum tomatoes, cut crosswise into ⅛-inch slices

 ¼ cup pumpkin seeds, toasted

Romaine lettuce has the stiffness it takes to stand up to this thick dressing.

1. Prepare the dressing: Place the ½ cup pumpkin seeds in a blender or food processor and grind to a medium-fine texture. Add the remaining dressing ingredients, except the oil, and process for a few seconds. With the motor running, add the oil in a stream. Process until smooth and emulsified. This dressing can be refrigerated, covered, for up to 2 days. Bring it to room temperature and whisk to re-emulsify before serving.

2. Remove the outer few leaves from the lettuce and cut off the dark green tops of the remaining lettuce. Cut the lettuce crosswise into ½-inch pieces, wash, and spin dry.

3. Place the lettuce in a large bowl. Add the tomatillos and tomatoes and mix well. Add the dressing and toss, making sure that all the lettuce is well coated. Serve in a large salad bowl or on plates, garnished with the remaining pumpkin seeds.

Note *To toast pumpkin seeds, preheat the oven to 350°. Spread the raw pumpkin seeds in a single layer on a baking sheet and bake, stirring twice, until the seeds are lightly browned, 7 to 10 minutes.*

indonesian cucumber salad

MAKES 3 CUPS; 4 TO 6 SERVINGS
AS A STARTER OR SIDE DISH

1 large English
(hothouse) cucumber,
peeled, seeded, and
cut into ¼-inch dice
(2 cups)

½ small red onion,
minced (½ cup)

½ small ripe mango,
pitted, peeled, and
cut into ¼-inch dice
(½ cup)

1 small serrano chile,
seeded and minced
(1½ teaspoons)

One ½-inch strip red
bell pepper, cut into
⅛-inch dice
(1 tablespoon)

3 tablespoons very
thinly sliced fresh mint
leaves

One ½-inch piece ginger,
peeled and grated
(1½ teaspoons)

⅓ cup unsweetened
coconut milk

2 teaspoons nam pla
(Thai fish sauce)

1 tablespoon freshly
squeezed lime juice

¼ teaspoon freshly
ground black pepper

½ teaspoon chile
(satay) oil

In Indonesia and Thailand, nam pla, a fermented anchovy sauce, is used instead of salt. This seasoning imparts a unique flavor that is not easily duplicated. This salad is very refreshing with any grilled fish or with Thai Chicken Satay.

Mix all the ingredients gently in a medium-size, nonreactive bowl. Refrigerate, covered, for at least 1 hour before serving and up to 6 hours.

moroccan black olive and orange salad

MAKES 4 SERVINGS AS A STARTER

- 4 large navel or blood orange segments, all membranes removed (2 cups)
- ½ cup oil-cured black olives, pitted and halved
- ½ small red onion, halved and sliced paper thin (½ cup)
- 1 to 2 teaspoons harissa
- ¼ teaspoon freshly ground black pepper
- ½ teaspoon kosher salt
- 2 tablespoons extra-virgin olive oil

I've eaten this salad since I was a child. The citrus flavor plays off the saltiness of the olives, while the harissa, which is a Moroccan chile paste, adds just the right amount of heat to offset the oranges' sweetness.

Mix all the ingredients gently in a medium-size, nonreactive bowl. Refrigerate, covered, for at least 1 hour and up to 3 hours before serving.

red onion

blood oranges

black pepper

moroccan carrot-cumin salad

MAKES ABOUT 2 CUPS; 4 SERVINGS
AS A STARTER OR SIDE DISH

- 6 medium-size carrots, peeled and cut into $\frac{1}{2}$-inch rounds
- $1\frac{1}{2}$ teaspoons kosher salt
- 3 tablespoons pure olive oil
- 1 large garlic clove, minced (1 tablespoon)
- $1\frac{1}{2}$ tablespoons ground cumin
- $\frac{1}{2}$ teaspoon freshly ground black pepper
- 1 tablespoon harissa
- 2 tablespoons freshly squeezed lemon juice
- $\frac{1}{2}$ teaspoon kosher salt
- 1 tablespoon chopped Italian (flat-leaf) parsley
- 2 tablespoons extra-virgin olive oil

Here's another salad I have been eating at relatives' homes ever since I was a child. The lemon juice makes this a very refreshing salad.

1. Place the carrots and $1\frac{1}{2}$ teaspoons salt in a medium-size saucepan, cover with water, and bring to a boil over medium heat. Reduce the heat to low and simmer the carrots until they are just tender, 5 to 7 minutes. Meanwhile, prepare an ice bath with about 4 cups of cold water and about 6 ice cubes.

2. When the carrots are done, drain them quickly, then plunge them into the ice bath to stop the cooking. Drain the cooled carrots.

3. Heat a large braising or frying pan over medium heat until hot. Add the pure olive oil, garlic, cumin, and black pepper, then add the carrots and cook, stirring occasionally, for about 5 minutes. Make sure the carrots are well coated with the spices.

4. Place the carrots in a large, nonreactive bowl and add the harissa, lemon juice, $\frac{1}{2}$ teaspoon salt, the parsley, and the extra-virgin olive oil. Mix well and refrigerate, covered, until cool. Serve chilled or at room temperature. The salad can be refrigerated for up to 1 day.

fava bean salad

Two   15-ounce cans fava
      beans, drained

  3   tablespoons minced
      onion

  2   small garlic cloves,
      minced (2 teaspoons)

½   teaspoon
      ground cumin

  1   tablespoon minced
      Preserved Lemons,
      rind only *(page 27)*

¼   teaspoon freshly
      ground black pepper

  2   tablespoons freshly
      squeezed lemon juice

½   teaspoon harissa

¼   cup extra-virgin
      olive oil

  1   tablespoon minced
      Italian (flat-leaf)
      parsley

This is one of my favorite summer salads; it goes especially well with grilled meats and vegetables. Favas are large beans with a thick skin. They can be eaten with or without their skins.

Mix all the ingredients in a medium-size, nonreactive bowl. Refrigerate, covered, for at least 1 hour and up to 6 hours before serving.

fresh fava beans, tomatoes, fennel, and capers

MAKES 2 CUPS; 4 SERVINGS
AS A STARTER OR SIDE DISH

- 1 tablespoon kosher salt
- 1 pound fava beans in the pod, shelled (1 cup)
- 1 very small fennel bulb, cut into matchstick strips
- 1 large plum tomato, seeded and cut into ¼-inch dice (½ cup)
- 2 teaspoons drained capers, rinsed
- ¼ teaspoon freshly ground black pepper
- ¾ teaspoon kosher salt

This is a wonderful salad using one of my favorite beans. They appear frequently in southern French and Italian cuisines. You must use favas immediately after peeling them, because they blacken quickly. Just after cooking, toss them with anything acidic, such as tomatoes, citrus juice, or vinegar.

1. Prepare an ice bath with about 4 cups of cold water and about 6 ice cubes. In a medium-size saucepan, bring 4 cups of water to a boil with the 1 tablespoon of salt. Add the beans and boil until they seem soft, but not mushy, when squeezed, about 2 minutes. Drain the beans and plunge them into the ice bath to stop the cooking. Drain the cooled favas, tear off the ends with the marking, and, from the other end, squeeze the beans out of their skins.

2. Toss the peeled fava beans with the remaining ingredients in a medium-size, nonreactive bowl. Serve immediately.

moroccan eggplant salad

MAKES ABOUT 2½ CUPS;
5 OR 6 SERVINGS AS A STARTER OR
SIDE DISH

One 1- to 1¼-pound
eggplant

1 tablespoon pure olive
oil

4 large plum tomatoes

2 small garlic cloves,
minced (2 teaspoons)

½ teaspoon ground
cumin

½ teaspoon ground
cayenne pepper

1 tablespoon minced
Preserved Lemons,
rind only *(page 27)*

2 tablespoons freshly
squeezed lemon juice

¼ teaspoon freshly
ground black pepper

½ teaspoon kosher salt

1 tablespoon minced
Italian (flat-leaf)
parsley

1 tablespoon plus 2
teaspoons extra-virgin
olive oil

This is one of the salads my grandmother made when I was a child. Grab a hunk of warm bread and dip into it! Roasting the eggplant and tomatoes concentrates their flavors.

1. Pierce the eggplant several times with a fork, then rub it all over with 2 teaspoons of the pure olive oil. Place the eggplant in a small shallow baking pan and roast it until it is tender and begins to shrink, about 45 minutes. Remove the pan from the oven and let the eggplant cool just enough so that you can handle it. (The eggplant will be easier to peel when it is still warm, so don't let it cool completely.) Peel the eggplant, then cut it in quarters lengthwise and remove the seeds. Chop the eggplant coarsely. You should have about 1½ cups of pulp.

2. While the eggplant is baking, rub the tomatoes with the remaining 1 teaspoon of pure olive oil and arrange them in a medium-size shallow baking pan. Roast them at the same temperature until the skins begin to split and the tomatoes are tender, about 25 minutes. Let the tomatoes cool, then peel and seed them. Chop them coarsely. You should have about ¾ cup of pulp.

3. Combine the roasted eggplant and tomatoes and the remaining ingredients in a medium-size, nonreactive bowl and mix well. Let the salad sit at room temperature for at least 1 hour before serving. Serve at room temperature.

tabbouleh

Makes 4 cups; 4 to 8 servings
as a starter or side dish

¾ cup fine or medium
cracked wheat
(bulgur)

1½ cups boiling water

3 tablespoons freshly
squeezed lemon juice

1 medium-size
garlic clove, minced
(1¾ teaspoons)

3 to 4 green onions, white
and light green parts
only, finely chopped
(¼ cup)

½ cup minced Italian
(flat-leaf) parsley

2 tablespoons chopped
fresh mint

½ teaspoon freshly
ground black pepper

2 teaspoons kosher salt

3 tablespoons
extra-virgin olive oil

2 small plum tomatoes,
seeded and cut into
chunks (¾ cup)

¼ small English
(hothouse) cucumber,
peeled, seeded, and
cut into chunks
(½ cup)

This is a wonderful dish based on a much underutilized grain—cracked wheat. The mint and the cucumber add a cool touch. Try this salad with Falafel, Hummus, and Moroccan Eggplant Salad for the full Mediterranean treatment, or serve it as a side dish with cold roast meats or chicken.

1. Place the cracked wheat in a large, nonreactive bowl. Pour the boiling water over the wheat, then cover the bowl and let the wheat absorb the water, about 1 hour. Let cool completely.

2. Add the remaining ingredients, except the tomatoes and cucumber, and toss well. Mince the tomatoes and cucumber in a blender or food processor, then stir them into the other ingredients. Refrigerate, covered, for at least 1 hour before serving and up to 6 hours.

fennel–red onion salad

2 large bulbs fennel, very thinly sliced (3 cups)

1 small red onion, very thinly sliced (1 cup)

2 small garlic cloves, minced (2 teaspoons)

3 tablespoons freshly squeezed lemon juice

1 tablespoon aged red wine vinegar

¼ teaspoon freshly ground black pepper

1 teaspoon kosher salt

¼ cup extra-virgin olive oil

2 tablespoons minced fennel fronds

The anise flavor of fresh fennel is one I never tire of. This salad always makes me want to go on a picnic. All you need is some cheese and wine and a shady spot.

Combine all the ingredients in a large, nonreactive bowl and mix well. This salad can be refrigerated, covered, for up to 4 hours. Serve at room temperature.

tomato, cucumber, feta, and mint salad

MAKES 3 CUPS; 3 TO 4 SERVINGS
AS A STARTER

1 large English
(hothouse) cucumber
peeled, seeded, and
cut into ¼-inch dice
(2 cups)

2 large plum tomatoes,
seeded and cut into
¼-inch dice (1 cup)

½ small red onion,
minced (½ cup)

2 tablespoons chopped
cilantro (fresh corian-
der)

6 tablespoons chopped
fresh mint

2 large garlic
cloves, minced
(2 tablespoons)

2 tablespoons freshly
squeezed lemon juice

2 tablespoons
extra-virgin olive oil

¼ teaspoon freshly
ground black pepper

1 teaspoon kosher salt

2½ ounces semi-firm feta
cheese, preferably
French, drained and
cut into ¼-inch dice
(½ cup)

This classic, very refreshing salad blends cool cucumbers and fresh mint with salty feta cheese. It's hard to improve on tried-and-true combinations. Try to find French feta cheese for this recipe; you will enjoy its silky taste.

Combine all the ingredients, except the cheese, in a medium-size, nonreactive bowl and mix well. Gently fold in the cheese to prevent it from crumbling too much. Let the salad sit at room temperature for about 10 minutes to meld the flavors before serving. The salad can be refrigerated, covered, for up to 2 hours.

grilled cactus and papaya salad

MAKES 4 TO 6 SERVINGS
AS A STARTER

12 ounces (4 pieces) cactus (nopale) pads, spines removed (*see* Note)

2 tablespoons pure olive oil

1 tablespoon Authentic Cafe Spice Mix (*page 30*)

12 ounces (about 12 cups) mixed salad greens

1 large ripe papaya, peeled, seeded, and cut into ¼-inch dice (2 cups)

8 radishes, thinly sliced

1 small red onion, very thinly sliced (1 cup)

4 plum tomatoes, cut into ¼-inch slices

1½ ounces queso cotija añejo, grated (¼ cup)

½ cup Chipotle Chile Vinaigrette (*recipe follows*)

The sweet papaya and pungent radishes in this salad set off one another, while the cactus adds a slight tang and a consistency similar to that of crisply cooked green beans. The smokiness of the Chipotle Chile Vinaigrette brings all the flavors together.

1. Prepare a fire in a barbecue grill or preheat the broiler. Oil the grill/broiler rack. Rub the cactus pads with the oil and sprinkle with the Authentic Cafe Spice Mix.

2. Place the cactus on the grill/broiler rack about 6 inches from the heat and cook just until it softens, about 3 minutes on each side. Do not wait for the cactus to brown. Cool slightly and cut into ¼-inch strips.

3. Combine the grilled cactus with all the remaining ingredients in a large bowl and mix well. Serve in a large salad bowl or pile onto plates.

Note *Gloves must be worn when handling cactus. Using a knife, cut out the spines, which are sometimes hard to see.*

Cooking Cactus

Cactus is a vegetable that is not widely used, and this is a shame because it is has a unique and delicious flavor, a sort of cross between green beans and okra. Like okra, it is also a bit slippery when cooked. Make sure to wear rubber gloves when cleaning the cactus pads; their spines are fine but painful.

chipotle chile vinaigrette

1 large plum tomato

¼ teaspoon pure olive oil

2 tablespoons champagne vinegar

1 tablespoon puréed chipotle chile en adobo *(see* Note, *page 37)*, or puréed dried morita chile *(see* Note, *page 141)*

1 small shallot, minced (1 tablespoon)

1½ teaspoons Dijon mustard

1 to 2 green onions, white and light green parts only, chopped (2 tablespoons)

2 tablespoons chopped cilantro (fresh coriander)

¾ teaspoon chopped fresh oregano or ⅜ teaspoon dried

¾ teaspoon chopped fresh marjoram or ⅜ teaspoon dried

½ teaspoon freshly ground black pepper

¾ teaspoon kosher salt

6 tablespoons extra-virgin olive oil

This vinaigrette goes well with Grilled Cactus and Papaya Salad; the smoked spicy flavor of the chipotle (or morita) chilies contrasts with the papaya's sweetness. Also, try this vinaigrette with cold corkscrew pasta (fusilli), mixed with diced tomatoes, toasted pine nuts, and fresh cilantro.

1. Preheat the broiler. Rub the tomato with the pure olive oil and put the tomato in a small shallow baking pan. Broil the tomato, turning it once, until the skin turns black and blisters, about 3 to 5 minutes on each side. Remove the pan and let the tomato cool for a few minutes. Peel, seed, and coarsely chop the tomato. You should have about ¼ cup.

2. Place all the ingredients, except the extra-virgin olive oil, in a blender or food processor and purée. With the motor running, add the extra-virgin oil in a thin stream. Process until smooth and emulsified. The vinaigrette can be refrigerated, covered, for up to 2 days. Bring it to room temperature and whisk to re-emulsify before serving.

shrimp, crab, and cabbage slaw

MAKES 4 OR 5 SERVINGS
AS A STARTER

4 cups boiling water

2 teaspoons kosher salt

½ pound raw small to medium-size shrimp, peeled and deveined

½ pound lump crabmeat, preferably Dungeness, carefully picked over

½ small head red cabbage, finely shredded (2 cups)

½ small head green cabbage, finely shredded (2 cups)

3 to 4 green onions, white and light green parts only, thinly sliced (¼ cup)

One 2-inch strip red bell pepper, minced (¼ cup)

1 tablespoon black sesame seeds, toasted (see Note, page 47)

Lemongrass Vinaigrette (recipe follows)

This fresh and simple slaw combines Thai ingredients to create a crunchy treat. Using fresh Dungeness crabmeat here makes all the difference.

1. Bring the water to a boil in a medium-size saucepan over high heat and add the salt. Drop the shrimp into the pan and cook until they just turn pink and are firm, 1 to 2 minutes. Do not overcook. Drain the shrimp immediately and run them under cold water to stop the cooking. Drain again and let the shrimp cool.

2. Place the cooled shrimp and all the remaining ingredients in a large bowl and mix well. Refrigerate, covered, for 1 hour before serving and up to 3 hours.

lemongrass vinaigrette

MAKES ABOUT 1 CUP

- 1½ lemongrass stalks, bottom 3 or 4 inches only, tough outer leaves removed, minced (3 tablespoons)

- 2 tablespoons nam pla (Thai fish sauce)

- 2 tablespoons plus 1 teaspoon freshly squeezed lime juice

- 2 tablespoons minced fresh mint leaves

- 1½ teaspoons mild honey, such as orange

- 5 or 6 large garlic cloves, minced (¼ cup)

- 1 medium-size serrano chile, seeded and minced (1½ teaspoons)

- ½ cup mild vegetable oil, such as peanut

This vinaigrette uses traditional Thai products in an updated Western context. It's also delicious tossed with cold capellini or fettuccine for a first course.

Place all the ingredients, except the oil, in a blender or food processor and blend for a few seconds. With the motor running, add the oil in a thin stream. Process until smooth and emulsified. This vinaigrette can be refrigerated, covered, for up to 2 days. Bring it to room temperature and whisk to re-emulsify before serving.

crispy calamari salad

MAKES 4 SERVINGS AS A MAIN COURSE OR 8 AS A STARTER

2 cups mild vegetable oil, such as corn

2 ounces rice noodles (*see* Note)

Six 3½- to 4-inch square won ton skins, cut into ¼-inch strips

Crust

1 cup rice flour

½ cup cornstarch

1 teaspoon baking powder

2½ teaspoons Special Szechwan Salt *(page 28)*

1 tablespoon black sesame seeds, toasted *(see* Note, *page 47)*

1 pound small or medium-size cleaned calamari, with tentacles, bodies sliced into ¼-inch rings (do not slice the tentacles)

1 cup milk, poured into a shallow bowl

1 pound fresh spinach, stems removed, washed and dried

1 small red onion, very thinly sliced (1 cup)

½ cup slivered blanched almonds, lightly toasted

1 small carrot, grated (1 cup)

Hoisin-Plum Dressing *(recipe follows)*

1 tablespoon white or black sesame seeds, toasted

This salad incorporates many flavors, textures, and temperatures: I find the cool spinach leaves to be a refreshing foil for the hot fried calamari; the sweet flavors are an equally nice complement for the sour.

1. Heat the oil to 375° in a medium-size saucepan over medium heat. Use a candy thermometer to verify the temperature. Add the rice noodles and fry for about 30 seconds. If the oil is at the right temperature, they will puff up immediately and turn a translucent white. Remove the noodles using tongs or a slotted spoon and drain them on paper towels. Break the noodles into bite-size pieces and set aside.

2. Fry the won ton skins in the same oil until golden brown, about 1 minute. Drain on paper towels.

3. Now prepare the calamari: Combine all the crust ingredients in a shallow bowl and mix well. Dredge the calamari in the crust mixture, then dip it in the milk. Dredge the calamari in the crust mixture again, and shake off any excess.

4. Fry the calamari in 3 or 4 batches until brown and quite crisp, about 1 minute per batch. Do not overcook or the calamari will be tough. Verify that the oil is still at 375° between batches. (If the oil is not hot enough, the calamari will take too long to cook and will toughen; if the oil is too hot, the crust will burn and the calamari may not be cooked enough.) Remove the calamari from the oil and pat dry on paper towels.

5. Toss the fried noodles and won ton strips and all the remaining ingredients, except the sesame seeds, together in a large bowl. Arrange this spinach salad on plates and top with the calamari. Sprinkle with the sesame seeds and serve immediately.

Note *Rice noodles usually come in 1-pound bags, so use one-eighth.*

hoisin-plum dressing

MAKES 1 CUP

5 tablespoons
Chinese plum sauce

¼ cup hoisin sauce

2 tablespoons Dijon
mustard

1 sliver ginger,
peeled and grated
(¾ teaspoon)

1 small garlic clove,
minced (¾ teaspoon)

2 tablespoons plus 2
teaspoons rice vinegar

1 teaspoon Vietnamese
chile-garlic paste

½ teaspoon freshly
ground black pepper

¾ teaspoon toasted
sesame oil

2 tablespoons mild
vegetable oil, such as
peanut or soy

This dressing is delicious with roasted duck or roasted game birds, such as quail, squab, or pheasant.

Place all the ingredients, except the oils, in a blender or food processor and process for a few seconds. With the motor running, add the oils in a thin stream. Process until smooth and emulsified. This dressing can be refrigerated, covered, for up to 2 days. Bring it to room temperature and whisk to re-emulsify before serving.

pepper-crusted seared rare tuna salad

MAKES 4 SERVINGS AS A
MAIN COURSE

1   cup freshly ground
    black pepper

2   teaspoons kosher salt

¼   cup mild vegetable oil,
    such as peanut

One 1-pound tuna steak,
     cut into 4 pieces, skin
     and bones removed

2   egg whites, lightly
    beaten in a shallow
    bowl

Salad

1   pound (about 12 cups)
    mixed baby greens

One 3 ½-ounce package
     enoki mushrooms,
     bottoms sliced off

¼   pound sunflower
    greens (sprouts)

1   small red onion, very
    thinly sliced (1 cup)

½   pound plum tomatoes,
    seeded and cut into
    ¼-inch dice (1 cup)

    Citrus-Tahini Dressing
    (recipe follows)

½   cup salted sunflower
    seeds, toasted (see
    Note)

Having a natural food store across the street from the restaurant not only provides access to different ingredients, it also stimulates my creative processes. I love to eat sushi and sashimi, so I came up with this recipe for a "hot sashimi" salad using enoki mushrooms and sunflower greens, which add a nutty flavor.

1. Mix the pepper and salt together in a shallow bowl.

2. Heat a large nonstick sauté pan or frying pan over medium heat. Add the oil and heat it, about 2 minutes. Dip the tuna in the egg whites. Dredge the tuna in the pepper-salt mixture, then place in the pan. Sear the tuna, turning it once with a large wide spatula, until crusty on the outside but still rare in the middle, about 1 minute on each side. If you want tuna cooked through, cook it for 4 to 6 minutes on each side, depending on the thickness. Remove the tuna from the pan and let it rest for about 30 seconds.

3. Meanwhile, toss all the salad ingredients, including the dressing, together in a large bowl. Arrange the salad on plates. Sprinkle with the sunflower seeds.

4. Using a thin sharp knife, slice the tuna into ¼-inch strips. Arrange the slices around the salad, standing them up around the greens. Serve immediately.

Note *To toast sunflower seeds, preheat the oven to 375°. Spread the seeds in a layer on a baking sheet and bake them, stirring once, until they begin to pop, 5 to 6 minutes.*

citrus-tahini dressing

MAKES ABOUT 1¼ CUPS

- 2 tablespoons tahini
- 1 sliver ginger, peeled and minced (¾ teaspoon)
- 2 tablespoons drained Japanese pickled (sushi) ginger, chopped
- 2 tablespoons freshly squeezed lemon juice
- 2 tablespoons freshly squeezed orange juice
- 2 tablespoons mirin
- ⅛ teaspoon freshly ground white pepper
- ½ teaspoon Japanese togarishi spice mix
- ½ teaspoon kosher salt
- ½ teaspoon toasted sesame oil
- ¾ teaspoon chile (satay) oil
- 6 tablespoons mild vegetable oil, such as soy or peanut

The unique combination of citrus flavors with Japanese and Middle Eastern ingredients makes this simple dressing very appealing. Try this dressing also with a cold seafood platter: poached shrimp, crab legs, steamed mussels, clams, etc.

Place all the ingredients, except the oils, in a blender or food processor and blend for a few seconds. With the motor running, add the oils in a thin stream. Process until smooth and emulsified. This dressing can be refrigerated, covered, for up to 2 days. Bring it to room temperature and whisk to re-emulsify before serving.

yin and yang chicken salad

MAKES 4 SERVINGS AS A
MAIN COURSE OR 8 AS A STARTER

Marinade

1 cup hoisin sauce

½ cup plum sauce

⅓ cup rice vinegar

1 teaspoon Vietnamese chile-garlic paste

One ¼-inch piece ginger, peeled and minced (1 teaspoon)

1 small garlic clove, minced (1 teaspoon)

½ teaspoon toasted sesame oil

1 teaspoon minced cilantro (fresh coriander)

¼ cup mild vegetable oil, such as soy

1 pound skinless, boneless chicken legs (about 4 thighs and 4 drumsticks)

2 cups mild vegetable oil, such as soy

18 small square won ton skins, cut into ¼-inch strips

¼ pound rice noodles

1 medium-size head iceberg lettuce, shredded (8 cups)

2 medium-size carrots, peeled and grated (1 cup)

¼ pound mung bean sprouts (2 cups)

¼ small head red cabbage, shredded (2 cups)

1½ ounces slivered almonds, slightly toasted (*see Note, page 34*) (¼ cup)

¾ cup Red Ginger Vinaigrette (*recipe follows*)

Named for the contrasting and complementary universal forces in Chinese philosophy, this sweet/tart, soft/crunchy, mild/spicy Chinese chicken salad is like no one else's.

The chicken must be marinated a day before serving. Do not be daunted by the number of ingredients in this recipe. And, although there is a fair amount of chopping involved, the final assembly is extremely simple (that is, everything is just tossed together), and the salad is very satisfying.

1. Combine the marinade ingredients in a large, nonreactive bowl and mix well. Place the chicken in the marinade, making sure that each piece is well coated. Refrigerate, covered, overnight and up to 24 hours.

2. About 1½ hours before serving, preheat the oven to 350°. Remove the chicken from the marinade. Do not scrape the marinade off the chicken. Arrange the chicken on a nonstick baking sheet and bake until just done, about 15 minutes. Let the chicken cool and cut it against the grain into ¼-inch strips.

3. Heat the 2 cups of vegetable oil to 375° in a medium-size shallow pan. Use a candy thermometer to verify the temperature. Add the won ton strips and fry them until golden, about 1 minute. Remove them with a slotted spoon and drain on paper towels.

4. Verify that the oil is still at 375°. Add the rice noodles and fry them for about 30 seconds. If the oil is at the right temperature, they will puff immediately and turn a translucent white. Remove the noodles using tongs or a slotted spoon and drain on paper towels. Break the noodles into bite-size pieces.

5. Place the baked chicken, fried won ton strips and noodles, and all the remaining ingredients in a large bowl and toss well with the Red Ginger Vinaigrette. Arrange the salad on plates, mounding the salad high, and serve immediately.

red ginger vinaigrette

MAKES 1 CUP

One 1/4-inch piece ginger, peeled and minced (1 teaspoon)

1/4 cup minced candied red ginger

2 tablespoons red candied ginger syrup

2 to 3 green onions, white and light green parts only, sliced (2 tablespoons)

1/3 cup aged red wine vinegar

2 tablespoons dark (Chinese) soy sauce

1/2 teaspoon sugar

2 tablespoons toasted sesame oil

I first tasted a version of this dressing at a Chinese dim sum bar in Los Angeles. The sweet ginger is the perfect foil for the vinegar. This vinaigrette is also good with whole fried catfish or whole steamed rock cod.

Place all the ingredients, except the sesame oil, in a blender or food processor and purée. With the motor running, add the oil in a thin stream. Process until smooth and emulsified. This dressing can be refrigerated, covered, for up to 2 days. Bring it to room temperature and whisk to re-emulsify before serving.

thai chicken salad

MAKES 8 SERVINGS AS A
MAIN COURSE OR 8 AS A STARTER

¼ cup pure olive oil

1 pound skinless,
boneless chicken
breast half, cut into
1-inch cubes

Lime-Chile Vinaigrette
(recipe follows)

6 ounces saifun (mung
bean, or glass,
noodles), soaked in
very warm tap water
for 20 minutes, then
drained (*see* Note)

8 cups mixed salad
greens

1 medium-size carrot,
grated (½ cup)

1 cup (about 2 ounces)
mung bean sprouts

¼ cup fresh basil,
stacked, rolled tightly,
and very thinly sliced

2½ ounces roasted
peanuts, chopped
(½ cup)

Saifun (mung bean, or glass, noodles), a common and delightful ingredient in Thai cooking, gives this salad an unusual texture. The preparation is quite simple, and the use of other ingredients that are key to Thai cuisine—chilies, citrus, and herbs—keep it light and fresh tasting. I love this combination of hot and cold elements.

1. Heat a large sauté pan or frying pan over medium heat. Add the oil and heat it, about 2 minutes. Add the chicken and cook, turning the pieces once, for 2 minutes.

2. Add ½ cup of the Lime-Chile Vinaigrette and continue cooking until the vinaigrette and chicken juices reduce slightly, making sure that the vinaigrette does not separate, about 1 minute.

3. In a large bowl, toss the next 5 ingredients with the remaining vinaigrette. Pull the glass noodles apart if they are knotted. Arrange this mixture on 4 large plates, or 8 smaller ones.

4. Spoon some of the chicken and its cooking liquid over each of the salads. Sprinkle with the chopped peanuts and serve immediately.

Note *Saifun is usually packaged in 8-ounce bags, with four 2-ounce bundles to a package. So, for this recipe, use 3 of those bundles.*

lime-chile vinaigrette

MAKES 1½ CUPS

1 lemongrass stalk,
bottom 2 inches only,
tough outer leaves
removed, minced
(1 tablespoon)

⅔ cup freshly squeezed
lime juice

¼ cup nam pla
(Thai fish sauce)

2 tablespoons sugar

1 teaspoon Vietnamese
chile-garlic paste

1 large garlic clove,
minced (1 tablespoon)

2 large or 3 small
serrano chilies,
seeded and minced
(4 teaspoons)

⅓ cup chopped fresh
basil leaves, packed

½ cup pure olive oil

Use this vinaigrette to marinate and baste a whole roast chicken for a Thai accent.

Place all the ingredients, except the oil, in a blender or food processor and purée. While the machine is running, add the oil in a thin stream. Process until smooth and emulsified. This can be refrigerated, covered, for up to 2 days. Bring it to room temperature and whisk to re-emulsify before serving.

MAKES 4 SERVINGS AS A
MAIN COURSE

¼ cup pure olive oil

1 pound skinless,
boneless chicken
breast, cut against the
grain into ¼-inch strips

2 tablespoons Authentic
Cafe Spice Mix
(page 30)

1 large corn ear, kernels
scraped from cob (see
Note, page 147), or
thawed frozen kernels
(1½ cups)

1 small red onion, very
thinly sliced (1 cup)

1 large poblano chile,
roasted, peeled, seeded
(page 92), and sliced
into ⅛-inch strips
(1 cup)

1 pound (about 12 cups)
mixed salad greens

¾ cup Lime-Cilantro
Dressing (recipe
follows)

Four 8-inch flour tortillas,
warmed

2 cups Authentic Cafe
Black Beans (page 200),
warmed

4 ripe plum tomatoes,
quartered lengthwise

4 tomatillos, husked and
quartered lengthwise

One ½-pound jicama,
peeled and cut into
½ x ½ x 2-inch sticks
(see Note)

¼ cup chopped cilantro
(fresh coriander)

This dish started out as a tostada and, with the same elements, evolved into a layered salad. It's our bestseller in the restaurant at lunch.

1. Heat a large nonstick sauté pan or frying pan over medium heat. Add the oil and heat it, about 2 minutes. Season the chicken with the Authentic Cafe Spice Mix and add the chicken to the pan. Cook, stirring often, for 2 minutes. Add the corn, red onion, and poblano chile and cook, stirring, for 3 more minutes.

2. In a large bowl, toss the greens with the dressing.

3. Place a warm tortilla on each plate. Spread one-quarter of the Authentic Cafe Black Beans over the center of each tortilla. Mound the greens over the beans, then spoon the chicken mixture over the greens. Place the tomatoes and tomatillos around the greens, then place the jicama sticks on top. Sprinkle with the cilantro and serve immediately.

Note *After peeling jicama, the woody layer just underneath should be cut away.*

lime-cilantro dressing

MAKES 1½ CUPS

- 2 medium-size shallots, minced (3 tablespoons)
- ¼ cup chopped cilantro (fresh coriander)
- ¼ cup freshly squeezed lime juice
- 1 tablespoon Dijon mustard
- 1 small garlic clove, minced (1 teaspoon)
- ½ teaspoon sugar
- ¼ teaspoon freshly ground white pepper
- ⅓ teaspoon kosher salt
- ¾ cup mild vegetable oil, such as soy
- 2 tablespoons pure olive oil

This fresh-tasting and light dressing adds a decidedly Southwestern accent to any salad or piece of grilled fish.

Place all the ingredients, except the oils, in a blender or food processor and process for a few seconds. With the motor running, add the oils in a thin stream. Process until smooth and emulsified. This can be refrigerated, covered, for up to 2 days. Bring it to room temperature and whisk to re-emulsify before serving.

warm smoked chicken salad

MAKES 4 SERVINGS AS A MAIN
COURSE OR 8 AS A STARTER

1 cup mild vegetable oil,
such as soy

Two 6-inch corn tortillas,
preferably homemade
(page 30), cut into
⅛-inch strips

1 pound (about 12 cups)
mixed salad greens

4 plum tomatoes,
quartered lengthwise

2 cups drained
Vegetable Escabeche
(page 205)

2 tablespoons pure
olive oil

1 pound skinless,
boneless smoked
chicken meat, cut
against the grain into
¼-inch strips

½ pound oyster
mushrooms, sliced

1 large red onion, very
thinly sliced (2 cups)

Red Pepper
Vinaigrette *(recipe
follows)*

It seems to me that the components in this salad create a very round flavor. The pickled vegetables and the smoky chicken, combined with the sweet roasted Red Pepper Vinaigrette, meld seamlessly together. The tortilla garnish adds a crunchy textural note.

1. Heat the vegetable oil to 375° in a small saucepan. Use a candy thermometer to verify the temperature. Fry the tortilla strips until crisp and golden, about 1 minute. Remove them with a slotted spoon and drain on paper towels. Set aside.

2. Arrange the greens on plates. Place the tomatoes around the greens, then spoon the Vegetable Escabeche between the tomatoes.

3. Heat a large nonstick sauté pan or frying pan over medium heat. Add the olive oil and heat it, about 1 minute. Add the chicken, mushrooms, and onion and cook, stirring occasionally, until the onion and mushrooms begin to soften, about 3 minutes. (The chicken has already been cooked during the smoking process; you are really only heating it and releasing its flavors here.)

4. Spoon the chicken mixture onto the greens. Drizzle with the Red Pepper Vinaigrette, or pass it separately. Top with the tortilla strips and serve immediately.

red pepper vinaigrette

MAKES ¾ CUP

1 large red bell pepper

5 tablespoons pure
  olive oil

2 small shallots

2 tablespoons plus 2
  teaspoons Spanish
  sherry vinegar

1½ teaspoons Dijon
  mustard

⅛ teaspoon freshly
  ground black pepper

½ teaspoon kosher salt

3 tablespoons plus
  1 teaspoon pure
  olive oil

2 tablespoons
  extra-virgin olive oil

This simple vinaigrette is full of flavor, thanks
to the roasting of the sweet red pepper.
Serve it with chilled asparagus or as a dip for
cold boiled or steamed whole artichokes.

1. Preheat the broiler. Rub the bell pepper with 1 teaspoon
of the pure olive oil and put it in a small baking pan. Broil the
pepper until the skin begins to blister, about 2 minutes on
each side. Place the pepper in a small, nonporous bowl, cover
with plastic wrap, and let it "sweat" for about 20 minutes.
Peel the thin outer skin from the pepper and remove the stem
and seeds. Cut the pepper into large chunks.

2. Place the pepper chunks and all the remaining ingredients,
except the remaining pure olive oil and the extra-virgin olive
oil, in a blender or food processor. Blend until smooth. With
the motor running, add the oils in a thin stream. Process until
smooth and emulsified. This dressing can be refrigerated,
covered, for up to 2 days. Bring it to room temperature and
whisk to re-emulsify before serving.

grilled chicken and gorgonzola salad

MAKES 4 SERVINGS AS A
MAIN COURSE

Four   6-ounce skinless,
       boneless chicken
       breast halves

2   tablespoons pure
    olive oil

¼   teaspoon kosher salt

Pinch   freshly ground black
        pepper

1   pound (about 12 cups)
    mixed baby greens

    Balsamic Vinaigrette
    (recipe follows)

1   small red onion, very
    thinly slice (⅔ cup)

    Candied Pecans
    (recipe follows)

6   ounces Gorgonzola
    cheese, crumbled
    (1½ cups)

4   plum tomatoes,
    quartered lengthwise

This salad combines several different spectra of flavor—smoky, sweet, and tangy—and texture: Gorgonzola, with its pleasant, creamy bite, is a perfect foil for the sugary, crunchy pecans.

1. Prepare a fire in a barbecue grill or preheat the broiler. Oil the grill/broiler rack. Rub the chicken with the oil, salt, and pepper.

2. Place the chicken on the grill/broiler rack about 6 inches from the heat and cook, turning it once with a large wide spatula, for about 3 minutes on each side. Remove the chicken from the heat, let it rest for about 30 seconds, and then cut it against the grain into ¼-inch strips.

3. In a large bowl, toss the greens with the Balsamic Vinaigrette and arrange on plates or a platter. Top the greens with the onion, Candied Pecans, and cheese. Place the tomatoes around the greens. Top with the chicken and serve immediately.

balsamic vinaigrette

Makes about 1¼ cups

- ¼ cup balsamic vinegar
- 2 medium-size shallots, minced (3 tablespoons)
- 1 tablespoon Dijon mustard
- ¼ teaspoon freshly ground black pepper
- ¼ teaspoon kosher salt
- ¾ cup pure olive oil

Fantastic with grilled vegetables, this extremely simple dressing can also be used to marinate the vegetables before grilling.

Place all the ingredients, except the olive oil, in a blender or food processor and process for a few seconds. With the motor running, add the oil in a thin stream. Process until smooth and emulsified. This dressing can be refrigerated, covered, for up to 2 days. Bring it to room temperature and whisk to re-emulsify before serving.

candied pecans

Makes about 1 cup

- 1 cup pecan halves
- 2 tablespoons packed light or dark brown sugar
- 1 tablespoon water
- ½ teaspoon kosher salt

These pecans are great for a sweet crunch with pancakes and waffles, or as a nibble with cocktails.

Preheat the oven to 325°. Mix all the ingredients in a small bowl, making sure that the nuts are well coated. Arrange the nuts in a single layer on a nonstick baking sheet and bake them until browned and crispy, 7 to 10 minutes. These burn easily, so watch them carefully.

marinated grilled skirt steak salad

MAKES 4 SERVINGS AS A
MAIN COURSE

Marinade

2 tablespoons heavy (Chinese) soy sauce

2 tablespoons balsamic vinegar

2 tablespoons champagne vinegar

1 small garlic clove, minced (1 teaspoon)

1 small serrano chile, seeded and minced (1$\frac{1}{2}$ teaspoons)

1 tablespoon minced cilantro (fresh coriander)

1 teaspoon sugar

$\frac{1}{4}$ teaspoon freshly ground black pepper

$\frac{1}{3}$ cup mild vegetable oil, such as soy

1$\frac{1}{2}$ pounds skirt steak, fat and tendons removed

1 pound (12 cups) mixed salad greens

Balsamic Vinaigrette (page 125)

1 small red onion, cut into $\frac{1}{8}$-inch slices (1 cup)

8 ounces feta cheese, crumbled (about 1$\frac{1}{2}$ cups)

24 Calamata olives, pitted and halved

4 plum tomatoes, quartered lengthwise

This salad requires some planning, as the skirt steak should marinate for at least 12 hours. It's well worth the wait, however, since the final assembly is quite simple and the meat is amazingly tender. If you do not have a barbecue grill, you can broil the steak with somewhat different, but still delicious, results. My friend, Jerry Burgos, came up with the marinade recipe.

1. Place all the marinade ingredients, except the oil, in a blender or food processor. Process for a few seconds to mix. With the blender or processor running, add the oil in a thin stream.

2. Place the marinade in a medium-size, nonreactive bowl with the steak (cut the steak to fit, if necessary), making sure that the meat is completely covered with the marinade. Refrigerate, covered, for at least 12 hours and up to 24 hours. Do not scrape the marinade off the steak before using. Discard any remaining marinade.

3. Prepare a fire in a barbecue grill, using fruitwood if possible, or preheat the broiler. Oil the grill/broiler rack.

4. Place the marinated steak on the grill/broiler rack about 6 inches from the heat and cook, turning it once, until medium-rare, 3 to 4 minutes on each side.

5. In a large bowl, combine the greens with the Balsamic Vinaigrette and mix well. Arrange the greens on plates and top with the onion, cheese, and olives. Place the tomatoes around the salad.

6. Cut the steak against the grain into $\frac{1}{4}$-inch slices. Lay the steak on top of the salads and serve immediately.

Fish and Seafood

We are fortunate to have an abundance of fish and seafood available to us. These include soft-shell crabs from Maryland, Gulf shrimp caught off the shore of Florida, crawfish from Louisiana, New Zealand red snapper, Mexican sea bass, and much, much more.

Fish and seafood lend themselves to a vast array of preparations, and we include a good number of these here. Make sure to find only the best fishmonger in your city or town, and use only the freshest fish and seafood available to you.

Whenever traveling, I always make it a point to go to the markets and check out the local catch. The diversity of fish and seafood available from all over the world never ceases to amaze me. And, I have found the simplest preparations to be the best.

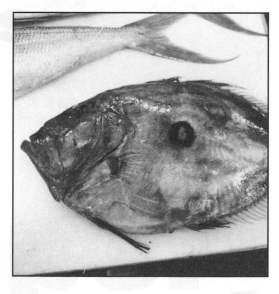

I love to cook fish quickly with some sort of nut or seed crust. Not only does this add new dimensions in flavor and texture to fish that may otherwise be considered mundane, it provides for a fish that is crisp on the outside and moist and tender inside. Many of the recipes, whether crusted or not, include a salad or side dish for a full meal on one plate.

From the Roasted Whole Red Snapper on a Moroccan Tomato, Black Olive, and Preserved Lemon Salad to the Pecan-Cornmeal-Crusted Catfish Club Sandwich, we will cook our way around the continents.

sautéed soft-shell crab sandwich

MAKES 4 SERVINGS

Crust

1 cup rice flour

½ cup cornstarch

1 teaspoon baking powder

1 teaspoon Szechwan peppercorns, toasted (see Box, page 131) and ground

½ teaspoon freshly ground black pepper

1 tablespoon kosher salt

4 very fresh soft-shell crabs, cleaned

1 cup milk, poured into a shallow bowl

½ cup mild vegetable oil, such as corn

4 large crusty rolls, or 1 baguette cut crosswise into 4 equal pieces

½ cup Pickled Ginger and Black Sesame Mayonnaise (recipe follows)

Fresh soft-shell crabs have a very short season starting mid-May, so grab them while you can. Here is a great sandwich that reminds me of the East Coast (while I was in Maryland I couldn't stop eating these crabs), but with an Asian flavor.

1. Combine all the crust ingredients in a shallow bowl and mix well. Dredge the crabs in the crust mixture, then dip them in the milk. Dredge the crabs in the crust mixture again, and shake off any excess.

2. Heat a large, nonreactive sauté pan or frying pan over medium heat. Add the oil and heat it until shimmering, or until 350°. Use a candy thermometer to verify the temperature. (This is a small amount of oil, so it should heat quickly. If the oil is the right temperature, the crabs should crackle when placed in the oil.) Add the crabs to the pan and cook, turning them once, carefully, with tongs, until quite crisp, about 3 minutes on each side. Remove the crabs to paper towels and pat dry.

3. Cut the rolls or baguette pieces in half horizontally, and spread each half with about 1 tablespoon of the Pickled Ginger and Black Sesame Mayonnaise. Place a crab in each roll and serve immediately.

pickled ginger and black sesame mayonnaise

MAKES ABOUT 1¼ CUPS

1 cup mayonnaise

2 tablespoons minced drained Japanese pickled (sushi) ginger, marinade reserved

1 tablespoon Japanese pickled (sushi) ginger marinade (*from above*)

1 green onion, white and light green parts only, minced (1 tablespoon)

1 tablespoon Japanese togarishi spice mix

1 teaspoon toasted black sesame seeds, toasted (*see* Note, page 47)

1 teaspoon chile (satay) oil

Combine all the ingredients in a small, nonreactive bowl and whisk together well. The mayonnaise can be refrigerated, covered, for up to 3 days.

fennel and coriander–crusted rare tuna with chick-pea, red onion, and fennel salad

MAKES 4 SERVINGS

Chick-pea salad

3 cups cooked chick-peas (garbanzo beans), drained (*see* Note)

1 large fennel bulb, cut into ¼-inch dice (1½ cups)

⅓ small red onion, cut into ⅛-inch dice (⅓ cup)

The chick-pea salad can be prepared ahead, and the tuna only takes a few minutes to prepare and cook, making this dish extremely simple to put together. Still, it's somewhat exotic. The combination of fresh fennel bulb and fennel seed is delicious.

1. Combine all of the salad ingredients in a medium-size, nonreactive bowl and mix well. This salad can be refrigerated, covered, for up to 6 hours. Bring it to room temperature before serving.

2 small garlic cloves,
   minced (2 teaspoons)

One 1-inch strip red bell
   pepper, minced
   (1 tablespoon)

½ teaspoon freshly
   ground black pepper

⅓ cup freshly squeezed
   lemon juice

2 tablespoons chopped
   fennel fronds

1 teaspoon kosher salt

⅓ cup extra-virgin
   olive oil

Fennel-coriander crust

¼ cup coarsely
   ground fennel

¼ cup coarsely
   ground coriander

1 tablespoon freshly
   ground black pepper

2 teaspoons kosher salt

2 teaspoons sugar

Four 8-ounce skinless,
   boneless tuna steaks,
   1 inch thick, trimmed
   of tendons and dark
   tissue

3 large eggs whites,
   lightly beaten in a
   shallow bowl

¼ cup pure olive oil

4 lemon wedges

2. Combine the crust ingredients in a shallow bowl, and mix well.

3. Dip the tuna steaks in the egg whites. Dredge the steaks in the crust mixture, and shake off any excess.

4. Heat a large nonstick sauté pan or frying pan over medium heat. Add the pure olive oil and heat it, about 2 minutes. Place the tuna steaks in the pan and cook, turning them once with a large wide spatula until the crust darkens somewhat and becomes crisp, and the fish is nearly opaque through, about 2 minutes on each side. If you want tuna cooked through, cook it for 4 to 6 minutes on each side, depending on the thickness.

5. Arrange the salad on dinner plates or shallow soup plates. Place a tuna steak on each salad and garnish with a lemon wedge. Serve immediately.

Note *Use two 15-ounce cans of chick-peas (garbanzo beans), or soak 1½ cups of dried chick-peas overnight, refrigerated, then cook them in 1½ quarts of water until tender, about 45 minutes. Add 2 teaspoons of kosher salt toward the end of the cooking time.*

Whole Spices: Even More Fragrance

When a recipe calls for ground spices, such as fennel or coriander, start with the whole spices. Just before using them, toast the seeds dry over low heat in a skillet to bring their oils to the surface. Then grind them.

Chermoula

2 cups packed coarsely chopped Italian (flat-leaf) parsley

2 cups packed coarsely chopped cilantro (fresh coriander)

10 large garlic cloves, chopped

½ cup freshly squeezed lemon juice

3 tablespoons champagne vinegar

¼ teaspoon ground turmeric

2 tablespoons sweet paprika

1 teaspoon ground cayenne pepper

1 tablespoon ground cumin

1 tablespoon freshly ground black pepper

1½ teaspoons kosher salt

1 cup extra-virgin olive oil

Four 8-ounce skinless halibut fillets, about 1 inch thick

Chermoula is a very aromatic Moroccan spice paste used as a sauce as well as for marinating. I first had a dish similar to this one, made with sea bream, in Rabat, Morocco. The ground spices permeate the fish, lending an exotic flavor to a thoroughly simple preparation.

1. Prepare the chermoula: Place the herbs, garlic, lemon juice, and vinegar in a food processor and process until pasty. Stir in the remaining ingredients by hand.

2. Place the halibut fillets in a medium-size shallow, nonreactive baking pan, and add half the chermoula. Make sure the fillets are completely covered with the sauce. Refrigerate, covered, for 4 to 6 hours, but not longer, or the vinegar and lemon juice will "cook" the fish. Refrigerate the remaining chermoula, covered, but serve it at room temperature.

3. Prepare a fire in a barbecue grill, or preheat the oven to 400°. Oil the grill rack.

4. Place the fillets on the grill rack about 6 inches from the heat and cook, turning once with a large wide spatula, just until opaque through, about 3 minutes on each side. Or place the fillets in a medium-size shallow baking pan (do not use the cold dish in which you marinated the fish as it may crack when you put it in the hot oven), and roast it until opaque through, 20 to 25 minutes.

5. Place the fish on plates and ladle the remaining chermoula over the top. Serve immediately.

red snapper with capers, olives, and lemon

MAKES 4 SERVINGS

Four 6-ounce skinless red
  snapper fillets

2 tablespoons pure olive oil

$1/4$ teaspoon kosher salt

$1/4$ teaspoon freshly ground
  black pepper

Vinaigrette

2 tablespoons champagne
  vinegar

2 tablespoons sherry
  vinegar

1 large shallot, minced
  (2 tablespoons)

$1/8$ teaspoon freshly ground
  black pepper

$1/4$ teaspoon kosher salt

$1/4$ cup mild vegetable oil,
  such as peanut

$1/4$ pound (about 4 cups)
  mixed salad greens

Sauce

2 tablespoons unsalted
  butter

2 tablespoons pure olive oil

2 tablespoons capers,
  rinsed and drained

2 small plum tomatoes,
  peeled, seeded, and cut
  into $1/8$-inch dice (1 cup)

10 Calamata olives, pitted
  and quartered

$1/4$ teaspoon freshly ground
  black pepper

3 tablespoons grated
  lemon zest

This dish combines many of the flavors of southern France. The simplicity of the dish is what makes it so good. Try it when you want a fine meal but don't have much time.

Whether you use a grater or a citrus zester to remove the lemon zest, make sure to use only the yellow part of the peel; the white part underneath will be bitter.

1. Preheat the oven to 400°.

2. Rub the fish with the oil, salt, and pepper. Place fillets in a medium-size shallow baking dish and bake them until the fish is opaque through, about 20 minutes.

3. Meanwhile, in a small bowl, whisk together all the vinaigrette ingredients, except the oil. Add the oil in a thin stream at the end. In a medium-size bowl, toss the salad greens with this vinaigrette, and arrange them on plates.

4. When the fish is nearly cooked, place all the sauce ingredients, except 1 tablespoon of the lemon zest, in a small saucepan and cook them, stirring occasionally, over low heat for 2 minutes.

5. Place 1 fish fillet on the greens on each plate. Spoon some of the sauce over the fish, then garnish with the reserved lemon zest. Serve immediately. Pass any remaining sauce separately.

walnut-crusted trout with braised fennel sauce

MAKES 4 SERVINGS

Braised Fennel Sauce
(recipe follows)

Crust

¾ cup ground walnuts
(*see* Note)

¼ cup fine dried bread crumbs

2 medium-size garlic cloves, minced
(1½ teaspoons)

⅛ teaspoon freshly ground black pepper

1½ teaspoons kosher salt

½ teaspoon ground fennel

1 small fennel bulb, cut lengthwise into
1/16-inch slices (1 cup)

½ teaspoon kosher salt

¼ teaspoon freshly ground pepper

Four 8-ounce trout fillets, skin left on

1 cup all-purpose flour, spread in a shallow bowl

4 large egg whites, lightly beaten in a shallow bowl

¼ cup mild vegetable oil, such as corn

1 tablespoon minced fresh fennel fronds

By using ground fennel seed in the walnut crust, you accentuate the braised fennel in the sauce and the sliced fresh fennel cooked inside the trout. The fish will absorb some of the sauce underneath, which will make it crisp on top, yet very moist on the bottom and throughout.

1. Warm the Braised Fennel Sauce in a medium-size saucepan over low heat, stirring occasionally.

2. Meanwhile, combine all the crust ingredients in a shallow bowl and mix well.

3. In a small bowl, toss the fennel with the salt and pepper. Arrange the trout fillets, skin side down, on a work surface. Place one-quarter of the fennel down the center of each trout fillet, then fold the fillet in half lengthwise with the fennel inside.

4. Dredge the folded trout fillets (which should have the skin side on the outside) in the flour, and shake off any excess. Dip them into the egg whites, then dredge them into the crust mixture.

5. Heat a large nonstick sauté pan or frying pan over low heat. Add the oil and heat it through, about 2 minutes. Cook the fish, turning it once with a large flat spatula, until the crust is golden brown, not blackened at all, and the fish is opaque through, about 6 minutes on each side.

6. Ladle some of the Braised Fennel Sauce on each of 4 plates or on a platter. Sprinkle the fennel fronds on top. Place the fish on the sauce and serve immediately. Pass any remaining sauce separately.

Note *To grind the walnuts, place them in a blender or food processor and pulse them a few times. Do not process continuously or the nuts will become oily. The walnuts may be coarsely ground for this recipe.*

braised fennel sauce

2 tablespoons pure olive oil

2 small fennel bulbs, outer tough leaves removed, cut lengthwise into $\frac{1}{16}$-inch slices (2 cups)

1 large garlic clove, minced (1 tablespoon)

1 teaspoon ground fennel

$\frac{1}{4}$ teaspoon freshly ground black pepper

$\frac{1}{2}$ teaspoon red chile flakes

3 cups chicken stock, preferably homemade (page 24)

$\frac{1}{2}$ teaspoon kosher salt

Using the different parts of the fennel bulb gives the sauce depth of flavor. This simple sauce is a natural with the walnuts in the crust of Walnut-Crusted Trout. Or, for a simple side dish, toss penne pasta in this sauce.

1. Heat a large, nonreactive saucepan over low heat. Add the olive oil and heat it, about 1 minute. Add the fennel and cook, stirring occasionally, until it begins to brown, about 7 to 10 minutes.

2. Add the garlic, ground fennel, pepper, and chile flakes. Cook, stirring, for 1 minute.

3. Increase the heat to medium, add the stock, and bring to a boil. Reduce the heat again to low and simmer until the liquid reduces by half, about 45 minutes. Add the salt. Using a blender, food processor, or hand-held (inversion) blender, purée the sauce until smooth.

4. Strain the sauce through a medium-mesh strainer or china cap. Discard the contents of the strainer or china cap. Serve immediately, or keep warm in a medium-size covered saucepan. The sauce can be refrigerated, covered, for up to 2 days.

China Cap (Conical Strainer)

This cone-shaped strainer, which may be made of fine wire mesh or a perforated sheet of stainless steel, is ideal for straining sauces and stocks. Because of its shape, the liquid flows along the outside of the strainer and pours from the bottom, allowing you to strain a large amount of liquid into a vessel with a relatively narrow opening.

grilled shrimp and scallop skewers with mussels, rapini, and mushrooms

MAKES 4 SERVINGS

2 large cloves garlic, minced (2 tablespoons)

2 stalks lemongrass, bottom 3 to 4 inches, outer leaves removed, minced (4 tablespoons)

1 tablespoon kosher salt

½ teaspoon freshly ground black pepper

¼ teaspoon toasted sesame oil

One 1¾-inch piece ginger, peeled and minced (5 teaspoons)

6 tablespoons extra-virgin olive oil

24 raw medium-size shrimp, shells on, butterflied

24 raw medium-size sea scallops, rubbery hinges removed

1½ pounds rapini, bottom 3 inches of stems trimmed

1½ teaspoons Vietnamese chile-garlic paste

2 ounces fresh shiitake mushrooms, stems removed, sliced ¼ inch thick

The rapini in this dish is reminiscent of Chinese broccoli, but the stalks are thinner, the plant is less leafy, and as a whole, it is much more tender. Rapini also has a slight bitterness, offsetting the other ingredients in the dish. Partially butterflying the shrimp—that is, cutting down their back two-thirds of the way through to their belly sides—allows the marinade to permeate completely.

1. In a medium-size, nonreactive bowl, combine 1 tablespoon of garlic, 2 tablespoons of lemongrass, 1 teaspoon of salt, the pepper, sesame oil, 3 teaspoons (1 tablespoon) of ginger, and ¼ cup of oil. Stir well, then place the shrimps and scallops in this marinade, making sure they are completely covered. Refrigerate the seafood, covered, for at least 2 hours and up to 4 hours.

2. Bring 12 cups of water and 2 teaspoons of salt to a rolling bowl in a large saucepan over high heat. Prepare an ice bath with 8 cups of water and 12 ice cubes. Plunge the rapini into the boiling water, making sure that it is completely submerged by pushing it down with a pair or tongs or a spoon. Boil the rapini for 1 minute, then remove it all at once with the tongs or with a slotted spoon, and place it directly in the ice water bath. Once the rapini is cold, drain it completely, squeezing out any excess water. Mound the rapini on a cutting board and cut them in half, just for ease in handling. This step may be done ahead, in which case you should refrigerate the rapini until it is to be reheated for serving.

One 8-ounce can straw
 mushrooms, drained
 (³/₄ cup)

 1 medium-size red bell
 pepper, cut length-
 wise into ¹/₈-inch
 slices (1 cup)

16 very fresh farm-
 raised green- or red-
 lip mussels,
 debearded, shells
 scraped clean

 2 tablespoons nam pla
 (Thai fish sauce)

¹/₄ cup Shrimp Stock
 (page 26) or chicken
 stock, preferably
 homemade *(page 24)*

 1 cup unsweetened
 coconut milk

 2 tablespoons freshly
 squeezed lime juice

Twelve 6-inch bamboo
 skewers, soaked in
 water for 8 hours
 and drained

¹/₂ teaspoon freshly
 ground black pepper

 4 teaspoons black
 sesame seeds,
 toasted *(see* Note,
 page 47*)*

3. Prepare a fire in a barbecue grill, or preheat the broiler. Oil the grill/broiler rack.

4. Heat a very large frying pan or a large shallow braising pan over low heat. Add the remaining 2 tablespoons of oil and heat it, about 1 minute. Place the remaining garlic, ginger (2 teaspoons), lemongrass, and the chile-garlic paste in the pan and cook, stirring constantly, until fragrant, about 1 minute.

5. Add the shiitakes, straw mushrooms, and bell pepper to the pan and cook until the shiitakes just begin to soften, about 1 minute.

6. Place the mussels in the pan, along with the drained rapini, and stirring constantly, cook for 30 seconds more.

7. Pour the nam pla, stock, coconut milk, and lime juice over the rapini and mussels, stir well, and raise the heat to medium. As soon as the liquid begins to boil, cover the pan and allow it to simmer for 3 minutes.

8. Meanwhile, remove the seafood from the marinade and thread 2 shrimp and 2 scallops, alternating, on each of the 12 skewers. Place the seafood skewers on the grill/broiler rack about 6 inches from the heat and cook, turning once, until the scallops are just opaque, and the shrimp shells just turn pink, about 1 minute on each side.

9. If all the mussels have opened, they can be served now. If not, cover the pan again and simmer for another minute or two. After a total of 5 minutes of simmering time, discard any still unopened.

10. Use a pair of tongs to place a mound of rapini in the middle of each of 4 soup plates. Spoon the cooking liquid and other vegetables around the rapini. Sprinkle ground pepper all over, and the toasted sesame seeds on the liquid. Place 3 skewers, points in the middle, ends radiating outward like the bottom of a peace sign, on each pile of rapini. Place the opened mussels between the skewers. Serve immediately.

green onion–black sesame catfish

MAKES 4 SERVINGS

Crust

2 bunches green onions,
white and light green
parts only, minced
(¹/₂ cup)

2 tablespoons black
sesame seeds, toasted
(see Note, *page 47)*

1 cup Pankow rice
bread crumbs

¹/₂ cup rice flour

¹/₄ teaspoon freshly ground
black pepper

1 tablespoon granulated
garlic

1 teaspoon kosher salt

One ³/₄-inch piece ginger,
peeled and minced
(2 teaspoons)

Four 6-ounce skinless
catfish fillets

1 cup rice flour, spread in
a shallow bowl

4 large egg whites, lightly
beaten in a shallow bowl

¹/₄ cup mild vegetable oil,
such as peanut

1¹/₂ recipe cups Green
Curry–Coconut Sauce
(recipe follows)

4 teaspoons black sesame
seeds, toasted

This is one of my favorite fish dishes. The Asian ingredients, especially the Japanese rice bread crumbs in the crust, create a crispy coating. The Green Curry–Coconut Sauce adds a sweet and fiery touch to this dish.

1. Combine the crust ingredients in a shallow bowl and mix well. Dredge the catfish fillets in the rice flour, and shake off any excess. Dip them in the egg whites. Dredge the fillets in the crust mixture.

2. Heat a large nonstick sauté pan or frying pan over medium heat. Add the oil and heat it, about 2 minutes. Add the fish and cook, turning it once with a large wide spatula, until the crust is golden and the fish is opaque through, about 4 or 5 minutes on each side. Remove the fish to paper towels and pat dry.

3. Ladle the Green Curry–Coconut Sauce onto plates. Place 1 catfish fillet on each plate, sprinkle the black sesame seeds onto the sauce, and serve immediately. Pass any remaining sauce separately.

green curry–coconut sauce

MAKES ABOUT 3 CUPS

½ cup mild vegetable oil, such as peanut

Green Curry Paste (page 29)

3 cups chicken stock, preferably homemade (page 24), or Shrimp Stock (page 26)

1 cup unsweetened coconut milk

2 tablespoons cornstarch

2 tablespoons water

This classic Thai sauce can be used in many ways. It is great with seafood, chicken, or vegetables. For one alternative, simmer some clams, mussels, and shrimp in this sauce until the clams and mussels open, and serve some steamed jasmine rice on the side. The coconut milk gives the sauce a rich and exotic flavor.

1. Heat a medium-size, nonreactive saucepan over low heat. Add the oil and heat it, about 2 minutes. Add the curry paste and cook, stirring constantly with a wooden spoon, for 2 minutes. The paste tends to burn quickly.

2. Increase the heat under the saucepan to medium and stir in the stock. Once the liquid begins to boil, reduce the heat again to low and simmer until the stock reduces by one-half, about 30 minutes.

3. Stir in the coconut milk; continue cooking and stirring over low heat until the sauce boils, about 5 minutes.

4. Meanwhile, in a small bowl, mix together the cornstarch and water. Just before the sauce comes to a boil, whisk in the cornstarch mixture. Let the sauce simmer over low heat for 1 minute. Serve warm.

sautéed catfish on cheddar cheese grits with pecan–morita chile sauce

MAKES 4 SERVINGS

Pecan–Morita Chile
Sauce *(recipe follows)*

2 cups Cheddar Cheese
Grits *(page 202)*

Four 6-ounce skinless
catfish fillets

1 teaspoon kosher salt

½ teaspoon freshly ground
black pepper

2 tablespoons pure
olive oil

This is a Southwestern take on a homey, Southern-style dish. Catfish lends itself to a variety of preparations, such as steamed, with Soy-Cilantro Sauce, or cornmeal-coated and fried, with Green Onion–Creole Mustard Dressing.

1. Warm the Pecan–Morita Chile Sauce and the Cheddar Cheese Grits in covered saucepans over low heat.

2. Sprinkle the catfish fillets with salt and pepper. Heat a large sauté pan or frying pan over medium heat. Add the oil and heat it, about 1 minute. Increase the heat to medium-high and cook the fish, turning it once with a large wide spatula, until golden brown and opaque through, about 5 minutes on each side.

3. Scoop the Cheddar Cheese Grits onto plates and spread the grits over the bottom. Place 1 catfish fillet on each, then ladle the sauce over the fish and around the grits. Serve immediately. Pass any remaining sauce separately.

pecan–morita chile sauce

MAKES ABOUT 2½ CUPS

2   tablespoons pure
      olive oil

¼   small onion, minced
      (¼ cup)

1   large garlic clove,
      minced (1 tablespoon)

3   tablespoons
      tomato sauce
      (not tomato paste)

4   cups chicken stock,
      preferably homemade
      (page 24)

2   cups shelled pecans,
      toasted and ground
      (see Note)

1½ tablespoons puréed
      dried morita chile (see
      Note) or chipotle chile
      en adobo (see Note,
      page 37)

1   teaspoon freshly
      ground black pepper

½   teaspoon kosher salt
      (optional, depending
      on your taste and
      saltiness of the
      chicken stock)

The idea for the sauce came from tasting peanut-chipotle sauces in Oaxaca, Mexico. Pair it also with grilled chicken, or pasta, sprinkled with goat cheese.

1. Heat a medium-size broad, shallow saucepan over low heat. Add the oil and heat it, about 1 minute. Add the onion and garlic and cook, stirring constantly, until translucent, about 2 minutes.

2. Add the tomato sauce and cook for 1 minute. Stir in the stock, pecans, chile, and black pepper. Simmer, uncovered, until the sauce reduces by about half, about 1 hour. Taste the sauce and add salt if needed. The sauce can be refrigerated, covered, for up to 2 days.

Note *To toast pecans, preheat the oven to 350°. Place the nuts on a baking sheet and bake, stirring once, until they give off a toasted aroma, about 10 minutes.*

To grind pecans, place them in small batches in a blender or in a food processor. Use pulse or rapid on/off switches to grind. Do not grind continuously, or the nuts will become oily.

To make puréed dried morita chile, toast the chilies for about 5 minutes in a dry skillet over low heat. Soak the toasted chilies in water for 25 minutes, then drain them, leaving a bit of water clinging to the chilies. Remove the chilies' stems and seeds, and purée them in a blender or food processor. Pour 1 teaspoon of olive oil on top and store any remaining purée in a covered jar, refrigerated, for up to 5 days.

roasted red snapper fillets and cactus with pasilla chile sauce

MAKES 4 SERVINGS

Pasilla Chile Sauce
(recipe follows)

Four 6-ounce skinless red
snapper fillets

½ pound cactus (nopale)
pads (about 3 thin
pads), spines removed
(see Note, page 108)

2 teaspoons kosher salt

1 teaspoon freshly
ground black pepper

3 tablespoons pure
olive oil

1½ ounces queso cotija
añejo, grated (¼ cup)

On my way back from Oaxaca, Mexico, I stopped off for two days in Mexico City and enjoyed a dish of layered red snapper fillets and cactus in a very fine restaurant. This dish is great with margaritas!

1. Preheat the oven to 400°. Warm the Pasilla Chile Sauce in a small covered saucepan over low heat, stirring occasionally.

2. Cut each snapper fillet in half, crosswise. Cut the cactus pads to the same size and shape as the fillets, making 8 pieces of cactus. It is okay to piece together scraps of cactus to form cactus pieces, if needed.

3. Sprinkle the fillets with salt and pepper. Spread half of the oil over the bottom of a small, shallow baking pan. Arrange 4 pieces of cactus on the bottom of the pan. Place 1 fillet on top of each, using the fillet that is the same size and shape as the cactus; then add another piece of cactus. Finish with a fillet of fish. Drizzle the remaining oil over the fish. Cover the baking pan with aluminum foil and roast until the fish is opaque through, 20 to 25 minutes.

4. Ladle the Pasilla Chile Sauce onto plates or a platter. Using a large wide spatula, carefully remove the fish "napoleons" from the pan and place on the sauce. Sprinkle each with 1 tablespoon of the cheese and serve immediately. Pass any remaining sauce separately.

pasilla chile sauce

MAKES ABOUT 1¼ CUPS

5 dried pasilla
negro chilies

4 large plum tomatoes

4 large cloves garlic,
peeled

½ medium-size onion,
unpeeled

2 tablespoons pure olive
oil

½ teaspoon ground
coriander

½ teaspoon ground
cumin

1 cup chicken stock,
preferably homemade
(page 24)

¼ teaspoon freshly
ground black pepper

1½ teaspoons kosher salt

2 tablespoons mild
vegetable oil, such as
corn

This rich-tasting chile sauce is the perfect foil
for the cactus in Roasted Red Snapper Fillets.

1. Preheat the oven to 400°.

2. Heat a large nonstick sauté pan or frying pan over low
heat. Place the dried chilies in the pan and press down with a
large wide spatula. Toast for 30 seconds on each side. Do not
walk away during this process as these chilies burn easily. If
they begin to smoke, avoid inhaling it. Remove the stems and
seeds from the chilies. In a small bowl, soak the chilies in hot
water for 20 minutes. Drain the chilies and chop them
coarsely.

3. Rub the tomatoes, garlic, and onion with the olive oil.
Arrange them in a small shallow baking pan or pie pan and
roast them for 5 minutes. Remove the garlic and continue
roasting the tomatoes and onion, until the tomatoes are soft
and their skins begin to split, an additional 15 minutes.
Remove the pan from the oven and let the vegetables cool.
Peel and chop the onion coarsely. Remove the skins and seeds
from the tomatoes. You should have about 1 cup of tomato
pulp.

4. Heat a small nonreactive saucepan over medium heat.
Place all the ingredients, except the salt and vegetable oil, in
the pan and bring to a boil. Simmer the mixture until it
reduces by half, about 30 minutes. Purée the sauce in a
blender or food processor, or with a hand-held blender. Strain
the sauce through a fine sieve into a bowl and add the salt.

5. Heat a large nonreactive skillet over medium heat. Add
the vegetable oil and heat it, about 1 minute. Add the strained
sauce, taking care to not let it splatter too much. Fry the
sauce, stirring constantly to keep it from burning, for 5
minutes.

sesame-crusted salmon fillet

MAKES 4 SERVINGS

Crust

3/4 cup sesame seeds, toasted (*see* Note, page 47)

1/4 cup black sesame seeds, toasted

One 1-inch piece ginger, peeled and grated (1 tablespoon)

1 teaspoon granulated garlic

1 teaspoon freshly ground black pepper

1 tablespoon kosher salt

Four 6-ounce salmon fillets, skin left on, scales removed

1 large egg white, lightly beaten in a shallow bowl

1/4 cup mild vegetable oil, such as peanut

Pan-Asian Guacamole (page 47)

While traveling in Hawaii, which I often do, I ate a dish similar to this one. This fish has a lovely, crisp crust on the outside, and is extremely moist on the inside. As the recipe is written, the fish will come out slightly underdone. You may adjust the baking time to suit your taste. Pan-Asian Guacamole is the perfect accompaniment to this crispy fish because of its Pacific flavors and its contrasting smoothness.

1. Preheat the oven to 400°. Combine all the crust ingredients in a shallow bowl and mix well.

2. Dip the skinless side of the salmon fillets into the egg white, then dredge in the crust mixture, and shake off any excess. Do not dip or coat the sides or skin of the fillets.

3. Heat a large ovenproof, nonstick sauté pan or frying pan over medium-high heat. Add the oil and heat it, about 2 minutes. Place the fish in the pan, skin side up, and cook, turning once with a large wide spatula, for about 3 minutes on each side.

4. Place the pan in the oven and bake until the fish is nearly opaque through, for 5 to 7 minutes, or about 10 minutes for fish cooked through.

5. Remove the pan fish from the oven and place the fish on plates or a platter. Serve immediately with a large dollop of the Pan-Asian Guacamole on the side. Pass any remaining Guacamole on the side.

potato-crusted sea bass and olive mashed potatoes with a saffron-fennel broth

Olive Mashed
Potatoes *(page 145)*

Saffron-Fennel Broth
(recipe follows)

Potato Crust

1 cup dried potato flakes

1½ teaspoons ground
fennel

¼ teaspoon granulated
garlic; or 1 very small
garlic clove, minced
(½ teaspoon)

½ teaspoon freshly
ground black pepper

1 tablespoon kosher salt

Four 6-ounce skinless
sea bass fillets, cut
1 inch thick

1 cup milk, poured into
a shallow bowl

6 tablespoons pure olive
oil

6 tablespoons unsalted
butter, cut into ½-inch
pieces

¼ cup minced fresh
fennel fronds

I like the idea of using ingredients two different ways within the same dish. Potato flakes in the crust keep the fish moist, while the crisp texture plays off the smooth mashed potatoes underneath. It may seem strange to use dry potato flakes, but they keep the crust even crisper than fresh potatoes.

1. Preheat the oven to 350°. Warm the Olive Mashed Potatoes and Saffron-Fennel Broth in covered saucepans over low heat.

2. Combine the crust ingredients in a shallow bowl and mix well. Dredge the sea bass fillets in the crust mixture, and shake off any excess. Dip the fillets in the milk and then dredge them again in the crust mixture.

3. Heat a large, ovenproof, nonreactive sauté pan or frying pan over medium heat. Add the oil and heat it, about 3 minutes. Add the fish and cook, turning once with a large wide spatula, for 3 minutes on each side. Place the pan in the oven and bake for 4 minutes.

4. To serve, place a scoop of mashed potatoes in large soup bowls. Bring the Saffron-Fennel Broth to a boil and whisk in the butter to thicken it. Remove it from the heat and add the fennel fronds. Pour the broth around the potatoes and place a piece of fish on top of each mound of mashed potatoes. Serve immediately. Pass any remaining broth separately.

saffron-fennel broth

2 tablespoons pure
olive oil

1 large or 2 small fennel
bulbs, thinly sliced
lengthwise

¼ teaspoon crumbled
saffron, preferably
Spanish

1 small garlic clove,
minced (1 teaspoon)

¼ teaspoon freshly
ground black pepper

1 teaspoon ground
fennel seed

2 cups chicken stock,
preferably homemade
(page 24)

1. Heat a medium-size, nonreactive saucepan over low heat. Add the oil and heat it, about 1 minute. Add the fennel, saffron, garlic, pepper, and ground fennel and cook, stirring, for 2 minutes. This will release the flavors of the saffron and fennel.

2. Add the stock and bring to a boil. Reduce the heat to low and simmer until the liquid reduces by one-third, about 20 minutes. The broth can be refrigerated, covered, for up to 2 days.

dinner at the authentic cafe

roasted sea bass with jalapeño-spiked corn sauce

MAKES 4 SERVINGS

Sauce

2 tablespoons mild vegetable oil, such as corn

2 to 3 medium-size shallots, minced (¼ cup)

2 small corn ears, kernels scraped from cob (*see* Note), or thawed frozen kernels (2½ cups)

½ small jalapeño chile, seeded and minced (1 teaspoon)

⅛ teaspoon freshly ground black pepper

1 cup water

½ teaspoon kosher salt

½ cup heavy cream (optional)

Four 8-ounce skinless sea bass fillets, about 1 inch thick

2 tablespoons olive oil

½ teaspoon freshly ground black pepper

1½ teaspoons kosher salt

This is a very simple dish that combines sweet corn and spicy jalapeño chilies. If you wish, you can add ½ cup of heavy cream to make the sauce richer. Shoestring sweet potato fries (placed on top of the fish) would be a great garnish.

1. Prepare the sauce: Heat a small, nonreactive saucepan over low heat. Add the vegetable oil and heat it, about 1 minute. Add the shallots and cook, stirring, until translucent, about 1 minute.

2. Purée half the corn kernels in a blender or food processor and set aside. Add the whole kernels to the saucepan and cook over low heat, stirring occasionally, until the corn releases some of its liquid, 6 to 8 minutes. Add the chile and ground pepper and cook, stirring, for 1 minute.

3. Add the water, puréed corn, and salt to the same pan. Add the cream now, if desired. Simmer the sauce until it reduces to 2 cups, slightly more with the cream, about 20 minutes.

4. While the sauce is simmering, prepare the fish. Preheat the oven to 400°.

5. Rub the fish fillets with the olive oil, pepper, and salt. Heat a large, ovenproof, nonreactive sauté pan or frying pan over a medium heat. Cook the fish for 2 minutes on each side, then place the pan in the oven and roast until the fish is opaque through, 15 to 20 minutes.

6. Ladle the sauce onto plates. Remove the fish from the oven and place 1 fillet on each plate. Serve immediately. Pass any remaining sauce separately.

Note *Peel away all the husk and the silk (the strings under the husk) from the corn ear. Cut the broad end of the ear flat and stand the ear on that end; the ear will not slip as long as the end is flat. Run the back of a knife blade straight down next to the cob and cut the kernels away.*

pecan-cornmeal-crusted catfish club sandwich

MAKES 4 SERVINGS

Crust

¹⁄₂ cup ground pecans
     (see Note, page 141)

³⁄₄ cup yellow cornmeal

 1   teaspoon dried thyme

¹⁄₂ teaspoon ground
     cayenne pepper

¹⁄₄ teaspoon freshly
     ground black pepper

 2   teaspoons
     onion powder

1¹⁄₂ teaspoons kosher salt

 1   tablespoon brown
     sugar, lumps removed

 8   slices bacon

Eight 3-ounce skinless
       catfish fillets

 1   cup milk, poured into
     a shallow bowl

¹⁄₄ cup mild vegetable
     oil, such as corn

¹⁄₂ cup Green Onion–
     Creole Mustard
     Dressing *(recipe
     follows)*

12   slices sandwich bread,
     lightly toasted

 8   mustard green leaves

Four ¹⁄₄-inch slices of large
      ripe tomato, such as
      Beefsteak

Using these traditional Southern ingredients and twisting them around a little to create this sandwich is what experimentation can produce.

1. Combine all the crust ingredients in a shallow bowl and mix well.

2. Preheat the oven to 400°. Place the bacon slices in a medium-size shallow baking pan and bake until crisp, 8 to 12 minutes. Remove the bacon to paper towels and pat dry. Discard the grease. If you prefer, you may pan-fry the bacon over low heat until it is crisp, 8 to 12 minutes. Pat dry on paper towels. Set aside.

3. Dredge the catfish in the crust mixture. Dip the fillets in the milk, then dredge them again in the crust mixture.

4. Heat a large sauté pan or frying pan over low heat. Add the oil and heat it, about 2 minutes. Add the catfish fillets and cook, turning them once with a large wide spatula, until the crust is golden and crisp and the fish is opaque through, 4 to 5 minutes on each side. Remove the fish to paper towels and pat dry.

5. Meanwhile, spread 1 tablespoon of the Green Onion–Creole Mustard Dressing on each of 8 slices of toast. Place a mustard green leaf on each of 4 of these slices. Cover each leaf with 2 catfish fillets, then 1 slice of dry toast. Top this with 2 slices of the bacon, crisscrossed, 1 slice of tomato, and another mustard leaf. Place the dressing-spread toast on top, cut the sandwich in half, and serve immediately.

green onion–creole mustard dressing

MAKES ABOUT ¾ CUP

1 tablespoon
Creole mustard

2 bunches green onions,
white and light green
parts only, chopped
(½ cup)

1 small garlic clove,
minced (1 teaspoon)

1 tablespoon plus
1 teaspoon
champagne vinegar

⅓ teaspoon minced
fresh thyme leaves or
1 pinch dried

Pinch freshly ground black
pepper

Pinch ground cayenne
pepper

⅓ teaspoon kosher salt

¼ cup pure olive oil

This is just a variation of a basic vinaigrette recipe.

Place all the ingredients, except the olive oil, in a blender or food processor and process for a few seconds. With the motor running, add the oil in a thin stream. Process until smooth and emulsified. This dressing can be refrigerated, covered, for up to 2 days. Bring it to room temperature and whisk to re-emulsify before serving.

seared mirin salmon on a papaya-noodle salad

1 cup mirin

2 tablespoons rice vinegar

One ⅛-inch slice ginger, peeled and minced (½ teaspoon)

2 tablespoons granulated sugar

1 teaspoon kosher salt

Four 6-ounce salmon fillets, skin on

Papaya-Noodle Salad (recipe follows)

2 tablespoons mild vegetable oil, such as peanut

16 drops chile (satay) oil

The buttery flavor and firm texture of Atlantic salmon lend themselves beautifully to marinating. Time-honored gravlax and smoked salmon prove the point. The inspiration for this dish came to me when eating salmon skin rolls at my favorite sushi bar.

1. Combine the mirin, vinegar, ginger, sugar, and salt in a small bowl and stir until the sugar and salt dissolve.

2. Place the salmon fillets in a single layer in a medium-size, nonreactive shallow bowl or a glass pie plate. Pour the mirin mixture over the fish. Cover with plastic wrap and refrigerate for 6 to 8 hours. (You can also place the fish and the mirin mixture in a large resealable bag to marinate.)

3. Just before serving, prepare the Papaya-Noodle Salad.

4. Preheat the oven to 350°.

5. Heat a large, ovenproof frying pan over medium heat. Heat the oil, about 1 minute. Drain the salmon (discard the mirin mixture) and place the fillets in the pan, skin side down. The oil will sputter, so be careful. Cook, turning carefully with a large wide spatula, about 3 minutes on each side. Then bake until cooked through, about 5 minutes. This will just cook fillets that are 1 inch thick. If fillets are thicker or thinner, or you prefer fish more or less cooked, adjust the baking time accordingly.

5. While the fish is baking, arrange the salad on plates. Garnish each with 4 drops of chile oil, placing the oil only on the liquid that is sitting on the plate. Remove the pan from the oven, and carefully place 1 salmon fillet, skin side down, atop each salad. Serve immediately.

papaya-noodle salad

MAKES 4 SERVINGS

Two 2-ounce bundles saifun
     (glass or mung bean
     noodles)

8 to 10 green onions, white and
         light green parts only,
         very thinly sliced
         diagonally ($^3/_4$ cup)

3 large carrots, peeled
   and cut into $^1/_{16}$-inch
   matchstick strips,
   3 inches long (1$^1/_2$ cups)

1 English (hothouse)
   cucumber, peeled,
   seeded, and cut into
   $^1/_{16}$-inch matchstick
   strips, 3 inches long
   (1$^1/_2$ cups)

1 large barely ripe papaya,
   peeled, seeded, and cut
   into $^1/_8$-inch matchstick
   strips (1$^1/_2$ cups)

1 tablespoon granulated
   sugar

1 tablespoon nam pla
   (Thai fish sauce)

One $^1/_2$- to $^3/_4$-inch slice
     ginger, peeled and
     minced (2 teaspoons)

2 small cloves garlic,
   minced (2 teaspoons)

3 tablespoons freshly
   squeezed lime juice

2 small serrano chilies,
   seeded and minced
   (2 teaspoons)

1 tablespoon minced
   cilantro (fresh coriander)

4 to 6 basil leaves, minced
        (2 tablespoons)

2 tablespoons mild
   vegetable oil, such as
   peanut

$^1/_3$ cup unsweetened
     coconut milk

This refreshing salad can also stand on its own as a starter. If you have a Japanese-style mandoline, use it to cut the carrots, cucumber, and papaya. This "plane" cutter is easy to use and will provide you with gorgeous, evenly cut fruits and vegetables. Simply place the vegetables on top of the flat part of the mandoline. Keep running them down across the blade, which can be adjusted for any thickness that you want. With various simple attachments, the mandoline will also cut even matchsticks, waffle-cut potatoes, or simply perfect slices.

1. Soak the saifun in 4 cups of warm tap water for 20 minutes. Drain and squeeze out any excess water. Cut the noodles in half to unknot them and make them easier to handle. Place them in a large, nonreactive bowl. Add the green onions, carrots, cucumber, and papaya to the noodles.

2. Place the remaining ingredients in a small, nonreactive bowl and whisk well. Pour over the noodles and toss gently to mix. Serve immediately.

Variation
Seared Mirin Salmon on a Papaya-Noodle Salad is equally delightful with scallops instead of salmon. For 4 servings, use 1 pound of medium-size (1$^1/_2$ inches in diameter) sea scallops, rubbery hinges removed. Marinate them as you would the salmon. Cook, stirring, for 3 minutes on each side, then serve. There is no need to bake the scallops.

roasted whole red snapper with moroccan tomato, olive, and preserved lemon salad

MAKES 4 SERVINGS

Salad

3/4 pound ripe plum tomatoes, seeded and cut into 1/2-inch dice (2 cups)

1/2 small red onion, cut into 1/8-inch dice (1/2 cup)

25 Moroccan black olives, pitted and halved

1/4 cup Preserved Lemons, rind only *(page 27)*, cut into 1/16-inch strips

2 large garlic cloves, minced (2 tablespoons)

2 tablespoons harissa

3/4 teaspoon freshly ground black pepper

1/4 teaspoon kosher salt

1/4 cup freshly squeezed lemon juice

1/4 cup extra-virgin olive oil

Two 1 1/2- to 2-pound whole red snappers, cleaned

1/4 cup extra-virgin olive oil

2 large garlic cloves, minced (2 tablespoons)

1 teaspoon salt

1/2 teaspoon freshly ground black pepper

1/2 teaspoon ground cumin

Roasting a whole fish, especially in a wood-burning oven, is one of the best ways to attain a moist and fragrant fish with a crisp skin. The use of these Moroccan ingredients in a modern way will play off this Mediterranean-style fish. The pairing of fish and salad makes for an extremely healthful combination.

1. Preheat the oven to 350°.

2. Mix all the salad ingredients together in a medium-size, nonreactive bowl. Let the salad sit for at least 15 minutes at room temperature to let the flavors meld.

3. Cut 2 diagonal slashes parallel to the gills on each side of each fish. Combine the oil, garlic, salt, pepper, and cumin in a small bowl, and rub this mixture all over the fish, including inside the slashes and the cavities.

4. Heat a large, ovenproof sauté pan or frying pan over medium heat. Place the fish in the pan and cook for 3 minutes on each side, then place the pan in the oven and roast the fish until opaque through, about 20 minutes.

5. Place the salad on a large serving platter and, with a large wide spatula, place the fish on the salad. Serve immediately.

Filleting Whole Cooked Fish without Fear

To fillet a whole fish at the table, first cut away the head and the tail. Cut down the center of the top side of the fish and lift away the fillet halves by gently running a knife between the flesh and the bone. Move these fillets to either side of the fish, then lift out the spine and bones.

Meat and Poultry

Growing up in Chicago, where my father, uncles, and grandfather were all butchers, left a lasting impression on me. Eventually, I too took up sausage making, which is an art in itself. From the Chicken Sausage with Serrano and Cilantro, to the Thai Green Curry and Jerked Pork Sausages, at the Authentic Cafe we carry on my family's tradition, but using nontraditional ingredients.

Most of the meat dishes at the restaurant appear as daily specials. And the offerings are eclectic, reflecting my fascination with foreign travel. Through the Marinated Skirt Steak with Chimichurri and Spice-Rubbed Pork Tenderloin, which is served on plantains, yuca, and sweet potatoes, we make our way to different exotic lands.

Compared to the meat dishes, poultry plays a larger part in the regular menu at the Authentic Cafe, where we use mostly chicken, duck, and Cornish hens. We are able to explore foods with depth of flavor and traditional ideas through such dishes as Yucatán Marinated Chicken in Banana Leaves and Brazilian Duck Braised in Orange, Olives, Almonds, and Currants.

wood-grilled marinated skirt steak with chimichurri sauce

MAKES 4 SERVINGS

Marinade

2 tablespoons heavy (Chinese) soy sauce

2 tablespoons balsamic vinegar

2 tablespoons champagne vinegar

1 small garlic clove, minced (1 teaspoon)

1 small serrano chile, seeded and minced (1½ teaspoons)

1 tablespoon minced cilantro (fresh coriander)

1 teaspoon sugar

¼ teaspoon freshly ground white pepper

⅓ cup mild vegetable oil, such as soy

Four 8-ounce pieces of skirt steak, fat and silver (tendons) removed

Garlic Mashed Potatoes (page 194)

Chimichurri Sauce (recipe follows)

One of the most popular dishes at the restaurant, this steak has a lot of flavor, especially if grilled over wood. The vinegars in the marinade help to tenderize the meat.

1. Place all the marinade ingredients, except the oil, in a blender or food processor. Process for a few seconds. With the motor running, add the oil in a thin stream and process just until the oil is incorporated.

2. Place the pieces of meat in a medium-size, shallow, nonreactive baking pan and pour the marinade over them. Make sure the meat is completely covered with the marinade. Refrigerate the meat, covered, for at least 6 hours, or overnight, if possible.

3. Prepare a fire in a barbecue grill, or preheat the broiler. Oil the grill/broiler rack. Warm the Garlic Mashed Potatoes in a covered double boiler over barely simmering water.

4. Remove the meat from the marinade and discard the marinade. Place the meat on the grill/broiler rack about 6 inches from the heat and cook, turning it once, to desired doneness, 3 to 5 minutes on each side for medium-rare, depending on the thickness of the meat.

5. Spoon the Garlic Mashed Potatoes onto plates or a platter and spread them out slightly. Place the meat on top of the potatoes, pour the Chimichurri Sauce over the meat, and serve immediately. Pass any remaining sauce separately.

chimichurri sauce

MAKES 1¼ CUPS

- 1½ cups packed Italian (flat-leaf) parsley
- ¼ cup fresh oregano
- 3 medium-size jalapeño chilies, seeded and chopped
- ½ small onion, chopped (½ cup)
- ¾ teaspoon freshly ground black pepper
- 3 tablespoons aged red wine vinegar
- 3 tablespoons freshly squeezed lemon juice
- 2 teaspoons kosher salt
- 6 tablespoons extra-virgin olive oil

This Argentinian sauce was made to be served with grilled steak, but it is also great in a sandwich with grilled vegetables. I have added chilies to the traditional sauce to give it some depth.

Place all the ingredients, except the olive oil, in a blender or food processor and process for a few seconds. With the motor running, add the oil in a thin stream and blend until smooth. This sauce can be refrigerated, covered, for up to 2 days. Serve at room temperature.

onion

oregano

jalapeño chilies

szechwan peppercorn new york steak with caramelized onions

Caramelized Onions

¼ cup pure olive oil

2 pounds (4 large) onions, very thinly sliced

Four 8-ounce New York (strip) or sirloin steaks

¼ cup pure olive oil

4 teaspoons Special Szechwan Salt (page 28)

Tomato and Ginger Salsa (recipe follows)

Vegetables will begin to caramelize when most of their liquid has evaporated and their natural sugars begin to brown. You will find the simple process for caramelizing onions in this recipe. Their sweetness complements the heat of the Asian-style salsa, which includes serrano chilies.

1. Prepare the caramelized onions: Heat a large sauté pan or frying pan over medium heat. Add the ¼ cup oil and heat it, about 2 minutes. Place the onions in the pan and cook, stirring often so the onions do not stick, until limp and golden, about 30 minutes. If the onions begin to burn, reduce the heat.

2. Meanwhile, prepare a fire in a barbecue grill, or preheat the broiler. Oil the grill/broiler rack. Rub the steaks with the remaining ¼ cup oil, then sprinkle them evenly with the Special Szechwan Salt. Do not do this more than 1 hour before cooking the steaks, or the salt will draw out their blood and they will be dry and tough.

3. Place the steaks on the grill/broiler rack about 6 inches from the heat and cook, turning them once, to desired doneness, 3 to 5 minutes on each side for medium-rare, depending on the thickness of the meat.

4. Arrange the caramelized onions on plates, top with the steaks, then spoon the Tomato and Ginger Salsa over the steaks. Serve immediately.

tomato and ginger salsa

MAKES ABOUT 2 CUPS

¾ pound plum tomatoes

3 to 4 green onions, white and light green parts only, very thinly sliced (¼ cup)

1 thin slice ginger, peeled and minced (¾ teaspoon)

1 small serrano chile, seeded and minced (1 teaspoon)

2 teaspoons minced cilantro (fresh coriander)

2 tablespoons mirin

½ teaspoon freshly ground black pepper

1 teaspoon kosher salt

Mirin is a Japanese rice cooking wine. It has a subtle, sweet flavor that is perfect for this salsa. Use this salsa the same way you would use a regular Mexican tomato salsa: as a dip, or with fish or chicken.

1. Prepare an 8-cup ice bath. Then, bring 8 more cups of water to a rolling boil in a large saucepan. Core the tomatoes, then cut an "x" in the bottom of each with a small pointed knife. Plunge the tomatoes into the boiling water and leave them until the skins start to peel, 15 to 20 seconds. Remove the tomatoes with a slotted spoon and place them immediately in the ice water to stop the cooking. Using a small knife, peel the tomatoes. Cut them in half horizontally and seed them. Cut the tomatoes into ¼-inch dice. You should have about 2 cups of tomatoes.

2. Combine the diced tomatoes with the remaining ingredients in a medium-size bowl and mix well. Let the salsa sit at room temperature for ½ hour to allow the flavors to meld. Serve at room temperature.

braised moroccan-style lamb shanks

MAKES 4 SERVINGS

Four	18- to 20-ounce lamb shanks
6	tablespoons pure olive oil
	Kosher salt
	Freshly ground black pepper
1	small onion, minced (1 cup)
1½	teaspoon ground cumin
¼	teaspoon crumbled saffron, preferably Spanish
¼	teaspoon ground cinnamon
One	1-inch piece ginger, peeled and minced (1 tablespoon)
10	large garlic cloves, peeled
½	cup dark seedless raisins
½	pound pitted dates (about 1⅓ cups)
½	pound dark dried figs, tough stems removed (about 1⅓ cups)
1	tablespoon harissa
5	cups water
1	cup freshly squeezed orange juice
	Basic Couscous (page 203)

The complex taste of this dish is the natural result of the sweet and spicy flavorings typically used in Moroccan cooking. The broth obtained after 2 hours of slow cooking is extremely rich and aromatic.

1. Preheat the oven to 350°. Rub the lamb shanks with the oil, then sprinkle with salt and pepper. Heat a large, oven-proof braising pan over high heat. Place the lamb shanks in the pan and cook, turning them with tongs, until brown on all sides, about 10 to 12 minutes. Reduce the heat to low and remove the lamb shanks to a plate.

2. Add the onion, cumin, saffron, cinnamon, 2 teaspoons of salt, 1 teaspoon of pepper, the ginger, and garlic to the pan and cook, stirring, for 2 minutes to release their flavors.

3. Place the lamb shanks back in the pan and surround them with the dried fruit. Add the harissa, water, and orange juice and stir the liquids to combine them evenly. Bring to a boil, cover the pan with a lid or with aluminum foil, and carefully place it in the oven. Bake the lamb until very tender, about 2 hours. (Check after 1 hour to verify that the lamb is at least three-quarters covered with liquid; if not, add water.)

4. Carefully remove the pan from the oven and serve with Basic Couscous on the side.

meatloaf on caramelized onions and vegetables

MAKES 5 SERVINGS

Caramelized Onions

¼ cup pure olive oil

2 tablespoons unsalted butter

4 or 5 sweet onions, such as Vidalias, Texas 10s, or Maui, sliced ⅛-inch thick (6 cups)

Meatloaf

1½ pounds ground chuck, preferably Black Angus

2 large eggs, lightly beaten

1 large carrot, peeled and minced (½ cup packed)

1 small onion, minced, excess juice pressed out (½ cup)

1 celery rib, minced (½ cup)

¼ cup evaporated milk (not sweetened condensed milk)

¼ cup unseasoned dry bread crumbs

¼ cup ketchup

4 small cloves garlic, minced (4 teaspoons)

4 leaves fresh sage, very thinly sliced (1 tablespoon)

The ultimate comfort food, this is our version of the American classic. There are three reasons for making individual loaves: The meat cooks faster and more evenly, so that there are no dry spots. There are no slicing and crumbling problems, which often happens with traditionally shaped meatloaves. And most important, everyone gets more of the crust!

1. Prepare the caramelized onions: Heat a large, nonreactive frying pan over low heat. Add the oil and butter and heat until the butter begins to bubble. Place all the onions in the pan and cook them, still over low heat, stirring from time to time, until they are limp and deep brown in color, about 30 minutes.

2. Preheat the oven to 350°.

3. Place all the meatloaf ingredients, except the oil, in a large mixing bowl and combine thoroughly with your hands. Knead the mixture for 2 minutes, making sure that there are no air pockets. This mixture must be compact.

4. Divide the meat mixture into 5 equal portions, about 1¾ cups each, then pat each into a miniloaf, about 3 x 5 inches on top and 1½ inches thick. Place the loaves a few inches apart in a large baking pan with a rim that is at least 1 inch high. Brush the loaves with the oil. Bake the loaves for 30 minutes at 350°, then increase the temperature to 400° and bake 10 minutes more.

1 tablespoon fresh
    thyme leaves, minced

¼ teaspoon freshly
    ground white pepper

2 teaspoons kosher salt

1 tablespoon pure
    olive oil

Authentic Cafe Mixed
Vegetables (*page* 189)

Meatloaf Sauce
(*recipe follows*)

5. To serve, arrange the carmelized onions on large plates, mounding them in the center. Spoon the Authentic Cafe Mixed Vegetables around the onions. Carefully remove the meatloaves from the baking pan with a large wide spatula (there will be a lot of juice in the pan, so be cautious), and place one atop each mound of onions. Ladle some of the Meatloaf Sauce over the meatloaf, letting it flow onto the vegetables. Serve immediately. Pass any remaining sauce separately.

meatloaf sauce

MAKES ABOUT 1¼ CUPS

2 tablespoons pure
    olive oil

1 large shallot, minced
    (3 tablespoons)

2 cups beef stock,
    preferably homemade

2 teaspoons minced
    fresh thyme leaves or
    1 teaspoon dried

2 leaves fresh sage,
    thinly sliced
    (2 teaspoons); or
    1 teaspoon dried,
    crumbled

½ teaspoon freshly
    ground black pepper

Kosher salt to taste

4 tablespoons unsalted
    butter, softened but
    not melted

This is a rich-tasting sauce that contains no flour or cream. Its flavor depends on starting with a good-quality stock and a few table-spoons of sweet butter whisked in at the end.

1. Heat a medium-size, nonreactive saucepan over low heat. Add the oil and heat, about 1 minute. Place the shallot in the pan and cook, stirring constantly, until translucent, about 1 minute.

2. Raise the heat to medium. Pour the stock into the pan and, if you are using dried herbs, add them now. Bring to a boil. Reduce the heat to medium-low and simmer the stock until it reduces by half, about 15 minutes.

3. Just before serving, reheat the sauce to very hot, if needed. Off the heat, whisk in the fresh herbs, if using, and the pepper. Taste the sauce and add salt, if desired. Quickly whisk in the butter, 1 tablespoon at a time. Once the butter has been added, serve the sauce immediately.

roast pork loin stuffed with raisins, dried peaches, escarole, and pistachios

Makes 4 to 6 servings

3 tablespoons pure olive oil

½ medium-size head escarole, cut into ¼-inch pieces (2 cups)

⅓ cup dark raisins

4 or 5 dried peach halves, cut into ¼-inch dice (⅓ cup)

1 cup boiling water

¼ cup toasted shelled pistachios, coarsely chopped (*see* Note)

¾ teaspoon freshly ground black pepper

1⅔ teaspoons kosher salt

One 2-pound pork loin roast, butterflied (there should be a thin layer of fat on top of the roast)

2 large cloves garlic, minced (2 tablespoons)

1 tablespoon minced fresh oregano or ½ tablespoon dried

½ cup medium-ground toasted pistachios, spread in a large shallow bowl

My father, who is a butcher, is always telling me that I should try stuffing certain cuts of meat, such as pork loin, for roasting. I have finally started listening to him. This preparation, filled with pleasantly bitter escarole and sweet dried fruit, brings out the best in pork.

If you have the time, deep-fry extremely thinly sliced or shoestring-cut parsnips and serve them on top of the loin slices. An inexpensive Japanese mandoline is a great tool to have on hand for just such a cutting task.

1. Preheat the oven to 350°.

2. Heat a medium-size frying pan over low heat. Heat 2 tablespoons of the oil, about 1½ minutes. Cook the escarole, stirring constantly, until it wilts, about 1 minute. Place the escarole in a medium-size mixing bowl and let it cool completely.

2. Place the raisins, peaches, and boiling water in a small, heatproof bowl. Let the fruit rehydrate for 10 minutes, then drain and cool. Add the fruit to the escarole.

3. Add the chopped pistachios, ¼ teaspoon of pepper, and ⅔ teaspoon of salt to the other stuffing ingredients and mix well.

4. Place the roast in a small shallow baking pan. In a small bowl, thoroughly combine the garlic, oregano, and the remaining pepper, salt, and oil. Spread this mixture all over the pork, including inside the butterfly cut. Pack the stuffing inside the roast. Tie it 3 times crosswise and twice lengthwise with kitchen string to keep the stuffing from falling out.

Authentic Cafe
Flageolet Beans
(page 199)

5. Roast the pork, covered with aluminum foil, for 1 hour. Remove the roast from the oven and take off the foil. Discard the string. Using tongs or 2 forks to move the roast, roll it in the ground pistachios. Place the roast back in the oven and roast, uncovered, until very slightly pink at the thickest part, about 20 minutes more. Let the roast rest, loosely covered with foil, for 20 minutes.

6. Spoon about $^3/_4$ cup of the Authentic Cafe Flageolet Beans onto each plate. Using a very sharp knife and holding one hand at the side of the roast to keep the stuffing from falling out, cut the roast into $^1/_2$-inch slices. Place 2 slices on each plate. Sprinkle with the remaining oregano and serve immediately.

Note *To toast shelled pistachios, spread them on a baking sheet and toast at 350° for 7 to 10 minutes, stirring twice during that time. If you need to grind them, make sure that they are cooled first, and process with pulses in a blender or food processor.*

Butterflying Pork Roast

If you buy your meat from a butcher, have him butterfly the roast. You can also do it yourself with a very sharp knife. Thinking of the roast as a cylinder laying on its side, cut the roast almost in half horizontally. To do this, cut parallel to the axis of the cylinder, stopping at about $^1/_2$ inch from the side opposite where you started. The roast can now be easily stuffed.

spice-rubbed pork tenderloin

Marinade

¼ teaspoon ground
  cinnamon

1 teaspoon ground
  cumin

2 teaspoons ground
  coriander

2 tablespoons ground
  ancho chile

½ teaspoon freshly
  ground black pepper

2 tablespoons packed
  light or dark brown
  sugar

1 tablespoon kosher salt

1 teaspoon dried
  oregano leaves

1 tablespoon freshly
  squeezed lime juice

¼ cup freshly squeezed
  pink grapefruit juice

1 tablespoon freshly
  squeezed orange juice

1 tablespoon
  extra-virgin olive oil

Four 6-ounce pieces of
  pork tenderloin, fat
  and silver (tendons)
  removed

2 medium-size
  (1½ pounds total)
  yams

¼ cup plus 1 teaspoon
  pure olive oil

In my opinion, a recipe approaches perfection when it possesses two characteristics: complexity of flavor and simplicity of preparation. This recipe is pretty close to that ideal. The tastes—tangy (citrus), spicy (chilies), and sweet (yams and plantains)—provide the depth of flavor, and after some very easy preparation, the dish takes about 15 minutes to put together.

Read the entire recipe first, then prepare, for instance, all the juices at one time, using what you need for the marinade and the rest for cooking the vegetables. This is a perfect meal for a winter evening. And don't worry about leftovers; slice the pork thinly for a delicious sandwich the next day.

1. Combine all the marinade ingredients in a medium-size shallow bowl and mix well. Take out ¼ cup of the marinade and refrigerate, covered, for later use. Rub the pieces of pork tenderloin all over with the marinade, then place them in the bowl. Refrigerate the meat, covered, for 2 to 6 hours. Turn the meat at least once.

2. Preheat the oven to 400° about 1½ hours (or even earlier) before serving.

3. Rub the yams with 1 tablespoon of the pure olive oil and place them in a small shallow baking pan. Roast the yams until a thin sharp knife easily pierces them, 50 to 55 minutes. They should, however, still be firm. Remove the yams, but leave the oven on. Let the yams cool, then peel them and cut them into ½-inch dice. You should have about 2 cups.

Mojo

4. While the yams are baking, rub the red bell pepper with 1 teaspoon of the pure olive oil and put it in a small, shallow baking pan. Roast it at the same temperature until the skin begins to char and blister, 20 to 25 minutes. Place the roasted pepper in a small bowl, cover with plastic wrap, and let it "sweat" for 20 minutes to loosen the skin. Peel the pepper and remove the stem and seeds, then cut it into ¼-inch dice. You will need 2 tablespoons. (Use any remaining pepper in a salad.) Set aside.

5. Meanwhile, place two-thirds of the contents of the bag of yuca in a small saucepan and cover with cold water. Add the 1 teaspoon of salt and 1 teaspoon of lemon or lime juice. Bring to a boil over high heat, then cover, reduce the heat to medium-low, and simmer the yuca until it is tender but not mushy, about 25 minutes. Drain, cool slightly, then split the yuca pieces lengthwise and remove the tough, stringy core from each piece. Cut the yuca into ½-inch dice. You should have about 2 cups.

6. Combine the mojo ingredients in a small bowl and mix well. Set aside. Remove the meat and the reserved marinade from the refrigerator.

7. Heat a very large nonstick sauté pan or frying pan over low heat. Add the remaining 3 tablespoons of pure olive oil and heat, about 2 minutes. Place the cut yuca and plantains in the pan and cook, stirring often, until the plantains begin to brown, about 15 minutes.

8. Meanwhile, heat another large nonstick sauté pan or frying pan with an ovenproof handle over medium-high heat. Remove the meat from the marinade and discard the marinade. Place the meat in the pan (it will sizzle if the pan is hot enough) and cook it, using tongs to turn it, until almost blackened, about 2 minutes on each side. Place the pan in the oven and roast the meat until firm to the touch, 10 to 12 minutes, depending on the thickness of the meat. Remove the pan from the oven and let the meat rest in the pan for 5 minutes while finishing the vegetables.

9. Once the plantains have begun to brown, add the roasted yams and bell pepper and cook, stirring, just to heat them through, for about 1 minute. Do not cook them so much that the yams begin to fall apart.

10. Add the mojo ingredients to the plantains, stir to mix all the vegetables, and then quickly remove the pan from the heat. Arrange the vegetables on plates, flattening the mound a bit.

11. Cut each piece of pork into 5 slices against the grain, and place them on top of the vegetables. Daub a bit of reserved marinade in the center of each slice of meat and serve immediately.

Note *If you wish to boil the full 20-ounce bag of yuca, do so. After removing the two-thirds or so that you will need for this recipe, refrigerate the rest. The next day, heat 1 tablespoon of pure olive oil in a nonstick frying pan. Sprinkle the yuca with kosher salt and freshly ground black pepper and cook, stirring, until lightly browned. Prepare a half recipe of Garlic-Citrus Sauce and pour it over the yuca. Stir for 30 seconds in the frying pan. You have now prepared yuca con mojo!*

jerked thick-cut pork chops

MAKES 4 SERVINGS

Four 10-ounce center-cut
pork chops, chine off

¼ cup mild vegetable oil,
such as corn or peanut

8 teaspoons Dry Jerk
Spice Rub *(page 32)*

Mashed Sweet
Potatoes *(page 196)*

Jerk Sauce
(recipe follows)

People just go crazy over this dish in the restaurant. The spiciness of the habañero chile on the pork chop is offset beautifully by the Mashed Sweet Potatoes underneath. Serve with Authentic Cafe Black Beans and fried plantains.

1. In a large shallow baking pan, rub the pork chops with the oil, then the Dry Jerk Spice Rub. Refrigerate the pork, covered, for at least 6 hours, or overnight, if possible.

2. Warm the Mashed Sweet Potatoes in a covered double boiler over barely simmering water.

3. Prepare a fire in a barbecue grill, using fruitwood, if possible, or preheat the broiler. Oil the grill/broiler rack.

4. Place the pork chops on the grill/broiler rack about 6 inches from the heat and cook, turning them once, until just cooked through, 4 to 7 minutes on each side, depending on the thickness of the chops.

5. Arrange the Mashed Sweet Potatoes on plates, spreading the potatoes out slightly, and set a pork chop on top. Ladle the Jerk Sauce around the potatoes. Pass any remaining sauce separately.

jerk sauce

MAKES 1½ CUPS

1½ teaspoons ground allspice

1½ teaspoons fresh thyme or ¾ teaspoon dried

¼ teaspoon ground cinnamon

¼ teaspoon ground nutmeg

1½ teaspoons freshly ground black pepper

1½ teaspoons kosher salt

2 to 3 medium-size garlic cloves, minced (1½ tablespoons)

1 tablespoon plus 1½ teaspoons mild honey, such as orange

2 tablespoons plus 2 teaspoons tamarind concentrate

¼ cup champagne vinegar

2 small serrano chilies, seeded and chopped (2 teaspoons)

½ small onion, chopped (½ cup)

1 bunch green onions, white and light green parts only, chopped (½ cup)

2 tablespoons heavy (Chinese) soy sauce

2 tablespoons pure olive oil

Although this sauce has many ingredients, the sauce as a whole has a very clean taste. While in Jamaica, I had the chance to taste many different versions of this sauce. I even went to the Negril Jerk Center, where they let their sauce sit in a carved-out allspice log. Here is the sauce I came up with: It is spicy, yet will have you wanting more because all your taste buds will be stimulated when eating this tropical dish.

Place all the ingredients in a blender or food processor and process until smooth. This sauce can be refrigerated, covered, for up to 3 days. Serve at room temperature.

jerk-spiced pork sausage

MAKES ABOUT 1 DOZEN SAUSAGES
(IN CASING) OR 1 DOZEN PATTIES

1¼ pounds very lean
boneless pork
shoulder, cut into
1-inch cubes

¼ cup crushed ice

¼ pound pork fat,
finely ground

3 tablespoons
Dry Jerk Spice Rub
(page 32)

2 to 3 green onions, white
and light green parts
only, very thinly sliced
(¼ cup)

1½ teaspoon kosher salt

2¼ teaspoons sugar

About 6 feet sheep or lamb
casing (optional)

This is just one of the sausages that my father makes at the restaurant. It makes a great filling for a Jamaican patty or, without the casing, for an empanada.

1. Using the large grate of a meat grinder, grind the pork and the ice together. In a chilled bowl, combine the chilled ground pork with the fat and the rest of the ingredients, except the optional casing. Mix well with a metal spoon (not with your hands or a wooden spoon).

2. To make patties, measure out 2¼-ounce, or about ¼-cup, portions of the mixture and form twelve ½-inch-thick patties, 2½ inches in diameter.

3. To make sausages in casings, place the casing on the end of the sausage stuffer and make 4-inch-long sausages, about 1 inch thick and weighing about 2½ ounces, twisting the casing between sausages. Once the sausages are formed, cut them apart. Prick 4 or 5 holes in the sausage casing with a needle before cooking.

4. Heat a large nonstick frying pan over medium heat. Place the patties in the pan and fry, turning them once with a large wide spatula, until browned and firm, about 4 minutes on each side. Remove from the pan with a slotted spatula, blot excess grease with paper towels, and serve immediately. Or fry the sausages in casings for a total of 8 to 10 minutes

Safe Sausages

Whenever making meat sausage, it is important to keep the mixture chilled at all times. Whenever possible, chill bowls before using them, and keep the mixture refrigerated before cooking, or cook it immediately after preparation.

yucatán marinated chicken in banana leaves

MAKES 4 SERVINGS

Marinade

2 cups freshly squeezed orange juice

1 cup freshly squeezed pink grapefruit juice

1 cup freshly squeezed lime juice

2 large garlic cloves, minced (2 tablespoons)

6 tablespoons achiote paste

1 tablespoon kosher salt

Two 3-pound frying chickens, each split into 2 halves, backs removed

Four 10 x 16-inch pieces of banana leaf, toasted (page 8)

Four 12 x 16-inch pieces of aluminum foil

¼ cup fruity pure olive oil

Baking the chicken in a banana leaf not only keeps it moist, it lends its unique flavor to the chicken. Fresh or frozen banana leaves are available in Latin markets. Serve steamed rice, Authentic Cafe Black Beans, and warmed fresh corn tortillas on the side.

For this recipe, you don't need to trim the tough, central stem of the banana leaves. It is more important to do this when making tamales, which are smaller and therefore require more flexibility in the leaves. (The stem is considerably less flexible than the leaf, even after toasting.)

1. Combine the marinade ingredients in a large, nonreactive, shallow baking pan and stir well, making sure to break up any lumps of achiote paste. Measure out 1 cup of the marinade for the sauce, and refrigerate it, covered, until ready to use. Stir the marinade before using.

2. Gently push your finger between the skin and flesh of the chicken halves to separate them slightly. Do not remove the skin. Place the chicken in the marinade, making sure that some of the marinade goes under the skin. The chicken should be completely covered. Refrigerate it, covered, for at least 6 hours, or overnight, if possible. Turn the chicken several times while marinating.

3. Preheat the oven to 350°. Remove the chicken halves from the marinade and discard the marinade. Lay each chicken half on a piece of toasted banana leaf and wrap the leaf around the chicken, making sure that it is completely covered. Enfold the banana-leaf package tightly in a piece of aluminum foil.

4. Place the 4 packages in a very large shallow roasting pan and bake for 1 hour.

5. Just before the chicken is ready, prepare the sauce: Remove the reserved cup of marinade from the refrigerator and heat it in a small, nonreactive saucepan over low heat. Just before the marinade comes to a boil, remove it from the heat and whisk in the olive oil.

6. Remove the chicken from the oven and carefully remove the aluminum foil, leaving the banana-leaf wrapping intact. Be aware that hot juices may have collected inside the foil. Place each chicken half on a plate and serve immediately. Let your guests remove the banana leaves, revealing the steaming chicken inside. Whisk the sauce again and serve it on the side.

pink grapefruit juice

achiote paste

banana leaf

peanut-crusted half chicken

MAKES 4 SERVINGS

Crust

2 cups roasted unsalted
  peanuts, coarsely ground
  (see Note)

1 cup rice flour

1/2 cup Pankow rice
  bread crumbs

1/4 cup packed light brown
  sugar or palm sugar

One 2-inch piece ginger, peeled
  and grated (2 tablespoons)

1 lemongrass stalk, bottom
  3 or 4 inches only, tough
  outer leaves removed,
  minced (2 tablespoons)

1 tablespoon kaffir lime, or
  2 teaspoons finely grated
  lime zest

2 large garlic cloves, minced
  (2 tablespoons)

1/2 teaspoon ground cayenne
  pepper

1 teaspoon freshly ground
  black pepper

1 tablespoon plus
  1 1/2 teaspoons kosher salt

Two 2 1/2-pound frying chickens,
  quartered, backs removed

1 cup rice flour, spread in a
  shallow bowl

6 large egg whites, lightly
  beaten in a shallow bowl

1/4 cup mild vegetable oil,
  such as peanut

Ketjap Manis–Chile Sauce
  (recipe follows)

1 tablespoon sesame seeds,
  toasted (see Note, page 47)

The natural oil from the peanuts in this flavorful crust, which combines many Asian flavors, provides you with a textured, crisp coating on the outside and extremely moist meat on the inside. (Everyone gets two chicken quarters, making half-chicken servings.) Serve this with Ketjap Manis–Chile Sauce.

1. Preheat the oven to 350°.

2. Combine all the crust ingredients in a large bowl and mix well, making sure to break up any lumps in the brown sugar.

3. Dredge the chicken pieces in the rice flour, dip them in the egg whites, then coat them with the crust mixture. As you work, make sure that all parts of the chicken (for example, under the wings) are coated.

4. Brush a baking sheet or large shallow baking pan with some of the vegetable oil and place the chicken, skin side up, on the sheet. Brush the chicken parts with the remaining oil. Cover with aluminum foil and bake for 45 to 50 minutes.

5. Remove the foil, increase the temperature to 400°, and bake until the crust is golden brown and crisp and the juices from one of the thighs run clear when the thigh is poked with a thin sharp knife, 15 to 20 minutes more.

6. Place the chicken on plates or a platter, top with Ketjap Manis–Chile Sauce and sprinkle with the sesame seeds. Serve immediately.

Note *Grind the peanuts in small batches in a blender or food processor, using several on/off pulses. If you run the processor continuously, you will end up with peanut butter.*

ketjap manis–chile sauce

1 cup ketchup

¼ cup ketjap manis

1½ tablespoons Vietnamese chile-garlic paste

One ½-inch piece ginger, peeled and minced (1½ teaspoons)

The mother of the chef where I first worked introduced me to ketjap manis and sambal, or chile paste. She was from the Philippines and her husband, who was also a chef, was Swiss. (This, believe it or not, is a very common pairing of cultures.) This sauce is delicious with Peanut-Crusted Chicken, Five-Spice Fried Calamari, or spring rolls.

Mix all the ingredients very well in a small, nonreactive bowl. The sauce can be refrigerated, covered, for up to 2 days. Serve it at room temperature.

jamaican-style jerk chicken

MAKES 4 SERVINGS

Two 2 ½-pound frying
 chickens, each cut into
 8 pieces, backs
 removed

¼ cup mild vegetable oil,
 such as corn or peanut

6 tablespoons Dry Jerk
 Spice Rub *(page 32)*,
 well-mixed

 Jerk Sauce *(page 168)*,
 at room temperature

Jerk Chicken on the Barbecue

You can use a Weber or any other kettle-style barbecue for this chicken. Leave the marination process the same. Heat half the barbecue with charcoal and wood, using fruitwood or allspice wood, if possible. Place a small flameproof pan of water next to the coals, then place the chicken on the rack, away from the fire. Cover and cook for 40 minutes. Turn the chicken over and grill for 20 minutes, then turn it over again and cook until the skin is crisp, about 15 minutes more (total cooking time: 1 hour and 15 minutes). Make sure that the grill is not too hot, so that the chicken cooks very slowly. The temperature inside the oven should be about 350°; put an oven thermometer inside the kettle to verify the temperature.

I ate at many jerk stands in Jamaica and tasted as many variations of jerk. Here is my recipe, which is both very aromatic and spicy. In Jamaica, jerk chicken and pork are grilled slowly over allspice wood, enhancing the flavors greatly.

1. Rub the chicken pieces with the oil, then with ¼ cup of the Dry Jerk Spice Rub. Gently push your finger between the skin and flesh of the chicken to separate them slightly. Do not remove the skin. Rub some of the oil and spice on the flesh underneath. Place the chicken in a large shallow baking pan and refrigerate, covered, for at least 6 hours or overnight, if possible.

2. Preheat the oven to 300°.

3. Arrange the chicken in a single layer, skin side up, on a baking sheet or in another large shallow baking pan. Sprinkle the chicken with the remaining 2 tablespoons of spice rub. Cover with aluminum foil and bake for 50 minutes.

4. Remove the foil, increase the oven temperature to 400°, and bake until the skin is dark brown and crisp, and the meat is cooked through and moist, 15 minutes more.

5. Serve the chicken immediately on plates or a platter with the Jerk Sauce on the side.

braised chicken for tacos

MAKES 4 SERVINGS

- 2 large plum tomatoes
- 2 tablespoons pure olive oil
- ¼ small onion, minced (¼ cup)
- 2 medium-size garlic cloves, minced (4 teaspoons)
- 2 teaspoons ground cumin
- ½ teaspoon minced fresh oregano or ¼ teaspoon dried
- ½ teaspoon freshly ground black pepper
- 3 tomatillos, husked and cut into ¼-inch dice
- 2 tablespoons puréed ancho chile (see Note)
- 2 teaspoons puréed chipotle chile en adobo (see Note, page 37)
- 2 cups chicken stock, preferably homemade (page 24)
- 1 teaspoon kosher salt
- ¼ cup minced cilantro (fresh coriander)
- 1 pound skinless, boneless chicken breast, cut against the grain into ¼-inch strips

  Cabbage Escabeche (page 71)
- 8 corn tortillas, preferably homemade (page 30)

This chicken mixture works for just about any quesadilla, taco, burrito, or enchilada recipe. It has a great smoky flavor and spicy heat from the chipotle chilies. To complete the meal, serve this chicken with warmed, fresh corn tortillas and Cabbage Escabeche.

1. Prepare a fire in a barbecue grill, or preheat the broiler. Oil the grill/broiler rack.

2. Place the tomatoes on the grill/broiler rack about 6 inches from the heat and cook until they begin to soften and the skins blacken, about 5 minutes. Let them cool, then remove the skins and seeds. You should have about ½ cup of pulp.

3. Preheat the oven to 350°.

4. In a large bowl, mix the tomatoes with all the remaining ingredients, except the Cabbage Escabeche and tortillas. Spread the tomato mixture in a single layer in a medium-size shallow roasting pan. Cover with aluminum foil and bake until the vegetables release their juices, about 1 hour.

5. Serve with the Cabbage Escabeche and corn tortillas.

Note *To make puréed ancho chile, toast the chilies for about 5 minutes in a dry skillet over low heat. Soak the toasted chilies in water for 25 minutes, then drain them, leaving a bit of water clinging to the chilies. Remove the chilies' stems and seeds, and purée them in a blender or food processor. Pour 1 teaspoon of olive oil on top and store any remaining purée in a covered jar, refrigerated, for up to 5 days.*

moroccan-style braised chicken

MAKES 4 TO 6 SERVINGS

¼ cup pure olive oil

Two 2½-pound frying chickens, quartered, backs removed

Kosher salt

Freshly ground black pepper

2 tablespoons ground cumin

1 teaspoon ground coriander

1 large or 2 small onions, cut into ¼-inch dice (2 cups)

½ teaspoon crumbled saffron threads, preferably Spanish

3 large garlic cloves, minced (3 tablespoons)

1½ cups pitted Spanish green olives, or cracked green olives, boiled twice (see Note)

1 teaspoon freshly ground black pepper

6 cups chicken stock, preferably homemade (page 24)

My grandmother would make this dish almost every Saturday for lunch when I was growing up. When I went to Morocco with my father, we ate this classic dish in the restaurant of the Hotel Tour Hassan in Rabat. It's one of their specialties.

The Preserved Lemons in this dish have a unique flavor, which is sour, yet salty, and cannot be easily replaced.

1. Preheat the oven to 350°.

2. Heat a large (at least 12-cup capacity), ovenproof braising pan over medium heat. Add the oil and heat it, about 2 minutes. Sprinkle the chicken on both sides with salt and black pepper. Place the chicken, skin side down, in the pan and cook, turning it once with tongs, until brown, about 5 minutes on each side. Remove the chicken to a plate.

3. Add the cumin, coriander, onions, saffron, garlic, olives, and 1 teaspoon pepper to the same pan. Reduce the heat to medium-low and cook, stirring, until the onions are translucent, about 2 minutes.

4. Place the browned chicken, skin side down, back in the pan and add the stock, Preserved Lemons, and lemon juice. Bring to a boil over medium heat, then cover the pan with a lid or with aluminum foil and place it in the oven. Bake for 1 hour.

5. After 1 hour, verify that the chicken is still at least three-quarters submerged. If not, add water. Remove the lid or foil and continue to bake for 45 minutes longer.

½ cup Preserved
Lemons, rind only
(page 27), cut into
⅛-inch slices

⅓ cup freshly squeezed
lemon juice

Basic Couscous
(page 203), made with
cooking liquid from
the chicken

3 tablespoons minced
Italian (flat-leaf)
parsley

5. About 15 minutes before serving time, prepare the Basic Couscous, replacing 1 cup of the required water with 1 cup of the chicken cooking liquid and reducing the salt by half.

6. Remove the chicken from the oven and serve it and its sauce in a large tureen with Basic Couscous on the side.

Note *If you use cracked green olives, which I prefer, boil them twice for 5 minutes, in fresh water each time. This will remove some of the bitterness.*

roasted half chicken stuffed with plantains, cornbread, and rum

MAKES 4 SERVINGS

Stuffing

2 tablespoons pure olive oil

2 very ripe plantains, cut into ½-inch dice

1 pound prepared cornbread (*see* Note)

½ cup unsweetened dried coconut flakes

1 small habanero chile, or 2 medium-size serrano chilies, seeded and minced

½ small red onion, cut into ¼-inch dice (½ cup)

3 tablespoons minced cilantro (fresh coriander)

One 1-inch strip red bell pepper, cut into ⅛-inch dice (2 tablespoons)

One 2-inch piece ginger, peeled and minced (2 tablespoons)

2 large garlic cloves, minced (2 tablespoons)

1 tablespoon freshly ground black pepper

2 teaspoons kosher salt

¼ cup freshly squeezed lime juice

¼ cup dark rum

2 tablespoons light brown sugar

After returning from a trip to Negril, Jamaica, I wanted to create a few dishes that would remind me of my eating experiences there. This recipe combines the best of Caribbean flavors. I love fried plantains, and the combination of them with rum and coconut is irresistible. Placing the stuffing under the skin of the halved chickens, rather than in the cavity of the whole bird, keeps the meat extremely moist and flavorful. Thanks to Frieda's Finest, a purveyor and packager of fine produce, herbs, and gourmet products, fresh or dried habanero chilies can be found in just about any large supermarket.

1. Preheat the oven to 350°.

2. Prepare the stuffing: Heat a medium-size sauté pan or frying pan, then add the oil and heat it, about 1 minute. Add the plantains to the pan and cook, stirring, until they are soft, 3 to 4 minutes. Place them in a large bowl.

3. Crumble the cornbread into the bowl with the plantains. Add the remaining stuffing ingredients and mix thoroughly.

4. Gently push your finger between the skin and flesh of the chickens to separate them slightly. Do not remove the skin. Gently pack the stuffing under the skin, making sure the stuffing is of an even thickness throughout. Brush the chickens with the oil, then sprinkle each half chicken with ½ teaspoon of the garlic. Season with salt and pepper.

Two 2¹/₂-pound broiler
   chickens, each split into
   2 halves, backs removed

2 tablespoons pure
   olive oil

2 small garlic cloves,
   minced (2 teaspoons)

   Kosher salt

   Freshly ground
   black pepper

   Garlic-Citrus Sauce
   (recipe follows)

4. Place the chickens in a large shallow baking pan and cover with aluminum foil. Bake for 45 minutes. Remove the foil and bake the chicken until the juices run clear when pricked, another 25 minutes. Serve immediately with the Garlic-Citrus Sauce on the side.

Note *Use your favorite cornbread recipe for an 8-inch square pan.*

garlic-citrus sauce

MAKES ABOUT ³/₄ CUP

¹/₃ cup freshly squeezed
   lime juice

¹/₄ cup freshly squeezed
   orange juice

¹/₄ cup freshly squeezed
   grapefruit juice

1 large clove garlic,
   minced (1 tablespoon)

¹/₂ teaspoon freshly
   ground black pepper

¹/₂ teaspoon kosher salt

¹/₄ cup extra-virgin
   olive oil

2 tablespoons
   minced cilantro
   (fresh coriander)

Try this sauce also with boiled yuca, or sweet potato pancakes.

1. Place the juices, garlic, and pepper in a small, nonreactive saucepan and simmer over medium heat until reduced by half.

2. Remove the pan from the heat and whisk in the salt and the oil. Add the cilantro, and use the sauce immediately.

chicken sausage with serrano and cilantro

MAKES ABOUT 1 DOZEN SAUSAGES
(IN CASING) OR 1 DOZEN PATTIES

1 pound skinless,
 boneless chicken
 thighs

3 ounces skinless,
 boneless smoked
 chicken, chopped

¼ cup crushed ice

¼ pound chicken fat,
 ground

1 large garlic clove,
 minced (1 tablespoon)

2 small serrano chilies,
 seeded and minced
 (1 tablespoon)

½ teaspoon minced
 fresh oregano

1 teaspoon ground
 cumin

3 tablespoons finely
 grated or minced lime
 zest

2 tablespoons
 minced cilantro
 (fresh coriander)

¼ teaspoon freshly
 ground black pepper

1 teaspoon kosher salt

5 tablespoons pine nuts,
 toasted (see Note)

About 6 feet of sheep or
 lamb casing (optional)

Sausage is very easy to make, which makes me wonder why more people don't try it at home. Here is one of several sausages we serve at the restaurant. Pan-fry them, as here, or cook them on the barbecue grill, if you like.

1. Trim the chicken thighs of any tendons and excess fat and cut it into chunks. Using the large grate of a meat grinder, grind the chicken breast, smoked chicken, and ice together.

2. In a large chilled glass or stainless-steel bowl, combine the chilled ground chicken with the fat and the rest of the ingredients, except the optional casing. Mix very well with a metal spoon (not with your hands or with a wooden spoon).

3. To make patties, measure out 2¼-ounce, or about ¼ cup, portions of the mixture and form 12 patties, 2½ inches in diameter and ½ inch thick.

4. To make sausages in casings, place the casing on the end of the sausage stuffer and make 4-inch-long sausages, about 1 inch thick and weighing about 2¼ ounces each, twisting the casing between sausages. Once the sausages are formed, cut them apart. Prick the casings with a needle 4 or 5 times before cooking.

5. Heat a large nonstick frying pan over medium heat. Place the patties in the pan and fry, turning them once with a large wide spatula, until browned and firm, about 4 minutes on each side. Remove them from the pan with tongs or a slotted spatula, blot excess grease with paper towels, and serve immediately. Or fry the sausages in casings for a total of 8 to 10 minutes

Note *To toast pine nuts, bake them in a 350° oven, stirring once, until fragrant and lightly browned, 5 to 7 minutes.*

thai green curry and apple chicken sausage

MAKES ABOUT 14 SAUSAGES IN CASINGS OR 14 PATTIES

1¼ pounds skinless, boneless chicken dark meat (about 5 drumsticks and 5 thighs)

¼ cup crushed ice

¼ pound chicken fat, finely ground

4 to 6 tablespoons Green Curry Paste (page 29)

1 small pippin apple, peeled, cored, and coarsely grated (½ cup)

1 teaspoon kosher salt

1 teaspoon granulated sugar

About 6 feet of sheep casing (optional)

This sausage is very good in a sandwich with caramelized onions (see Szechwan Peppercorn New York Steak over Caramelized Onions. It is also delicious cut up and mixed with scrambled eggs.

1. Using the large grate of a meat grinder, grind the chicken and the ice together. In a large chilled glass or stainless-steel bowl, combine the chilled ground chicken with the fat and the rest of the ingredients, except the optional casing. Mix well with a metal spoon (not with your hands or a wooden spoon).

2. To make patties, measure out 2¼-ounce, about ¼ cup, portions of the mixture and form 14 patties, ½ inch thick and 2½ inches in diameter.

3. To make sausages in casings, place the casing on the end of the sausage stuffer and make 4-inch-long sausages, about 1 inch thick and weighing about 2½ ounces each, twisting the casing between sausages. Once the sausages are formed, cut them apart. Prick the casings with a needle 4 or 5 times before cooking.

4. Heat a large nonstick frying pan over medium heat. Place the patties in the pan and fry, turning them once with a large wide spatula, until nicely browned and firm, about 4 minutes on each side. Remove from the pan with a slotted spatula, blot excess grease with paper towels, and serve immediately. Or fry the sausages in casings for a total of 8 to 10 minutes.

spicy marinated game hens on rice noodles

MAKES 4 SERVINGS

Marinade

1/2 cup freshly squeezed lime juice

2 tablespoons nam pla (Thai fish sauce)

2 kaffir lime leaves, chopped, or the finely grated zest of 2 limes

1 large garlic clove, minced (1 tablespoon)

One 1/2- to 3/4-inch piece ginger, peeled and minced (2 teaspoons)

1 tablespoon Vietnamese chile-garlic paste

1/2 teaspoon freshly ground black pepper

2 tablespoons mild vegetable oil, such as soy

1 teaspoon toasted sesame oil

2 tablespoons minced cilantro (fresh coriander)

4 Cornish hens, cleaned

1/2 pound dried Thai rice noodles, fettuccine thickness

2 teaspoons kosher salt

Transparent rice noodles have a silky quality that I like to use with game hens. The contrasting Thai flavors provide a push-and-pull on your taste buds. Roasting the game hens keeps the birds moist, while the skin gets crispy. The finished dish has an extremely fresh taste.

1. In a large bowl, combine all the marinade ingredients and mix well. Place the hens in the marinade, making sure to spoon some of the liquid into each bird's cavity. Refrigerate, covered, for at least 6 hours, or overnight, if possible. Turn the birds once during this time so that they marinate evenly.

2. Preheat the oven to 350°.

3. Place the birds in a large shallow roasting pan and spoon the marinade over them and into their cavities. Cover and roast for 30 minutes. Remove the cover and baste the hens, then roast them until their legs seem loose and the juices are clear, not red, when a small knife is inserted in the thickest part of a thigh, about 30 minutes more.

3. While the hens are roasting, soak the rice noodles for 20 minutes in warm water, then drain them. In a large saucepan, bring 8 cups of water to a boil with the salt. Add the rice noodles and cook them until tender but quite elastic, about 5 minutes, then drain them.

¼ cup mild vegetable oil, such as soy

2 small garlic cloves, minced (2 teaspoons)

One ½- to ¾-inch piece ginger, peeled and minced (2 teaspoons)

1 large serrano chile, seeded and minced (1 tablespoon)

½ lemongrass stalk, bottom 3 or 4 inches only, tough outer leaves removed, minced (1 tablespoon)

1 cup (about 2 ounces) sugar snap peas, stem and string along the back of each pod removed

½ red bell pepper, cut into ⅛-inch strips (½ cup)

1 cup canned whole baby corn, drained, or fresh baby corn cooked

One 8-ounce can straw mushrooms, drained (¾ cup)

1 cup canned unsweetened coconut milk

3 tablespoons nam pla (Thai fish sauce)

¼ cup freshly squeezed lime juice

2 tablespoons minced cilantro (fresh coriander)

4. Heat a wok or large frying pan over medium heat. Add the oil and heat it, about 2 minutes. Add the garlic, ginger, chile, and lemongrass and cook, stirring, until fragrant, about 30 seconds. Add all the vegetables and stir-fry for 1 minute. Add the coconut milk, nam pla, and lime juice, bring to a boil, and simmer the liquid for 1 minute to thicken. Toss in the drained noodles and stir to coat them. Add the cilantro.

5. Using tongs, arrange a bed of noodles and vegetables on plates or a platter. Place the roasted hens on top of the noodles and serve immediately.

duck braised in orange, olives, almonds, and currants

MAKES 2 TO 4 SERVINGS

One 4- to 5-pound duck, quartered (back removed)

1 cup all-purpose flour

1/8 teaspoon freshly ground black pepper

1/2 teaspoon kosher salt

2 tablespoons pure olive oil

1/2 small onion, minced (1/2 cup)

2 small plum tomatoes, seeded and chopped (3/4 cup)

2 tablespoons zante currants or chopped dark raisins

2 tablespoons sweet sherry

2 small serrano chilies, seeded and minced (2 teaspoons)

1/4 teaspoon freshly ground black pepper

Finely grated zest of 1 large orange (prepare before juicing the orange)

3/4 cup freshly squeezed orange juice

1/4 cup blanched almonds, toasted (page 34) and ground

3/4 teaspoon minced fresh thyme or 1/4 teaspoon dried

3/4 teaspoon minced fresh oregano or 1/4 teaspoon dried

3/4 cup whole green olives, with pits

2 tablespoons chopped cilantro (fresh coriander)

The combination of the currants, chilies, and oranges gives this dish a nice balance. The ground almonds lend a nutty flavor, and thicken the sauce as well.

1. Preheat the oven to 350°.

2. Remove the excess skin and fat from the duck thighs. Prick the duck skin all over with a fork to let the fat drain during cooking. Combine the flour, pepper, and salt in a shallow bowl, and dredge the duck in this mixture.

3. Heat a large braising pan over medium heat. Add the oil and heat it about 1 minute. Place the duck quarters in the pan, skin side down, and cook, turning them once, until brown, about 10 minutes on each side. Remove the duck and place it on a plate.

4. Drain all but about 2 tablespoons of fat from the pan. Add the onion and cook, stirring, until lightly browned, about 5 minutes. Add the remaining ingredients, except the duck and cilantro, and bring to a boil. Reduce the heat to low and simmer for 5 minutes.

5. Put the duck back in the pan, skin side up. Cover and place the pan in the oven. Bake until the duck is extremely tender, about 1 1/2 hours.

6. Remove the pan from the oven and uncover. Place the duck quarters on a platter. Skim the fat off the sauce, then stir the cilantro into the sauce. Pour this over the duck and serve immediately. Be sure to tell your guests that the olives have pits.

Vegetables, Side Dishes, and Condiments

I've always said that it is the small things that have to be taken care of, and these small things usually add zest to any meal.

My aunts used to have many side dishes, which they referred to as "just a little something." Today I cook the same way, if only to bring those days and memories back to life.

Try the Moroccan-Spiced Potato and Chick-Pea Stew with a side of Basic Couscous. How about the Eggplant Pancakes with Oregano and Goat Cheese with some grilled lamb? These are the combinations that I remember from my childhood in Chicago, trying the various foods with my father at my side.

sautéed okra with tomatoes and corn

MAKES 4 SERVINGS

- 2 tablespoons pure olive oil
- 1 large shallot, minced (2 tablespoons)
- 1/2 pound okra, trimmed and cut into 1/4-inch rounds (2 cups)
- 2 plum tomatoes, seeded and cut into 1/4-inch dice (1 cup)
- 1 small ear corn, stripped (1/2 cup)
- 2 teaspoons Authentic Cajun Spice Mix (recipe follows)
- 1/2 teaspoon fresh thyme leaves, or 1/4 teaspoon dried
- 1/4 teaspoon freshly ground black pepper
- 1/2 teaspoon kosher salt

Okra is enjoyed in many parts of the world, from India to the southern United States. Because this particular preparation involves quick-cooking, the okra does not have time to get slimy, which is what offends many people. Try this with traditional Southern dishes, such as fried chicken, chicken-fried steak, or fried catfish. It is also a fresh, light foil for pork chops, barbecued ribs, or a hearty turkey loaf.

1. Heat a large frying pan over low heat. Heat the oil until hot, about 1 minute.

2. Cook the shallot, stirring constantly, until translucent, about 1 minute.

3. Add the okra and cook, stirring, for 30 seconds.

4. Increase the heat to medium. Place the tomatoes in the pan and cook, stirring, until they begin to exude their juices, about 1 minute.

5. Add the remaining ingredients to the pan and, still stirring, cook until the corn deepens slightly in color and begins to give off some of its juice. Serve immediately.

authentic cajun spice mix

MAKES ABOUT ½ CUP

- 2 tablespoons sweet paprika
- 4½ teaspoons kosher salt
- 2 teaspoons onion powder
- 2 teaspoons garlic powder
- 2 teaspoons ground cayenne pepper
- 1½ teaspoons ground white pepper
- 1½ teaspoons dried thyme leaves
- 1½ teaspoons dried oregano leaves
- 1½ teaspoons ground black pepper
- 1½ teaspoons brown sugar

Keep some of this spice mix for whenever you have the urge for intense, peppery heat. Be careful when you open the container, as the dust alone can send you reeling.

Combine all the spices in a small bowl. Store in a covered jar or another airtight container. Stir before using.

stir-fried coconut-ginger green beans

MAKES 4 SERVINGS AS A SIDE DISH

- ¾ pound fresh green beans, cut into 1-inch pieces
- ½ lemongrass stalk, bottom 3 or 4 inches only, tough outer leaves removed, minced (1 tablespoon)
- 1 small garlic clove, minced (1 teaspoon)
- 1 thin slice ginger, peeled and minced (½ teaspoon)
- ¼ teaspoon ground coriander
- ⅛ teaspoon ground caraway
- ¼ teaspoon ground cumin
- ⅛ teaspoon ground nutmeg
- 2 large serrano chilies, seeded and minced (2 tablespoons)
- 2 tablespoons nam pla (Thai fish sauce)
- ¾ cup unsweetened coconut milk

Dry stir-fried green beans have a pleasant charred flavor that goes well with coconut milk. Make sure to get your wok very hot first.

1. Heat a wok until very hot. Add the green beans and stir over high heat until beginning to char, about 3 minutes.

2. Add the lemongrass, garlic, ginger, coriander, caraway, cumin, nutmeg, and chilies. Stir-fry for 30 seconds.

3. Add the nam pla and coconut milk and stir for 1 minute more. Serve family-style on a platter.

authentic cafe
mixed vegetables

MAKES ABOUT 3½ CUPS;
5 SERVINGS AS A SIDE DISH

2 tablespoons pure
olive oil

2 small shallots, minced
(3 tablespoons)

1 tablespoon minced
fresh thyme or
½ tablespoon dried

3 medium-size carrots,
peeled and minced
(1¼ cup)

3 celery ribs, minced
(1¼ cup)

¾ pound peas in the
shell, shelled; or
1 cup thawed frozen
shelled peas

1 small sweet onion,
minced (1 cup)

¼ teaspoon freshly
ground black pepper

½ teaspoon kosher salt

These vegetables, a best-ever version of the '50s classic, are still a great match for meatloaf.

1. Heat a large frying pan over medium heat. Add the oil and heat it, about 1 minute. Add the shallots and, if using, the dried thyme and cook, stirring constantly, until translucent, about 1 minute. Add the carrots and celery and cook, stirring, until the celery just begins to soften, about 2 minutes.

2. Place the peas and onion in the pan and cook, stirring constantly, until the onion is translucent and the peas are just barely cooked, about 1½ minutes. Stir in the pepper, salt, and fresh thyme, if using. Serve immediately.

baked sun chokes with tomatoes, lemon, and sage

MAKES 4 TO 6 SERVINGS AS A
SIDE DISH

- 2 tablespoons pure olive oil
- 1 small onion, chopped (1 cup)
- 2 teaspoons minced fresh sage or 1 teaspoon dried
- 2 large garlic cloves, minced (2 tablespoons)
- 2 pounds whole sun chokes, peeled
- 3/4 pounds plum tomatoes, peeled, seeded, and quartered (2 cups)
- 1 teaspoon freshly ground black pepper
- 1/4 cup freshly squeezed lemon juice
- 2 teaspoons kosher salt

My grandmother always cooked with sun chokes, which have a nutty flavor. They can be baked, as here, or they can be boiled and mashed like potatoes. They are also delicious raw in salads. If you do cook them, make sure not to overcook them, as they will fall apart.

1. Preheat the oven to 350°.

2. Heat a large, nonreactive, ovenproof braising pan over medium heat. Add the oil and heat it, about 1 minute. Add the onion and, if using, dried sage and cook, stirring, until translucent, about 2 minutes. Reduce the heat to low, add the garlic and cook, stirring, for 1 minute more. Add the sun chokes, tomatoes, and pepper and cook, stirring, for 2 minutes.

3. Cover the pan with a lid or with aluminum foil and bake until the sun chokes are soft but still hold their shape, 40 to 45 minutes. Remove the cover and add the lemon juice, fresh sage, if using, and salt. Mix gently. Serve warm.

Peeling Tomatoes

To peel tomatoes, bring a pot of water to a boil; prepare an ice bath as well. Cut a shallow "x" in the skin at the bottom of each tomato. Drop the tomatoes into the boiling water and leave them there until the skin begins to peel, for about 20 seconds. Remove them with a slotted spoon or skimmer and add them immediately to the ice bath. The cold water will loosen their skins. You should be able to peel the tomatoes easily.

eggplant pancakes with oregano and goat cheese

Makes sixteen 3-inch pancakes;
4 or 5 servings as a side dish

One 1¼-pound eggplant

1 tablespoon pure olive oil

Dry ingredients

¾ sifted all-purpose flour

¼ teaspoon freshly ground black pepper

1½ teaspoons kosher salt

½ teaspoon baking powder

2 teaspoons red chile flakes

Wet ingredients

2 large eggs

1 cup milk

2 tablespoons freshly squeezed lemon juice

2 tablespoons extra-virgin olive oil

1 medium-size garlic clove, minced (1½ teaspoons)

¼ teaspoon freshly ground black pepper

½ teaspoon kosher salt

1 teaspoon minced fresh oregano

¼ cup crumbled goat cheese

These pancakes make a great side dish, especially with lamb or chicken. Make sure that the eggplant is roasted until it is very soft.

1. Preheat the oven to 400°. Rub the eggplant with the oil, then prick it several times with a fork. Place the eggplant in a small shallow baking pan and bake until it is soft, about 45 minutes. Let the eggplant cool slightly, then peel and seed it. In a small bowl, mash the pulp coarsely. You should have about 1½ cups of pulp.

2. Combine the dry ingredients in a medium-size bowl.

3. Beat the eggs lightly in a large bowl. Add the milk, then the rest of the wet ingredients, as well as the garlic and the remaining pepper and salt. Add the eggplant pulp to this and mix well. Add the combined dry ingredients to the eggplant mixture and mix thoroughly. Let this mixture sit at room temperature to allow the flour to absorb the liquid.

4. Heat a large cast-iron or nonstick skillet or griddle over medium-low heat. Ladle 1 ounce, or 2 tablespoons, of batter for each pancake into the skillet, spacing well apart. The pancakes will spread to about 3 inches in diameter. Cook, turning them once, until they are golden brown and set, about 1 minute on each side. The eggplant will keep them rather soft. Turn the pancakes only once to prevent them from getting tough.

5. As they are done, place the pancakes on an ovenproof platter. Keep the prepared pancakes warm in a 200° oven while preparing the rest. Garnish the pancakes with the minced oregano and goat cheese and serve.

grilled eggplant and potato gratin

MAKES 4 SERVINGS AS A
STARTER OR SIDE DISH

Four ⅓-inch lengthwise
slices of eggplant,
unpeeled (about
½ eggplant)

1 teaspoon kosher salt

¼ cup pure olive oil

¼ teaspoon freshly
ground black pepper

2 cups Garlic Mashed
Potatoes (page 194),
warmed

¼ pound fresh mozza-
rella cheese, cut into
¼-inch slices

4 teaspoons Calamata
Olive, Currant, and
Oregano Relish
(page 204)

This is a great winter first course, or a side dish with roasted leg of lamb. Make sure to salt the eggplant. This will cause it to release excess water and will prevent it from absorbing too much oil during cooking.

1. Sprinkle the eggplant with the salt and lay the slices in a single layer in a colander to drain for 20 to 30 minutes. Meanwhile, preheat the oven to 400°.

2. Pat the eggplant dry with paper towels. Brush it with the oil and sprinkle with pepper. Heat a large skillet over medium heat. Add the eggplant and cook, turning it once, until soft and golden brown, about 2 minutes on each side. (You can also grill or broil the eggplant.)

3. Place 1 slice of eggplant on ovenproof plates, or lay all the eggplant in a shallow, ovenproof serving dish. Top the eggplant slices with the Garlic Mashed Potatoes, spreading it out slightly, then place the sliced cheese on top. Bake until the cheese melts, about 10 minutes.

4. Place a teaspoon of Calamata, Olive, Currant, and Oregano Relish on the the cheese and serve immediately.

eggplant and couscous napoleon

MAKES 4 SERVINGS AS A
MAIN COURSE

One 1-pound eggplant
    (not a Japanese
    eggplant), unpeeled,
    cut crosswise into
    1/2-inch-thick rounds

  2 tablespoons
    kosher salt

  1 small red bell pepper

1/2 teaspoon pure
    olive oil

1/4 cup extra-virgin
    olive oil

  2 cups Basic Couscous
    (page 203), warmed

1 1/4 cups Moroccan
    Eggplant Salad
    (page 104), at room
    temperature

This layered dish, recalling a napoleon, makes a light, yet very nutritious vegetarian meal. In addition to absorbing less oil during cooking, eggplant that has been salted before being cooked is also less bitter.

1. Sprinkle the eggplant with the salt and lay the rounds in a single layer in a colander to drain for 20 to 30 minutes. Pat the eggplant dry with paper towels.

2. Preheat the broiler. Rub the bell pepper with the pure olive oil and put it in a small shallow baking pan. Broil the pepper, turning it on all sides, until the skin begins to blacken and blister, about 2 minutes on each side. Place the pepper in a small bowl, cover with plastic wrap, and let it "sweat" for 20 minutes. Peel the pepper and remove the stem and seeds, along with any white membrane from inside the pepper. Cut it into $1/16$-inch dice. Put the diced pepper in a small bowl, and mix it with 1 tablespoon of the extra-virgin olive oil. Set aside.

3. Brush the eggplant with the remaining extra-virgin olive oil. Heat a large skillet over medium heat. Add the eggplant and cook, turning it once, until soft and lightly browned, about 2 minutes on each side. (You can also grill or broil the eggplant.)

4. Place 1 round of eggplant on each plate. Spread 3 tablespoons of the Basic Couscous, then 2 tablespoons of the Moroccan Eggplant Salad on the eggplant round. Top with another round of eggplant and repeat the layering process, finishing with a round of eggplant. Place 1 tablespoon of diced red pepper on top of each "napoleon" and serve immediately.

garlic mashed potatoes

MAKES ABOUT 4 CUPS;
4 SERVINGS AS A SIDE DISH

2 pounds Idaho
   potatoes, peeled

2 tablespoons plus
   2 teaspoons kosher
   salt

8 cups cold water

¼ cup unsalted butter,
   room temperature

3 large garlic
   cloves, minced
   (3 tablespoons)

½ cup half-and-half,
   heated in a small
   saucepan until
   bubbles appear
   around the edge

⅓ teaspoon freshly
   ground black pepper

These potatoes are very easy to make. I prefer to use Idaho potatoes as they will give the mashed potatoes a light texture.

1. Place the potatoes, 2 tablespoons of the salt, and the water in a large saucepan. Bring to a boil over high heat, then reduce the heat to medium and simmer the potatoes until they offer no resistance when tested with a thin sharp knife, 30 to 40 minutes.

2. Drain the potatoes and place them in a large bowl. Use a food mill, potato masher, or a heavy whisk to mash the potatoes. Do not place them in a food processor or electric mixer, or the potatoes will be heavy and gluey.

3. Add the butter and continue to mash, then add the rest of the ingredients, including the remaining 2 teaspoons salt, and mix thoroughly. Serve immediately, or keep the potatoes warm in a covered double boiler over barely simmering water. Fluff with a large spoon before serving.

olive mashed potatoes

MAKES ABOUT 3 CUPS;
3 OR 4 SERVINGS AS A SIDE DISH

1 pound red potatoes, unpeeled

1 tablespoon plus ¼ teaspoon kosher salt

8 cups water

6 tablespoons unsalted butter, at room temperature, cut into ½-inch pieces

½ cup heavy cream

½ teaspoon freshly ground black pepper

½ cup oil-cured black olives, pitted and quartered

While traveling in Marrakech, Morocco, I went daily to the market, known as the Jamal Ef Na Souk. In those stalls, I tasted the different olives, nuts, and other foods, which gave me the idea of adding these intensely flavored olives to our own mashed potatoes. The olives in this recipe are slightly shriveled and quite pungent.

1. Place the potatoes, 1 tablespoon of the salt, and the water in a large saucepan. Bring to a boil over high heat, then reduce the heat to medium and simmer the potatoes until they offer no resistance when tested with a thin sharp knife, 30 to 35 minutes.

2. Drain the potatoes and place them in a large bowl. Use a food mill, potato masher, or a heavy whisk to mash the potatoes, leaving the skin on. Do not place them in a food processor or electric mixer, or the potatoes will be heavy and gluey. It is all right if some lumps remain, and these potatoes should be rather stiff, not liquid.

3. Add the butter and continue to mash. Stir in the cream, pepper, and remaining ¼ teaspoon salt. Gently fold in the olives at the end. Serve immediately, or keep the potatoes warm in a covered double boiler over barely simmering water. Fluff with a large spoon before serving.

mashed sweet potatoes

MAKES ABOUT 3½ CUPS;
3 OR 4 SERVINGS AS A SIDE DISH

2 pounds sweet
potatoes, unpeeled

3 tablespoons unsalted
butter, at room
temperature

2 tablespoons pure
maple syrup

2 teaspoons kosher salt

⅓ teaspoon freshly
ground black pepper

½ cup half-and-half,
heated in a small
saucepan until
bubbles appear
around the edge

Maple syrup adds a nice, yet subtle, touch to these mashed potatoes.

1. Preheat the oven to 400°.

2. Place the sweet potatoes in a medium-size shallow baking pan and bake until they offer no resistance when tested with a thin sharp knife, about 1 hour. Let the potatoes cool slightly but peel them while they are still warm. The skins will have separated from the flesh, so they will be quite easy to peel.

3. Place the potatoes in a large nonporous bowl. Use a food mill, potato masher, or a heavy whisk to mash the potatoes. Do not place them in a food processor or electric mixer, or the potatoes will become soupy.

4. Add the butter and continue to mash, then add the rest of the ingredients and mix thoroughly. Serve immediately, or keep warm in a covered double boiler over simmering water. Fluff with a large spoon before serving.

sweet potato and roasted corn relish

Two ¾-pound sweet potatoes

1 small ear yellow or white corn, husk and silk removed

½ cup plus 2 teaspoons pure olive oil

1½ teaspoons puréed chipotle chile en adobo (see Note, page 37) or puréed dried morita chile (see Note, page 141)

½ small red onion, cut into ⅛-inch dice (½ cup)

One 1-inch strip red bell pepper, minced (2 tablespoons)

½ cup freshly squeezed lime juice

3 tablespoons minced cilantro (fresh coriander)

1 teaspoon freshly ground black pepper

1 tablespoon kosher salt

I especially like to serve this salad with something spicy. Roasting the potatoes and corn, rather than boiling them, brings out their natural sugars and intensifies the flavor.

1. Preheat the oven to 400°.

2. Place the sweet potatoes in a small shallow baking pan and bake until they offer no resistance when tested with a thin sharp knife, about 50 minutes. Let the potatoes cool slightly, but peel them while they are still warm. Let them cool completely, then cut the potatoes into ½-inch dice. You should have about 2 cups.

2. Meanwhile, rub the corn with 2 teaspoons of oil and roast it in a small shallow baking pan until the corn begins to brown, 20 to 30 minutes. Let the corn cool and then scrape the kernels off the cob with a sharp knife. You should have about 1 cup of kernels.

3. Place the diced sweet potatoes, corn kernels, and the rest of the ingredients, including the ½ cup oil, in a large, nonreactive bowl and mix well. Refrigerate, covered, for at least 1 hour, but no longer than 4 hours, to let the flavors meld.

moroccan-spiced potato and chick-pea stew

MAKES 4 SERVINGS AS A MAIN DISH

2 medium-size red potatoes, unpeeled

2½ teaspoons kosher salt

¼ cup pure olive oil

½ small onion, chopped (½ cup)

1 large garlic clove, minced (1 tablespoon)

¼ teaspoon crumbled saffron threads, preferably Spanish

½ teaspoon freshly ground black pepper

1 teaspoon ground cumin

One ¼-inch piece ginger, peeled and minced (1 teaspoon)

1 pound plum tomatoes, seeded and cut into ⅓-inch dice (2¼ cups)

¾ cup water

1½ cups cooked chick-peas (garbanzo beans), drained (see Note)

1 to 2 teaspoons harissa

1 tablespoon chopped fresh mint

1 tablespoon chopped cilantro (fresh coriander)

I try to re-create flavors from my childhood whenever I get the chance. This dish consists of two simple, inexpensive staples that were common in my grandmother's house. Serve this stew over Basic Couscous for a hearty vegetarian main course.

1. Place the potatoes in a small saucepan and cover them with water. Add 1 teaspoon of the salt and bring to a boil over high heat. Reduce the heat to medium and simmer until the potatoes offer no resistance when tested with a thin sharp knife, about 30 minutes. Drain the potatoes and let them cool. Without peeling them, cut them into ½-inch dice.

2. Heat a large, nonreactive saucepan over medium heat. Add the oil and heat it, about 2 minutes. Add the onion, garlic, saffron, pepper, cumin, and ginger and cook, stirring, for 2 minutes.

3. Add the tomatoes and simmer for 2 minutes more. Place the water, diced potatoes, chick-peas, harissa, and the remaining 1½ teaspoons salt in the pan and bring to a boil. Reduce the heat to low and simmer, stirring occasionally, for 20 minutes.

4. Adjust the seasonings, especially the salt and harissa. Serve garnished with the mint and cilantro.

Note *If using dried chick-peas, soak ¾ cup of the peas in 3 cups of water overnight, refrigerated. The next day, rinse the chick-peas, and place them in a large saucepan with 4 cups of fresh water. Bring to a boil, then reduce the heat to medium-low and simmer until the chick-peas are tender, 30 to 40 minutes. Drain and add 2 teaspoons of kosher salt. Adding the salt at the end prevents the skins of dried peas and beans from hardening.*

authentic cafe flageolet beans

MAKES 4 CUPS; 4 TO 6 SERVINGS

1 cup dried
   flageolet beans

4 cups cold water

2 tablespoons pure
   olive oil

One $\frac{1}{4}$-inch slice pancetta,
   cut into $\frac{1}{4}$-inch dice
   ($\frac{1}{2}$ cup)

1 large onion, cut into
   $\frac{1}{4}$ inch dice (2 cups)

3 medium-size cloves
   garlic, minced
   ($4\frac{1}{2}$ teaspoons)

$\frac{1}{2}$ teaspoon freshly
   ground black pepper

3 cups chicken stock,
   preferably homemade
   (page 24)

1 tablespoon minced
   fresh oregano or
   $\frac{1}{2}$ tablespoon dried

These small, pale green dried beans are a traditional favorite in France. They are delicious with any roast meat or poultry.

1. Soak the flageolets in the water, refrigerated, for at least 4 hours, or up to 12 hours. Drain. You should have 3 cups of soaked beans.

2. Heat a large, nonreactive saucepan over low heat. Heat the oil until hot, about 1 minute. Add the pancetta and cook, stirring constantly, until it begins to get crisp around the edges, about 2 minutes.

3. Add the onion and cook, stirring, until translucent, about 5 minutes.

4. Add the garlic, pepper, drained beans, stock, and, if using, the dried oregano. Increase the heat to medium and bring to a slow boil. Reduce the heat to medium-low and simmer the beans until tender, about $1\frac{1}{4}$ to $1\frac{1}{2}$ hours. Some liquid will remain and the beans will be whole. Taste the beans and add salt, if desired. Stir in the fresh oregano, if using, and serve.

authentic cafe black beans

MAKES 8 CUPS;
16 SERVINGS AS A SIDE DISH

½ large onion, peeled

3 plum tomatoes

5 tablespoons mild
vegetable oil, such as
corn

4 large whole
garlic cloves

2 tablespoons
Authentic Cafe
Spice Mix *(page 30)*

3 tablespoons puréed
ancho chile *(see* Note,
page 175)

2 teaspoons puréed
chipotle chile en
adobo *(see* Note,
page 37)

1 medium-size serrano
chile, seeded and
minced

¼ teaspoon dried
oregano

2 bay leaves

1 tablespoon kosher salt

1 pound dried black
beans

12 cups cold water

Like all my recipes, these beans are lard-free. But they are still extremely rich and creamy. To replace the smokiness and depth of flavor that pork products give the beans as they are cooked in Mexico, I have added grilled tomatoes and onions to the recipe. Grilling the vegetables also complements the smokiness of the chipotle chile en adobo.

If, however, you do not have a barbecue grill, rub the onion and tomatoes with oil, and roast them at 400° for 20 minutes, then broil them until slightly blackened, about 5 minutes.

1. Prepare a fire in a barbecue grill. Oil the grill rack.

2. Rub the onion and tomatoes with 4 teaspoons of the oil. Place the vegetables on the grill rack about 6 inches from the heat and cook until soft and slightly blackened. (They will not be done at the same time.) Place the vegetables in a small bowl and let them cool. Seed and chop the tomatoes; you should have about 1 cup. Chop the onion; you should have 1 cup as well.

2. Meanwhile, preheat the oven to 400°. Rub the garlic cloves with 2 teaspoons of the oil and arrange them in a small shallow baking pan. Roast them until soft and slightly browned, about 15 minutes. Let the garlic cool. Chop the garlic, then add it to the tomatoes and onion.

3. Heat a large stockpot (with at least a 6-quart capacity) over low heat. Add the remaining 3 tablespoons of oil and heat it , about 2 minutes. Add the grilled vegetables and all the other ingredients, except the beans and water, and cook, stirring, for 5 minutes.

4. Add the beans and water and increase the heat to medium. Once the liquid begins to boil, reduce the heat to low and skim the foam off the surface. Simmer the beans, stirring frequently to prevent sticking, until the liquid reduces by about half, 3 to 3½ hours. The liquid should be quite creamy, but the beans will remain whole.

5. Let the beans cool completely before refrigerating. They can also be frozen. (Resealable bags are ideal for this; you can freeze the beans in small quantities this way.) Thaw frozen beans overnight in the refrigerator.

cheddar cheese grits

MAKES ABOUT 4 CUPS;
4 SERVINGS AS A SIDE DISH

1½ cups milk

1½ cups water

¼ teaspoon kosher salt

¾ cup Quick Grits

½ teaspoon freshly
ground black pepper

4 ounces Tillamook
cheese or sharp white
Cheddar cheese,
grated (1 cup)

Not only is this the perfect accompaniment for Sautéed Catfish with Pecan-Morita Sauce, it makes for a delicious breakfast with lots of staying power.

1. Bring the milk, water, and salt to a boil in a large saucepan over medium heat. Reduce the heat to low and stir in the grits. Cook, stirring constantly with a wooden spoon, over low heat for 5 to 7 minutes.

2. Remove the pan from the heat and stir the pepper and cheese into the grits. Stir until the cheese is completely melted. Serve immediately.

basic couscous

2 tablespoons pure
olive oil

½ small onion, minced
(½ cup)

1 large garlic clove,
minced (1 tablespoon)

1 teaspoon ground
cumin

¼ teaspoon crumbled
saffron, preferably
Spanish

¼ teaspoon freshly
ground black pepper

2 teaspoons kosher salt

2¼ cups water or chicken
stock, preferably
homemade (page 24)

¼ cup extra-virgin
olive oil

1½ cups instant couscous

Traditionally, couscous is prepared by steaming the grain twice in a *couscoussière*, a specialized double steamer whose perforated steaming basket holds the grain above bubbling broth or a stew. In this recipe, we use instant couscous for the sake of saving time, but we still steam the couscous to finish the preparation.

1. Heat a medium-size saucepan over medium heat. Add the pure olive oil and heat it, about 1 minute. Add the onion and cook, stirring, for 1 minute.

2. Add the garlic and cook, stirring constantly, for about 15 seconds. Add the cumin, saffron, pepper, and salt and, still stirring, cook for 1 minute.

3. Add the water or stock and extra-virgin oil and bring to a boil. Stir the couscous into the liquid, remove the pan from the heat, and cover. Let the couscous stand for 10 minutes to absorb the liquid. Uncover and fluff with a fork to separate the grains.

4. Cover the holes of a steamer basket with a clean, wet, lint-free towel. Place the couscous in the basket and steam it over simmering water for 20 minutes. This will make the couscous moist. Serve immediately.

calamata olive, currant, and oregano relish

MAKES 1½ CUPS

1 cup currants

¾ cup pitted
  Calamata olives

5 large garlic cloves

4 cured anchovy fillets

2 tablespoons mild
  honey, such as orange

1 teaspoon freshly
  ground black pepper

⅓ cup fresh oregano
  leaves

⅓ cup extra-virgin
  olive oil

This condiment is similar to *tapenade*, the smooth spread of black olives and capers from Provence, but with a slightly sweet twist. Not only is it delicious simply spread on a slice of crusty bread, it also makes a wonderful topping for roasted poultry.

1. Soak the currants in warm water for 10 minutes. Drain.

2. Place the currants, olives, garlic, anchovies, honey, pepper, and oregano in a blender or food processor and purée coarsely.

3. With the motor running, add the oil and process for about 20 seconds. The condiment can be refrigerated, covered, for up to 5 days.

vegetable escabeche

Makes 3 cups, drained

2 large carrots, peeled and cut into ¼-inch dice (2 cups)

1 cup cider vinegar

¼ teaspoon freshly ground black pepper

1 cup water

1 tablespoon kosher salt

½ medium-size red bell pepper, cut into ¼-inch dice (⅓ cup)

½ medium-size yellow bell pepper, cut into ¼-inch dice (⅓ cup)

2 medium-size serrano chilies, stems removed, quartered lengthwise (leave the seeds)

3 large garlic cloves, peeled

Pickled vegetables are used in many cultures. I remember when my father would take me to traditional, old-style Italian markets with sawdust on the floor. We would see large glass jars full of pickled vegetables like these.

1. Place the carrots in a medium-size, nonreactive, heatproof bowl. Combine the vinegar, black pepper, water, and salt in a small saucepan and bring to a boil. Pour this hot mixture over the carrots. Let cool.

2. Add the peppers, chilies, and garlic to the bowl and mix well. Refrigerate, covered, for 1 day and up to 4 days. Before serving, drain the escabeche that you will be using, leaving the rest in the marinade. Remove the serrano chile strips and garlic cloves (place them back in the marinade, if any vegetables are left, or discard).

mango vinaigrette

MAKES ABOUT 2 CUPS

1 medium-size ripe mango, peeled, seeded, and cut into small dice (1 cup)

3 medium-size shallots, minced (¼ cup)

¼ cup mango vinegar or champagne vinegar

1 tablespoon chopped cilantro (fresh coriander)

¼ teaspoon freshly ground black pepper

1 teaspoon kosher salt

1 small habanero chile, seeded and minced (1 teaspoon); or 2 small serrano chilies, seeded and minced (2 teaspoons)

¾ cup mild vegetable oil, such as peanut

Use this spicy-sweet dressing in a salad with grilled chicken or shrimp.

Place all the ingredients, except the oil, in a blender or food processor and purée. With the motor running, add the oil in a thin stream. The vinaigrette can be refrigerated, covered, for up to 1 day. Bring to room temperature and whisk to re-emulsify before serving.

Desserts

Just about everybody likes to end a meal with a dessert of some sort, whether it's rich and decadent or light and fruity. The desserts at the Authentic Cafe fall into both categories, although they tend to be more homey, less eclectic.

Many people seem to think of themselves as either "cooks" or "bakers," but not both, for some reason. Maybe it's because baking requires a bit more precision, or conversely, savory recipes often seem to be more adaptable, therefore leaving more room for creativity.

I, of course, believe that a recipe—any recipe—should serve as a guideline and, hopefully, as an inspiration. I encourage you to try these recipes, whether you think of yourself as a "cook" or a "baker," and to let your imagination run wild. Stretch the recipes, and yourselves, to the limit.

mango-raspberry napoleon

MAKES 4 SERVINGS

2 sheets phyllo dough

3 tablespoons unsalted
   butter, melted and
   cooled

1 tablespoon powdered
   sugar, plus additional
   for dusting

2 large ripe mangos

¼ cup granulated sugar

1 to 2 tablespoons freshly
   squeezed lime juice

1 cup very cold
   heavy cream

½ pint raspberries or
   blackberries

   Berry Coulis
   (recipe follows)

4 fresh mint leaves

The classic napoleon, or *millefeuille*, consists of layers of puff pastry filled with pastry cream. In this updated and immeasurably simpler version, phyllo dough stands in for the puff pastry and a mango mousse replaces the traditional pastry cream.

1. Preheat the oven to 375°.

2. Lay 1 sheet of phyllo on a flat work surface. (Be sure to cover the second sheet, first with waxed paper, then with a damp towel, to prevent it from drying out.) Brush the sheet generously with melted butter. Carefully lay the second sheet on top, making sure to match the edges. Run your hand over the top of the dough to force out as much air as possible. Brush the top with the rest of the butter.

3. Cut the dough in half crosswise. Since all companies make their dough a slightly different size, use a ruler to find the halfway point. It is important that both halves be exactly the same size.

4. Lay one half on top of the other, again matching the edges. Cut twelve two-layer rectangles, approximately 2 x 3½ inches each. Lay the dough rectangles in a single layer on a nonstick or foil-lined baking sheet. They may be close together, but not touching. Dust the tops lightly with powdered sugar. Bake until golden brown, 10 to 12 minutes. Let the pastry cool completely on the baking sheet. The layers may separate when you try to move the rectangles. Don't worry, you can put them back together when assembling the pastries. These rectangles can be made up to 24 hours ahead and stored at room temperature in an airtight container. They must, however, be completely cooled before storing and must also be stored in a single layer.

5. Lay 1 mango on its side and, with a thin sharp knife, cut horizontally through the fruit, cutting just above the large flat pit in the middle. Turn the mango over and repeat this step. Cut away the pulp that is around the perimeter of the pit. Cut all the pulp away from the skin. Repeat this with the other mango.

6. Place all the pulp in a blender or food processor and purée until smooth. Press the purée through a medium-mesh strainer. You should have about $1\frac{1}{3}$ cups of strained purée.

7. Stir the sugar and lime juice (adjust the latter to the sweetness of the mangos) into the mango purée. The purée can be refrigerated, covered, for up to 24 hours.

8. Just before serving, whip the cream with the 1 tablespoon of powdered sugar until very stiff, but not grainy. Gently fold in the mango purée with a large wide rubber spatula. Before the purée is completely incorporated, fold in the berries.

9. Assemble the napoleons: Spread about 2 heaping table-spoons of the mango mousse on each of 4 of the phyllo rectangles, then top each one with another rectangle (if the layers of any of the rectangles are separating, just line them up, or stick them together with some of the mousse). Repeat this, finishing with a pastry rectangle. Dust the tops with powdered sugar.

10. Set each napoleon on a large plate. Ladle about $\frac{1}{4}$ cup of the Berry Coulis around each napoleon. Garnish with mint and serve. Pass any remaining sauce separately.

Fabulous Phyllo

Made only from flour, water, and a little salt, phyllo dough is rolled and stretched to an amazing thinness. It must be stretched, and not only rolled, so that the gluten in the flour will not develop too much; this would result in a tough dough. Because of this thinness, it dries out very quickly, and you must keep unused sheets covered, first with waxed paper, then with a slightly damp towel. Phyllo can be re-frozen if tightly wrapped, first in plastic, then in foil. If this sounds like a task, it is nothing compared to the one involved in making fresh phyllo or puff pastry.

berry coulis

1 pint red berries, mixed or a single type

3 to 4 tablespoons granulated sugar, depending on the sweetness of the berries

1 to 2 tablespoons freshly squeezed lemon juice, or to taste

This sauce will enable you to use up those berries that are no longer presentable, but are not yet moldy. *Coulis* (pronounced "coo-lee") is a French term for a puréed and strained sauce, usually uncooked. The sauce can be sweet or savory. In this case, you can use a mixture of berries, such as strawberries, blackberries, and raspberries, or just one type of berry, for a cleaner taste. Do not use blueberries, however, because they contain more pectin and will not make a smooth sauce.

Purée the fruit in a blender or food processor. Strain through a medium-mesh strainer or a china cap. Add the smaller amount of sugar and lemon juice and taste, adding more if necessary. The sauce can be refrigerated, covered, for up to 2 days. Stir before using.

raspberries

strawberries

blackberries

bananas in phyllo

MAKES 4 SERVINGS

4 tablespoons (½ stick) unsalted butter

½ cup packed dark brown sugar

4 slightly underripe bananas, cut into ½-inch chunks

¼ cup brandy or Cognac

4 sheets phyllo dough

6 tablespoons (¾ stick) unsalted butter, melted and cooled

Powdered sugar for dusting

Brandied Caramel Sauce (recipe follows), warmed

This simple dessert can be prepared ahead and then baked while you are eating the main course.

1. Heat a large, heavy, nonreactive sauté pan or frying pan over a medium heat. Melt the 4 tablespoons butter in the pan, but do not let it brown. Add the brown sugar and whisk the mixture until smooth. Let the mixture bubble for about 20 seconds.

2. Place the bananas in the pan and stir with a wooden spoon until all the pieces are coated with the sugar-butter mixture. Raise the heat to medium-high and cook, stirring the bananas until the mixture bubbles, about 2 minutes.

3. Add the brandy and continue to cook over medium heat for 30 seconds to evaporate the alcohol. (The flavor of the brandy will remain.)

4. Place this mixture in a large bowl in a single layer, and let it cool to room temperature. This can be prepared ahead and refrigerated, covered, for up to 1 day.

5. If you are planning to bake the pastries immediately, preheat the oven to 350°. Otherwise, do so 15 minutes before baking.

6. Place 1 phyllo sheet on a flat work surface. (Be sure to cover the remaining sheets, first with waxed paper, then with a damp towel, to prevent them from drying out.) Brush the sheet with melted butter, then holding the edges of a short end, fold it in half crosswise and brush the top with more butter. Pile one-quarter of the banana mixture in the center of the dough, then gather the dough up around the filling to form a small bundle, allowing the edges to flop down around the filled part of the dough. Repeat with the remaining 3 sheets of dough and the rest of the filling.

7. Place the pastries at least 3 inches apart (to ensure even browning; these will not spread) on a nonstick or foil-lined baking sheet. Drizzle the remaining butter over the tops, then dust with the powdered sugar.

8. Bake the pastries until they are an even, golden brown, about 20 minutes.

9. Ladle some of the Brandied Caramel Sauce on dessert plates and place 1 banana pastry on top. Serve immediately. Pass any remaining sauce separately.

The Art of Cooking Sugar

Whenever boiling sugar, it is important to not stir or move the saucepan until the sugar begins to boil clear; there should be no visible crystals. It is equally important to wash down any crystals clinging to the inside of the pan at the beginning of the process, as these crystals can "seed" the sugar solution, causing it to continually crystallize, even though the temperature is increasing.

If your syrup turns cloudy—an indication of crystallization—add a few drops of lemon juice, which will break down the crystals and, hopefully, stop further crystallization. If the syrup continues to crystallize, start the process over with fresh ingredients in a clean saucepan.

brandied caramel sauce

Makes about 1¼ cups

1 cup granulated sugar

1 teaspoon lemon juice or 1 tablespoon light corn syrup

¼ cup water

1 cup heavy cream

1 to 2 tablespoons good-quality brandy

Be very careful when preparing this sauce, or anything else with caramel. Sugar begins to caramelize at about 300°. Resist the temptation to dip your finger in and taste the caramel, or you could suffer severe burns.

A heavy stainless-steel-lined aluminum saucepan is ideal for caramelizing sugar because it conducts the heat quickly but will not react with the caramel.

1. Place the sugar, lemon juice or corn syrup, and water in a small, heavy, nonreactive saucepan. Stir with a spoon so that all the sugar is dampened. Place the pan over low heat, and wash down any crystals on the side of the pan with a clean pastry brush dipped in water. Do not stir or move the pot until the sugar mixture begins to boil.

2. Once the syrup boils and is clear, swirl the pot every few minutes to ensure even heating. Watch the syrup closely once the sugar begins to take on color.

3. Let the caramel reach a deep color. As it approaches the proper caramelization for this sauce, the bubbles will become much smaller and the syrup will boil much faster. Do not, however, boil the caramel until it begins to smoke. This would yield a bitter-tasting caramel.

4. Remove the pan from the heat and quickly and carefully whisk in half the cream. Stand back as you do this, as the difference in temperature between the caramel and the cream will cause the sauce to boil and spatter furiously. Whisk in the remaining cream. Let the sauce cool for about 10 minutes, then stir in the brandy.

5. The sauce can be refrigerated, covered, for up to 1 week. Stir the sauce and heat it over low heat before serving.

ginger-orange flan

Caramel

  1 cup granulated sugar

¼ cup water

  2 teaspoons freshly
      squeezed lemon juice

2⅔ cups milk

1⅓ cups heavy whipping
      cream

      Zest of 2 large oranges
      (*see* Note), left in strips

One 2-inch piece ginger,
      peeled and chopped
      (2 tablespoons)

  1 cup granulated sugar

  6 whole large eggs

  4 large egg yolks

Flan is a traditional caramelized custard found throughout Latin America. The French version is *crème renversée* or *crème au caramel*.

1. Make the caramel: First prepare an ice bath. Place about 6 ice cubes in a bowl into which you can easily dip the base of a small saucepan, and cover the ice with water. Combine the sugar, water, and lemon juice in a small, heavy, nonreactive saucepan. Mix with a wooden spoon so that all the sugar is moistened and there are no lumps. Place the pan over low heat, then wash down any crystals clinging to the inside of the pan with a clean pastry brush that has been dipped in water. Do not stir or move the pot until it begins to boil clear.

2. Once the sugar begins to caramelize, watch it closely. Swirl the pot to ensure even caramelization. Once the caramel is a dark brown, but not black or smoking (when the caramel has reached the right degree of cooking, the bubbles will become very small and the liquid will boil very fast), turn off the heat and dip the base of the pan in the ice bath for 5 seconds. This will stop the caramel from cooking any further. Be careful, however, as the ice bath will immediately steam when it comes into contact with the hot pan.

3. Remove the pan from the ice bath, dry the bottom with a towel (so that no water drips into the mold), and pour the caramel into the bottom of an 8-cup soufflé dish or another deep porcelain or glass mold with straight sides. Turn the mold while the caramel is still liquid so that the bottom is completely covered. Set aside. (To clean the saucepan, boil water in the pan to dissolve the caramel.)

4. Preheat the oven to 350°. Combine the milk, cream, orange zest, ginger, and ½ cup of the sugar in a large saucepan. Heat the mixture over medium heat until bubbles form around the edge. Turn off the heat, cover the pot, and let the mixture steep for 20 minutes.

5. Meanwhile, whisk together the whole eggs, the egg yolks, and the remaining $\frac{1}{2}$ cup sugar. Slowly whisk the steeped liquid into the egg mixture. Keep the mixture moving the entire time so that the eggs do not cook, but try not to create too much foam. Strain the mixture through a medium-mesh strainer or a china cap into the prepared mold.

6. Place the mold into a large flat-bottomed roasting pan and fill the pan with hot (not necessarily boiling) water to about $\frac{1}{2}$ inch below the level of the custard. Carefully place the pan in the oven and bake until a thin sharp knife inserted in the center of the flan comes out clean, about 1 hour and 10 minutes. The custard may still jiggle a bit—this is okay.

7. Remove the pan from the oven and the mold from the pan and let the flan cool to room temperature. Refrigerate the flan, covered, for at least 6 hours, or overnight, if possible. (The caramel will become more liquid, and therefore easier to unmold, the longer the flan sits in the refrigerator.)

8. To unmold the flan, run a thin sharp knife up against the inside of the mold. Place a high-rimmed serving platter over the mold, then invert. Lift away the mold. The caramel will spill around the flan. Serve the flan in wedges.

Note *Use only the orange-colored part of the zest, as the white pith beneath will be bitter. The zest is easily removed with a zest stripper or with a sharp paring knife.*

A Gentle Bath for Cooking

Custards and creams are usually baked in a hot water bath or *bain-marie* (so called because Queen Marie Antoinette allegedly bathed in the palace kitchen's hot water after the staff finished serving meals). The technique promotes slow, even heating of the custard and prevents a hard, thick crust from forming on top.

It is important to start with hot water; since water is denser than air, hot water conducts heat more effectively than hot air. This way, the sides of the custard (or whatever you are baking), will cook before the top, which is only in contact with hot air, can begin to brown or burn.

authentic rice pudding

4 cups milk

1 vanilla bean,
split lengthwise

Two 3-inch cinnamon
sticks

½ cup Japanese
(short-grain) rice (do
not use converted or
long-grain rice)

4 large whole eggs

4 large egg yolks

¾ cup granulated sugar

8 tablespoons (1 stick)
unsalted butter,
softened but not
melted

1 teaspoon pure
vanilla extract

½ teaspoon ground
nutmeg

2½ ounces dark raisins
(½ cup)

2 cups whipped cream .
or 1½ cups chilled
heavy cream

Most rice puddings are baked, and consequently may be dry. This extremely creamy version is cooked on the stove, much like a *crème anglaise*. It resembles Mexican *arroz con leche.* Be sure to follow the directions for cooling the pudding once it is prepared. While the egg yolks should be fully cooked, you are better off chilling a custard of this type as quickly as possible to avoid microbial growth.

1. Pour the milk into a large, nonreactive saucepan. Scrape the vanilla seeds into the milk, then add the bean to the milk as well. Add the cinnamon sticks and rice, and bring to a boil over medium heat, stirring often to prevent the rice from sticking. Once the milk boils, reduce the heat to low and simmer until the rice is just tender, about 15 minutes. Stir from time to time with a wooden spoon.

2. When the rice is almost ready, place the whole eggs and egg yolks in a large, nonreactive bowl with the sugar and whisk immediately to prevent the sugar from "cooking" (hardening) the eggs.

3. Place the butter in another large, nonreactive bowl and set aside.

4. When the rice is cooked, pour all of the rice-milk mixture into the eggs and whisk well. Pour this back into the saucepan and cook over medium-low heat, stirring constantly with a wooden spoon. Lift the spoon from time to time to check if the liquid coats the back of the spoon. Cook the custard until it begins to thicken. Do not let it boil or it will curdle (although the rice starch will curtail this to some extent). When the rice grains start remaining on the surface of the custard, it is done. (If you have a candy thermometer, it should register 170° to 175°.)

5. Immediately pour the custard over the butter and whisk thoroughly. Remove the cinnamon sticks and vanilla bean, scraping any remaining seeds back into the custard. (You can set the bean aside for a minute to cool.) Whisk in the vanilla extract and nutmeg. Stir in the raisins.

6. Pour the pudding into a medium-size, nonreactive metal bowl. Scrape any remaining pudding from the bowl into the container with a rubber spatula, then leave the spatula in the pudding. Place this bowl in a larger bowl filled with 4 cups of ice water and a dozen ice cubes. Stir every few minutes until the pudding is cool. Refrigerate, covered, for at least 2 hours before serving. This pudding can be made up to 2 days ahead. Serve in sundae glasses with whipped cream or chilled heavy cream.

mexican chocolate cake

MAKES 8 TO 10 SERVINGS

1½ ounces (1½ squares) unsweetened chocolate

2 teaspoons instant coffee granules

2 tablespoons boiling water

½ cup sour cream

2 cups sifted all-purpose flour

1 teaspoon baking soda

½ teaspoon baking powder

1 teaspoon ground cinnamon

Pinch ground cloves

8 tablespoons (1 stick) unsalted butter, at room temperature

1 cup granulated sugar

2 large eggs

1 teaspoon pure vanilla extract

3 ounces dark raisins (⅔ cup)

8 ounces pecan halves (2 cups)

8 ounces pitted dates, chopped (1 cup)

6 ounces semisweet chocolate morsels (1 cup)

This dense, moist cake is almost like a fruit-cake. It is packed with dried fruits, pecans, and chocolate chips. The cake is best when made a day ahead and will keep for 5 days at room temperature if wrapped in plastic.

1. Preheat the oven to 350°. Adjust a rack to divide the oven in half. Butter a 9 x 5 x 3-inch loaf pan.

2. Place the unsweetened chocolate in a small, heatproof bowl and set in a saucepan filled one-third with barely simmering water. When the chocolate is almost melted, stir it and remove the bowl from the water bath.

3. In a small bowl, dissolve the instant coffee in the boiling water. Whisk this into the melted chocolate. The chocolate may thicken and appear dry. Immediately whisk in the sour cream (the chocolate will relax again), stirring until smooth.

4. Sift together the flour, baking soda, baking powder, cinnamon, and cloves onto a sheet of waxed paper and set aside.

5. In the large bowl of an electric mixer, or with a hand-held electric mixer, beat together the butter and sugar at medium speed until light and fluffy. Beat in the eggs, one at a time, scraping the bowl with a rubber spatula between additions. Add the vanilla extract.

6. Reduce the speed to low and add the sifted dry ingredients in 3 batches, alternating with the chocolate mixture in 2 batches. Mix only until incorporated and scrape the bowl after each addition.

7. Mix in the remaining ingredients, except the ice cream and Warm Chocolate Sauce, by hand, using a rubber spatula or a wooden spoon. Mix only until the ingredients are evenly distributed.

8. Spoon the batter into the loaf pan and smooth the top even. Bake until a cake tester inserted into the middle comes out barely dry (there may be some melted chocolate morsel that sticks to the tester—check that there are no wet crumbs), about $1\frac{1}{2}$ hours. The cake will form a heavy crust during baking. If the crust begins to burn, cover the top of the cake loosely with aluminum foil.

9. Cool the cake in the pan on a wire rack for about 10 minutes. Holding the pan with oven mitts, turn the cake out onto the rack, turn it right side up, and cool completely. Wrap in plastic until serving.

10. To serve, cut cut the cake into $\frac{1}{2}$-inch slices with a serrated knife. Lay 2 slices on each plate, place a scoop of coffee ice cream on top, and drizzle about 3 tablespoons of Warm Chocolate Sauce over the cake and the ice cream. Serve immediately.

warm chocolate sauce

MAKES $1\frac{1}{2}$ CUPS

$\frac{3}{4}$ cup milk

2 tablespoons heavy cream

9 ounces bittersweet chocolate, coarsely chopped

2 tablespoons unsalted butter, softened, but not melted

This sauce is actually a classic *ganache*: chocolate melted in cream or milk. Try stirring 2 tablespoons of this sauce into a cup of hot milk or half-and-half for an absolutely decadent cup of hot chocolate.

1. Heat the milk and cream in a small saucepan over medium heat until bubbles appear around the edge.

2. Place the chocolate in a small or medium-size bowl. Pour the hot liquid over the chocolate and whisk until completely smooth. Let the sauce cool for 10 minutes at room temperature.

3. Whisk the butter into the cooled sauce. (If you whisk the butter into chocolate that is too hot, the butter may separate.) Use the sauce immediately, or let it cool completely and store in a covered jar, refrigerated. Reheat gently in a double boiler or small, heatproof bowl set in simmering water. Do not boil.

lemon pound cake

MAKES 10 TO 12 SERVINGS

3 cups sifted
   all-purpose flour

2 teaspoons
   baking powder

1 teaspoon baking soda

½ pound (2 sticks)
   unsalted butter, at
   room temperature

2 cups granulated sugar

4 large eggs, at room
   temperature

   Finely grated zest of
   2 lemons

1 cup buttermilk, at
   room temperature

Glaze

¼ cup freshly squeezed
   lemon juice

⅔ cup granulated sugar

   Blueberry Compote
   (recipe follows)

Pound cake has always been one of my favorite desserts. This lemon version is very tart and moist. Try to make it a day ahead to let the flavors mature.

1. Preheat the oven to 350°. Lightly butter a 9-inch tube pan (or, if you have a 10 x 3-inch springform pan with a tube bottom—and these are often fluted as well—use that). Dust the inside of the pan with flour, invert the pan, and tap out any excess.

2. Sift together the flour, baking powder, and baking soda. Set aside.

3. In the large bowl of an electric mixer, or with a hand-held electric mixer, beat together the butter and sugar at medium speed until light and fluffy, about 5 minutes. Mix in the eggs 2 at a time, scraping down the bowl with a rubber spatula between additions. Beat in the lemon zest.

4. Reduce the mixer's speed to low and add the sifted dry ingredients in three batches, alternating with the buttermilk, starting and ending with the dry ingredients. Mix only until smooth after each addition, and scrape down the bowl between additions.

5. Spoon the batter into the prepared pan and smooth the top with a rubber spatula. Knock the pan lightly a few times on a countertop to bring any air bubbles to the top. Bake until the top springs back when touched and a toothpick stuck into the thickest part of the cake comes out dry, 1 hour to 1 hour and 10 minutes.

6. Remove the cake from the oven and let it sit in the pan on a wire rack for 5 minutes. Run a thin knife or metal spatula between the outside of the cake and the pan. Invert the cake onto a rack or a platter.

7. While the cake is still hot, prepare the glaze: In a small bowl, stir the glaze ingredients together. Liberally brush the glaze all over the top and sides of the cake, as well as in the hole in the center. Use all the glaze. Let the cake cool completely, then wrap it in plastic and let it mellow for at least 12 hours, or up to 3 days.

8. Cut the cake into $\frac{1}{2}$-inch slices and serve 3 or 4 slices per person with Blueberry Compote on top or on the side.

blueberry compote

MAKES ABOUT 3 CUPS

2 pints fresh blueberries or two 12-ounce packages frozen (no need to thaw them)

$\frac{1}{2}$ cup granulated sugar, or to taste, depending on the sweetness of the berries

2 tablespoons freshly squeezed lemon juice

$\frac{1}{2}$ teaspoon ground dried ginger (optional)

This compote is delicious served over ice cream or with Lemon Pound Cake. The natural pectin in blueberries keeps it thick.

1. Place all the ingredients in a medium-size, nonreactive saucepan and mix well. Heat over low heat, stirring often.

2. Once the compote comes to a boil, simmer until it begins to thicken, about 20 minutes. Remove the pan from the heat. The compote will thicken more as it cools. Serve warm, at room temperature, or chilled. The compote can be refrigerated, covered, for up to 3 days.

pine nut shortbread cookies

MAKES ABOUT 4 DOZEN
2-INCH COOKIES

8 tablespoons (1 stick)
  cold unsalted butter,
  diced

½ cup granulated sugar

2½ ounces ground
  blanched almonds
  (½ cup)

2 large eggs, 1 whole,
  1 separated

1 teaspoon pure vanilla
  extract

4 ounces pine nuts

½ cup raw (turbinado-
  style) sugar, spread in
  a large shallow bowl

Everyone seems to love shortbread. These fragile, buttery pine nut cookies will melt in your mouth. They have a raw sugar crust around the outer rim, while the pine nuts actually remain rather soft. They're great with tea or Authentic Rice Pudding.

1. Preheat the oven to 350°. Adjust the racks to divide the oven into thirds.

2. In the large bowl of an electric mixer, or with a hand-held electric mixer, beat together the butter, granulated sugar, and almonds at low speed until the butter is completely broken up and the mixture resembles coarse cornmeal.

3. Lightly beat the whole egg with the egg white in a small bowl. Add the vanilla extract, then pour this mixture into the batter and mix just until the dough comes together, still at low speed. Add the pine nuts and mix only until evenly incorporated.

4. Flour a work surface very lightly. Divide the dough in half, and with each half form a log, about 8 inches long and 1½ inches in diameter. Make sure that there are no air pockets in the logs. Wrap them separately in waxed paper and refrigerate until firm, at least 1 hour. At this point, you may choose to freeze one of the logs. You may do so for up to 1 month, but wrap the dough again in aluminum foil. Thaw it overnight in the refrigerator before proceeding. The unfrozen dough can be refrigerated for up to 1 day.

5. Spread the raw sugar in an 8-inch line on your work surface. Remove the chilled dough from the refrigerator and carefully unwrap it. Mix the remaining egg yolk with 1 teaspoon cold water in a very small bowl or a ramekin. Brush the dough evenly with the beaten egg, then roll it in the raw sugar, making sure that it is covered evenly. Repeat this with the other log, if desired.

6. Using a sharp chef's knife, slice the dough into ⅓-inch-thick rounds. Place them on nonstick or foil-lined baking sheets, spacing 2 inches apart. These will spread slightly. Bake until the rims are golden and the pine nuts are very lightly browned. Turn the pans and/or switch between racks to ensure even baking.

7. Cool these cookies on the pan, placed on wire racks. Do not attempt to remove them from the pan when they are still hot, as they will break. Once cooled, remove the cookies with a wide spatula and store in an airtight container for up to 1 week.

lemon-anise biscotti

2¾ cups sifted
all-purpose flour

1 teaspoon baking
powder

1 tablespoon plus
1½ teaspoons
whole anise seed
(not star anise)

½ pound (2 sticks)
unsalted butter, at
room temperature

⅔ cup granulated sugar

Finely grated zest of
1 lemon (grate the zest
before squeezing the
lemon)

2 large eggs, 1 whole,
1 separated

1 teaspoon pure vanilla
extract

2 tablespoons milk

1 tablespoon freshly
squeezed lemon juice

1 teaspoon water

Biscotti literally means "cooked twice," and these cookies are, indeed, cooked twice: once in a long strip, then again once the strip is cut up into cookies. Biscotti are usually very crisp, often hard, and rarely have much butter, if any. These, however, are crisp and crunchy, fairly delicate, and quite rich (i.e., they are made with butter). The lemon and anise flavors are subtle and complementary.

These cookies, which are great for dipping in tea or coffee, improve with age, and will last up to two weeks in an airtight container. This recipe is a gift from pastry chef Susan Inahara.

1. Preheat the oven to 350° and place a rack one-third from the top of the oven.

2. Sift together the flour and baking powder. Stir in the anise seed, then set aside.

3. In the large bowl of an electric mixer, or with a hand-held electric mixer, beat the butter and sugar together at medium speed until well mixed, about 3 minutes. Beat in the lemon zest.

4. Add the whole egg and the egg white and mix well at low speed. Scrape down the bowl with a rubber spatula as needed. Add the vanilla extract.

5. Combine the milk and lemon juice in a small bowl. Still at low speed, add the dry ingredients in two batches, alternating with the milk mixture. Mix only until smooth and scrape down the bowl after each addition.

6. Line a large baking sheet with aluminum foil. Divide the dough into 2 or 3 portions. (This will depend on the size of the baking sheet.) On a lightly floured work surface, roll each portion into a log, $1\frac{1}{2}$ inches in diameter and not longer than the length of the baking sheet. Make sure that there are no air pockets in the dough. Place the logs at least 5 inches apart on the baking sheet, and flatten them into strips, approximately $\frac{1}{2}$ inch thick and $2\frac{1}{2}$ inches wide. Make these as even as possible.

7. Stir together the egg yolk and water in a small bowl, and brush the tops of the strips evenly with this egg wash. Bake until the strips are an even golden brown and the tops spring back when touched (the tops may split while baking—this is okay), 20 to 25 minutes. Turn the pan to ensure even baking, if necessary. Remove the baking sheet from the oven and let it cool on a wire rack for about 10 minutes.

8. Place 1 of the still-warm strips on a large cutting board: First turn it on its side, then transfer it to the cutting board; the strip will not bend and break this way. Using a serrated knife, cut the strip crosswise into $\frac{3}{4}$-inch slices. Place these, on their sides, back on the foil-lined baking sheet. (There's no need to change the foil.) The biscotti may be very close together. Cut the remaining strip(s).

9. Bake the biscotti until the cut sides are lightly browned and the cookies no longer feel soft, 7 to 10 minutes more. Let the cookies cool completely still on the baking sheet, then store in an airtight container for up to 1 week.

macadamia and white chocolate chip cookies

MAKES 3 DOZEN 3-INCH COOKIES

2½ cups sifted
   all-purpose flour

1 teaspoon
   baking powder

1 teaspoon baking soda

½ pound (2 sticks)
   unsalted butter, at
   room temperature

¾ cup granulated sugar

¾ cup dark brown sugar

2 large eggs

1 teaspoon pure vanilla
   extract

2 cups (6 ounces) white
   chocolate chips or two
   3-ounce bars of white
   chocolate, cut up

1 cup unsalted maca-
   damia nuts, toasted
   (see Note) and
   coarsely chopped

These sinfully rich cookies are crunchy and chewy at the same time. Make a double batch and freeze half the batter for when you get the urge.

1. Preheat the oven to 350° and adjust the racks to divide the oven in thirds. Sift together the flour, baking powder, and baking soda and set aside.

2. In the large bowl of an electric mixer, or with a hand-held electric mixer, beat together the butter and the sugars at medium speed until light, about 5 minutes.

3. Add the eggs, one at a time, mixing well and scraping down the bowl with a rubber spatula after each addition. Add the vanilla extract.

4. At low speed, add the sifted dry ingredients in 3 additions, mixing only until incorporated after each. Scrape the bowl with a rubber spatula between additions.

5. Add the white chocolate and macadamia nuts at one time, mixing only until incorporated. (Overmixing will build up the gluten in the flour and make the cookies tough.) Using a large rubber spatula, finish mixing by hand.

6. Drop slightly heaping 2-tablespoon portions of the dough on nonstick, buttered, or foil-lined baking sheets, spacing 3 to 4 inches apart. You should be able to make 1 dozen cookies on a standard 12 x 16-inch baking sheet.

7. Bake the cookies, turning the baking sheets and switching them between the upper and lower racks as needed to ensure even browning, until the cookies are an even golden brown, 12 to 14 minutes.

dinner at the authentic cafe

8. Remove the baking sheets from the oven and cool the cookies still on the sheets on a wire rack for about 3 minutes. Using a wide spatula, carefully transfer the cookies to a wire rack to cook completely.

9. The cookies can be stored in an airtight container for up to 1 week, if they last that long.

Note *To toast macadamia nuts, arrange them on a baking sheet and bake, stirring twice, in a 350° oven until evenly browned, 7 to 10 minutes.*

coconut-macadamia cream pie

MAKES ONE 10-INCH PIE;
8 SERVINGS

Filling

1 cup medium-shredded coconut

1 cup unsalted macadamia nuts

2 cups milk

½ cup plus 2 tablespoons granulated sugar

4 large or extra-large egg yolks

6 tablespoons plus 2 teaspoons sifted all-purpose flour

1 teaspoon powdered gelatin, softened in 2 teaspoons cold water

½ teaspoon pure vanilla extract

2 tablespoons dark rum (optional)

Authentic Cafe Pie Crust *(page 230)*

1 cup very cold heavy cream

2 tablespoons powdered sugar

Very few people make cream pies at home, and this is indeed a shame. They are actually quite simple to make, although they do require some planning because they take time to set up. This is a variation on the coconut cream pie theme. Toasting the coconut and the macadamias intensifies their flavors considerably.

1. Preheat the oven to 350°.

2. Prepare the filling: Spread the coconut on a baking sheet and bake, stirring once, until golden, about 7 minutes. Let the coconut cool and break apart any lumps.

3. Spread the macadamia nuts on a baking sheet and bake at the same temperature, stirring twice, until light brown, about 10 minutes. Let the nuts cool and cut each nut into about 3 pieces.

3. In a small, nonreactive saucepan, heat the milk with half the sugar over medium heat until bubbles form around the edge. Reduce the heat to low.

4. Meanwhile, whisk the egg yolks in a small bowl. Add the remaining sugar and whisk until pale yellow. Add the flour and whisk until smooth.

5. Pour about one-third of the hot milk into the egg mixture, whisking until smooth. Immediately pour this mixture into the milk in the saucepan, whisking constantly. The mixture should thicken immediately. Once this pastry cream has come to a boil, let it boil for about 10 seconds, still whisking to prevent it from sticking.

6. Using a rubber spatula, scrape this pastry cream into a large, shallow, nonreactive bowl. Whisk in the gelatin and cover with waxed paper, pressing the paper directly on the surface of the cream to prevent a crust from forming. Let the pastry cream cool for about 30 minutes.

7. Remove the waxed paper from the cream and scrape off any cream that has stuck to it. Whisk in the vanilla and the rum, if desired. Fold in the coconut and nuts. Pour this mixture into the Authentic Cafe Pie Crust and smooth the top. Refrigerate, uncovered, for at least 3 hours, and up to 8 hours. Cover with plastic wrap after 1 hour.

8. Just before serving, whip the cream and the powdered sugar until stiff but not grainy. If you know how to use a pastry bag, fit one with a large star tip and pipe rosettes of whipped cream on the top of the pie. Otherwise, just spoon dollops of the whipped cream on the pie and serve. Use a sharp knife dipped in hot water to cut the pie.

coconut

cream

dark rum

banana-chocolate cream pie

Filling

2 cups milk

½ cup plus 2 tablespoons sugar

4 large or extra-large egg yolks

6 tablespoons plus 2 teaspoons sifted all-purpose flour

½ teaspoon pure vanilla extract

1 cup (6 ounces) semi-sweet chocolate chips or finely chopped semisweet chocolate

2 ripe bananas

Authentic Cafe Pie Crust *(recipe follows)*, baked and cooled

1 cup very cold heavy cream whipped until stiff with 2 tablespoons powdered sugar

This variation of Coconut-Macadamia Cream Pie is so good I'm including it here, too.

1. Prepare the filling as for Coconut-Macadamia Cream Pie, but omit the coconut and macadamias. While the hot pastry cream is still in the saucepan, add the vanilla and the chocolate, whisking until the chocolate is completely melted. Cool the pastry cream in a shallow, nonreactive bowl as above, about 30 minutes.

2. Peel the bananas and slice them in half lengthwise. Cut them in half again crosswise. Spread about ½ inch of filling over the bottom of the Authentic Cafe pie crust. Place the banana quarters on this cream, packing them in as tightly as possible. Cover the bananas with the remaining cream and smooth the top. Refrigerate, covered, for at least 2 hours (the chocolate helps the cream set up), and up to 8 hours. Top with whipped cream and serve.

authentic cafe pie crust

This is a simple flaky pie crust that is good for any cream or fruit pie. It contains no lard or vegetable shortening—just butter. Use it whenever you need a prebaked sweet pie crust.

1¼ cups sifted
     all-purpose flour

     Pinch of salt

1   tablespoon sugar

¼   pound (1 stick) very
     cold unsalted butter,
     cut into ¼-inch dice

3 to 4 tablespoons to ¼ cup
        ice water

1. Place the flour, salt, and sugar in a medium-size bowl and combine with a whisk. Add the butter, and using a pastry blender or your fingers, blend the butter into the flour until there are no lumps left and the mixture resembles coarse cornmeal.

2. Add the water, a little at a time, and stir with a fork just until the mixture comes together. The amount of water required will depend on the temperature of your kitchen and the ingredients. (The higher the temperature, the less water you will need, since the butter will begin to melt.) Do not overmix, and try to not add too much water.

3. Turn the dough onto a lightly floured work surface. Knead the dough briefly and then shape it into a disk, approximately 6 inches in diameter and ½ inch thick. Regrigerate, covered, until firm, 30 to 60 minutes.

4. Place the chilled dough on a lightly floured work surface and sprinkle the top lightly with flour. Roll the dough quickly and evenly (overworking the dough will build up the gluten in the flour and will result in a tough crust that shrinks when baked) into a round, about 14 inches in diameter and about ⅛ inch thick. Fold the dough in quarters and place the pointed end in the center of a 10-inch pie dish. Unfold the dough and fit it gently into the pie dish, taking care to ease it—not stretch it—into the corners. (Once again, stretching the dough will cause it to shrink when baking.) Trim the dough flush with the lip of the pie dish. Roll the raw edge slightly under toward the pie dish and crimp the edge decoratively. Freeze the unbaked pie shell for 30 minutes to relax the dough. (This will also prevent it from shrinking during baking.)

5. Preheat the oven to 375°. Line the chilled pie shell with foil, pressing the foil right up against the dough, and place about 2 cups of pie weights, rice, or dried beans inside the shell. Spread the weights, whatever they may be, throughout the bottom and up against the sides of the shell. Bake for 20 minutes. Remove the weights, which may be re-used, and the foil, and bake the shell until golden brown, an additional 10 to 15 minutes. If any air is trapped under the crust, it will cause the dough to blister. Gently pierce these blisters with a thin knife to release the air. Cool the baked pie shell before using.

caramelized pineapple tacos with red fruit salsa

Taco shells

3 tablespoons sugar

1 tablespoon all-purpose flour

2 large egg whites (2 fluid ounces)

1 tablespoon unsalted butter, melted and cooled

½ teaspoon pure vanilla extract

2 tablespoons coarsely chopped pine nuts

Salsa

1 pint strawberries, wiped clean (*see* Note), hulled and quartered

½ pint raspberries

¼ cup minced fresh mint

2 tablespoons granulated sugar, or to taste

2 tablespoons freshly squeezed lemon juice or tequila

½ teaspoon ground ginger

This dessert comprises four elements, which can all be prepared ahead of time and assembled just before serving. The "taco" shells are made from traditional French *tuile* batter. The recipe actually makes 6 shells, but they break easily, and you may be forced to eat a couple while preparing this dessert.

1. Prepare the taco shells: Preheat the oven to 350°, and lay a *clean* broomstick across the tops of two kitchen chairs. Combine the sugar and flour in a small bowl and mix with a wire whisk. Add the egg whites, butter, and vanilla and mix until smooth, then stir in the pine nuts.

2. Make 2 shells at a time: Generously butter a baking sheet, or if possible, line the sheet with baking parchment and butter it. Place 2 dollops, each one consisting of 1 tablespoon plus 1 teaspoon of batter on the sheet, spacing about 8 inches apart. Using the back of a fork dipped in water, spread the batter into a round, 6 inches in diameter. Do not worry if the edges are slightly uneven.

3. Bake the shells until evenly browned, 5 to 7 minutes. Remove the pan from the oven, and using a large wide spatula, lift the soft disks off the pan and lay them over the broomstick. The nuts should be on the outside of the shell, not facing the broomstick, and the shell should be folded in half as much as possible. Let the shells cool while you finish spreading and baking the rest.

4. Store the cooled shells (they must be completely cooled or they will become soggy) in a single layer in an airtight container for up to 24 hours.

Pineapple filling

2 tablespoons unsalted butter

½ large pineapple, peeled, cored, and cut into wedges, ½ inch thick and 1 inch wide (3 cups)

¼ cup packed light brown sugar

One ½- to ¾-inch piece ginger, peeled and minced (2 teaspoons)

2 tablespoons dark rum

1 pint vanilla ice cream

4 mint leaves

5. Prepare the salsa: Combine all the salsa ingredients in a medium-size, nonreactive bowl and mix well. Taste the mixture and add more sugar, if desired. Refrigerate, covered, for at least 2 hours, but not more than 12, or the berries will turn mushy.

6. Prepare the pineapple filling: Heat a large, nonreactive sauté pan or frying pan over medium heat. Add the butter and let it brown slightly. Place the pineapple in the pan and cook it, stirring often with a wooden spoon, until its juice evaporates and the pineapple begins to brown, about 15 to 30 minutes, depending on the juice content of the pineapple.

7. Once the pineapple begins to caramelize, add the brown sugar, stirring to coat all the pineapple. Add the ginger and continue to cook, stirring, until the sugar does not appear to be grainy, 5 to 7 minutes.

8. Add the rum and cook until it is almost completely evaporated, about 2 minutes. The pineapple filling can be refrigerated, covered, for up to 24 hours. Warm the filling in a large sauté pan or frying pan over medium heat just before serving, if needed.

9. To serve, measure out four 4-ounce, or ½-cup, scoops of ice cream and place on chilled dessert plates. Spoon one-quarter of the pineapple filling into each taco shell, then spoon some of the salsa over that, and prop the taco against the ice cream. Place some of the salsa on the plate, around the ice cream. Place a mint leaf on top, and serve immediately.

Note *If your strawberries are very sandy, wash them, but dry them thoroughly before proceeding. If they remain wet, the salsa will be mushy.*

mango-banana upside-down cake

MAKES 8 SERVINGS

- 4 tablespoons (½ stick) unsalted butter
- ¼ cup packed dark brown sugar
- 1 large medium-ripe mango, peeled, seeded, and cut into 8 long wedges
- 1 medium-ripe banana, peeled and cut into ½-inch rounds
- ½ cup coarsely chopped pecans
- 1½ cups sifted all-purpose flour
- 1 teaspoon baking powder
- ¼ teaspoon baking soda
- ¾ cup sugar
- ¼ pound (1 stick) cold unsalted butter, cut into ½-inch dice
- ½ cup sour cream
- 3 large or extra-large egg yolks
- 1 teaspoon pure vanilla extract

  Vanilla ice cream

This cake is so rich and moist, it's almost like a pudding. Serve it warm or at room temperature with vanilla ice cream. Besides mangos and bananas, try other fruit combinations, such as apple-cranberry (great for the holidays), pear-blueberry, or the ever-popular pineapple-cherry, for which I heartily recommend you use fresh, not canned, fruit.

Use a heavy enamel-coated cast-iron skillet, or a heavy stainless-steel-lined aluminum skillet. These materials conduct the heat efficiently and let the fruit caramelize, while the enamel or stainless steel prevents them from reacting with the iron or aluminum.

1. Preheat the oven to 350°.

2. Heat a 9-inch (measure at the top) enameled cast-iron skillet, or a stainless-steel-lined aluminum skillet, over medium heat. Add the butter and let it melt. Add the brown sugar and whisk until smooth. Let the butter and sugar become frothy, still whisking. Remove the pan from the heat and make sure that the butter and sugar are spread evenly over the bottom.

3. Arrange the mango wedges in a pinwheel pattern on top of the brown sugar mixture. Place a banana round between wedges, then fill in the gaps with the chopped pecans.

4. Sift together the flour, baking powder, and baking soda, then place these ingredients in the large bowl of an electric mixer. Add the sugar and the cold butter. Mix at low speed until the butter is completely broken up and the mixture resembles coarse cornmeal. Increase the speed to medium and, once the mixture comes together, continue beating at medium speed for about 30 seconds.

5. Whisk together the sour cream, egg yolks, and vanilla extract in a separate bowl and add this mixture all at once to the ingredients in step 4. Continue mixing on medium speed for about 15 seconds. Scrape down the bowl with a rubber spatula, and mix for an additional 15 seconds.

6. Spoon the batter over the fruit in the pan, taking care not to disrupt the arrangement of the fruit. Smooth the top of the batter with a rubber spatula. Bake until a toothpick inserted in the middle of the cake just comes out dry, 30 to 40 minutes. Do not overbake.

7. Remove the cake from the oven and run a thin knife around the edge to loosen it. Remember, this pan is still extremely hot. Very carefully, invert a platter over the pan and invert the cake onto the platter. Use the pan to center the cake on the platter, then remove the pan. If any fruit has stuck to the pan, remove it with a spatula and place it on the cake.

8. Serve hot or at room temperature with vanilla ice cream.

Index